OTHER OWNERSHIP RIGHTS

WATER RIGHTS

1. Riparian Doctrine: Water belongs to the owners of land bordering the watercourse.
   a. Natural Flow: Riparian owner is entitled to water without diminution in its quantity.
   b. Reasonable Use: Riparian owner must share with other riparian owners and is entitled only to reasonable use.
2. Prior Appropriation Doctrine: An individual may divert and use water whether or not she borders the watercourse; individual rights are established by actual use.

RIGHT TO LATERAL AND SUBJACENT SUPPORT

Strict liability for owner of land whose excavations cause a neighboring parcel to subside, or which damage buildings on adjacent land.

GIFTS

IN GENERAL

1. *Definition:* A gratuitous voluntary lifetime transfer of property from a donor to donee.
2. Requirements:
   a. Present intent to make a gift;
   b. Delivery by donor; and
   c. Acceptance by donee
3. Classification:
   a. *inter vivos:* Made during donor's lifetime; irrevocable unless donor retains right to revoke.
   b. *gifts causa mortis:* Lifetime gift by donor in contemplation of impending death.
      i. Contemplation of impending death;
      ii. Automatic revocation if donor survives peril;
      iii. Ambiguity of donor's intent; and
      iv. Death from different peril.

INTEREST IN LAND: ESTATES

TYPE		
PRESENT POSSESSORY ESTATES – *Property intere...*		*...ossession*
FEE SIMPLE ABSOLUTE:	Right given by...	E
FEE SIMPLE DETERMINABLE:	Right given by a...	E
FEE SIMPLE ON CONDITION SUBSEQUENT:	Right given by a grantor	E
FEE TAIL (FEE SIMPLE CONDITIONAL):	Right given by a grantor	E
LIFE ESTATE:	Right given by a grantor	E
CONCURRENT ESTATES – *Property interest in land currently possessed by several individuals at the same time, p...*		
TENANCY IN COMMON:	Deed, will, or law of intestate succession	E c n
JOINT TENANCY:	Deed and will, but not by intestate succession; requires the following Four Unities: 1. Time: Co-tenants acquire at same time 2. Title: Interests acquired under same instrument 3. Interest: Co-tenants have exactly same interest 4. Possession: Co-tenants each have possession of entire estate	E c h S i c
TENANCY BY ENTIRETY:	Deed, will, or law of intestate succession	E c n
LEASEHOLDS (LANDLORD AND TENANT) – *Interest in land according to the terms of a lease agreement, in th...*		
PERIODIC TENANCY:	Created by lease; contractual agreement	F n
TENANCY FOR YEARS:	Created by lease; contractual agreement	F c
TENANCY AT WILL:	Created by lease; contractual agreement	F t
TENANCY AT SUFFERANCE:	Created by operation of law when tenant wrongfully remains in possession after end of lawful lease term	H e
FUTURE INTERESTS – *An interest in property that is not presently possessory, but will come into possession s...*		
REVERSION (IN GRANTOR):	Automatically at end of transferred estate or by express reservation by grantor after transferring title	E t
POSSIBILITY OF REVERTER (IN GRANTOR):	Occurrence of event terminating a fee simple determinable	E g
RIGHT OF ENTRY (IN GRANTOR):	Occurrence of condition terminating a fee simple on condition subsequent	E g
EXECUTORY INTEREST (IN GRANTEE):	Occurrence of condition as specified by grantor	E g
REMAINDERS (IN GRANTEE):	Occurrence of limitation (not a condition) terminating a prior possessory estate simultaneously created	A c s

b. Interest in Property: A BFP has superior rights to others claiming an interest in the same property, including the actual owner, where the BFP takes possession in good faith and pays value.

2. Adverse Possessor (AP):
   a. *Definition*: One who takes possession contrary to the possessory rights of another. Requires that possession by the AP throughout the entire statutory period required be:
      i. Actual; open and notorious; exclusive; continuous; and hostile under Claim of Right.
   b. Interest in Property: Adverse possessor acquires superior title good against all the world.

LANDLORD AND TENANT

THE LEASE

The interest in property between a landlord and tenant is controlled by the lease.

1. For a proper lease:
   a. Formal lease requirements:
      i. Identification of landlord and tenant;
      ii. Adequate description of the premises;
      iii. Amount of rent/dates to pay rent (if no rent amount, reasonable value); and
      iv. Duration of lease.
   b. Statute of Frauds (if lease > 1 year):
      i. Must be in writing; and
      ii. Signed by the party to be charged.
2. The lease terms create the type of estate ("leasehold").
   a. Periodic Tenancy: Right to occupy tenancy for fixed period (year, month, week, or day).
   b. Tenancy for Years: Right to occupy tenancy beginning on a fixed date and ending on a fixed date.
   c. Tenancy at Will: Right to occupy tenancy "at will" as long as both landlord and tenant so desire.
   d. Tenancy at Sufferance: Holdover tenant is treated as trespasser and evicted, or new periodic tenancy is imposed.
3. The lease defines rights and duties between Landlord and Tenant.
   a. *Example*: All L's duties are done in exchange for T's payment of rent, if landlord breaches duties, tenant can withhold rent, if T breaches duties (e.g., fails to pay rent), L can evict.
   b. Lease terms/duties are independent:
      i. Failure to perform by one party does not excuse other party from performing.
      ii. Exception: if warranty of habitability is breached.
4. Other legal considerations arising from lease:
   a. Assignments/Subleases (see chart on p.1)
   b. Fixtures: Personal property or chattels that have been permanently attached to land:
      i. Common Law: Becomes property of landlord.
      ii. American courts: Look to objective intent of tenant, determined by: manner of attachment, damage from removal, fixture in context of property. *Sigrol Realty Corp. v. Valcich*, 11 N.Y.2d 668, 180 N.E.2d 904, 225 N.Y.S.2d 748 (1962).

iii. Trade fixtures: Used to carry on a trade or business; tenant can remove but is responsible for any damage. Restatement of Property: all fixtures installed by T are trade fixtures.

LANDLORD'S RIGHTS / REMEDIES

1. Security deposit: L retains amount of posted deposit for T's costs and damages.
2. Rent acceleration clause: If T defaults on rent, all future rents become immediately due and payable.
3. Sue for unpaid rent: In the absence of an acceleration clause, L may only sue for the rental amount owed for the current lease period.
4. Eviction: If T materially breaches any lease term, including failure to pay rent timely; may evict by: ejectment, self-help (physical ouster), or summary proceedings.

DUTIES OF LANDLORD

1. Duty to Deliver Possession:
   a. Right to Possess: Breach if someone has superior right to possess at time of commencement of lease; T not required to move in
   b. Actual Possession: Under English Rule, L must deliver actual possession. *Dieffenbach v. McIntyre*, 208 Okla. 163, 254 P.2d 346 (1952); under American Rule (minority), L's not required to deliver. *Hannan v. Dusch*, 154 Va. 356, 153 S.E. 824 (1930).
2. Covenant of Quiet Enjoyment (implied): L promises that neither L nor third party will interfere with T's use and enjoyment of premises.
   a. Actual Eviction: Physical expulsion or exclusion from possession.
   b. Partial Eviction: Denial of possession for only part of the premises.
      i. Common Law: T's obligation to pay entire rent is suspended until possession of entire premises restored.
      ii. Restatement: T can abate rent or terminate lease and seek damages; cannot remain in possession and pay no rent.
   c. Constructive Eviction: L wrongfully performs or fails to perform some duty that substantially deprives T of use and enjoyment of premises.
      i. Common Law: L has no duty to repair premises unless L & T so agree; Statute/Case Law: L makes reasonable repairs. *Chambers v. N. River Line*, 179 N.C. 199, 102 S.E. 198 (1920).
3. Warranty of Fitness for Particular Purpose (implied):
   a. Common Law: In the absence of express lease provision, no warranty by L that premises would be fit for any purpose. *Anderson Drive-In Theatre Inc. v. Kirkpatrick*, 123 Ind. App. 388, 110 N.E.2d 506 (1953).
   b. Exceptions: Short-term lease of furnished residence and building under construction when rented. *Ingalls v. Hobbs*, 156 Mass. 348, 31 N.E. 286 (1892).
4. Warranty of Habitability (implied): L required to take all reasonable action to maintain premises in habitable condition, including duty to repair residential leases only; for commercial leases, implied warranty of suitability for intended commercial purpose. *Davidow v. Inwood North Professional Group*, 747 S.W.2d 373 (Tex. 1988).

5. Retaliatory eviction: L may not evict T, refuse to renew lease, terminate a periodic tenancy, or increase T's rent in retaliation for T's prior actions. *Edwards v. Habib*, 397 F.2d 687 (D.C. Cir. 1968).
   a. Not applicable to commercial leases.
   b. Tenant bears burden of demonstrating retaliatory motive of landlord.

LANDLORD'S TORT LIABILITIES

Generally, L not liable to T or third parties for injuries sustained on the premises.
1. Exceptions:
   a. Common Areas. *Johnson v. O'Brien*, 258 Minn. 502, 105 N.W.2d 244 (1960).
   b. Latent Defects: L fails to disclose.
   c. Negligent Repairs: Only if L voluntarily undertakes to make repair.

DUTIES OF TENANT

1. Duty to Pay Rent: T's obligation to pay rent is independent of L's duties; therefore T must continue to pay rent even if L fails to fulfill duties, unless warranty of habitability is breached.
2. Duty to Take Possession: No duty unless express or implied in lease.
3. Restrictions on use of leased premises:
   a. Cannot use property for illegal purpose
   b. Cannot commit waste (see "Doctrine of Waste" section under "Concurrent Estates").
4. Duty to Repair: No duty unless T expressly agrees; if premises completely destroyed, T might be obligated to rebuild.
5. Duty to Deliver Premises at End of Lease:
   a. T must give premises over timely or be treated as a holdover.
   b. Wrongful Abandonment: If T fails to pay rent and abandons the premises, L may:
      i. Accept the abandonment as a surrender and end the lease,
      ii. Leave premises vacant and sue for rent owed, or
      iii. Re-let premises to minimize T's damages.

TENANT'S RIGHTS / REMEDIES

1. Remain in possession, and
   a. Abate rent, or
   b. Suspend rent
2. Terminate lease, and
   a. Sue for damages, or
   b. Quit premises.

REAL COVENANTS & EQUITABLE SERVITUDES

EQUITABLE SERVITUDES

1. Generally, same as real covenants except that no privity is required;
2. Therefore, must be enforced in equity.
3. Creation: *Tulk v. Moxhay*, 2 Phillips 774, 41 Eng. Rep. 1143 (Ch. 1848).
   a. Express agreement.
   b. Implied:
      i. Implied Reciprocal Agreement.
      ii. Common Scheme.
      iii. Subdivision Plat.
      iv. California rule: will not be enforced unless in deed. *Werner v. Graham*, 181 Cal. 174, 183 P. 945 (Cal. 1919).

Real Covenants & Equitable Servitudes continues on page 3

LAWS AFFECTING INTERESTS

DESCRIPTION OF PROPERTY

1. Metes and bounds.
2. Government survey.
3. Reference to plat/map.
4. Resolving inconsistencies:
   a. Natural monuments.
   b. Artificial monuments.
   c. References to adjacent tracts.
   d. Courses/directions.
   e. Distances.
   f. Area or quantity.
   g. Place names.

TYPES OF DEEDS

1. General Warranty Deed (contains six covenants of title):
   a. Covenant of Seisin: Promise by grantor who owns property to be conveyed.
   b. Covenant of Right to Convey: Promise grantor has power and legal ability to convey property.
   c. Covenant of Against Encumbrances: Promise property is free from encumbrances.
   d. Covenant of Quiet Enjoyment: Promise no third party with legal claim of superior title against grantee and that grantor will compensate grantee for losses incurred as a result.
   e. Covenant of Warranty: Promise grantor will defend against superior claims and will compensate grantee for losses incurred as a result.
   f. Covenant of Further Assurances: Promise grantor will do whatever is reasonably necessary to perfect title if title is defective.
2. Special Warranty Deed: Same covenants as general warranty, but only for the period of time that the grantor owned the property.
3. Quitclaim Deed: Contains no warranties and gives whatever interest in property grantor may have.

ZONING

1. Enacted pursuant to state police power for health, welfare, and safety of community.
2. Prevents certain use of property in favor of public good.
3. May be challenged on constitutional grounds or where benefit is primarily for private, and not public, interests.

NUISANCE

Owner of land may sue for interference with the use and enjoyment of her property. At common law, applied to noise, aesthetic harms, environmental changes, etc.

1. Private nuisance: substantial and unreasonable interference with the private use and enjoyment of another's land. *Hendricks v. Stalnaker*, 181 W.Va. 31, 380 S.E.2d 198 (1989).
   a. Interference must be substantial.
   b. Defendant's conduct must be intentional and unreasonable:
      i. Gravity of the harm outweighs utility, or
      ii. Utility outweighs harm, but harm is serious. *Boomer v. Atlantic Cement Co.*, 26 N.Y. 2d 219, 309 N.Y.S.2d 312, 257 N.E. 2d 870 (N.Y. 1970).
2. Public nuisance: harm to the community's use or enjoyment of public land.

3. Defense to a Nuisance Claim:
   a. Coming to the nuisance.
   b. Contributory negligence.
   c. Assumption of the risk.
4. Remedies for Nuisance:
   a. Enjoin D from acting, and
   b. Require D to pay.

THE REAL ESTATE CONTRACT

The sale of land is accompanied by a contract binding the buyer and seller to perform. Requires (must comply with Statute of Frauds):
1. Names of buyer and seller,
2. Description of realty to be sold,
3. Essential terms of the sale, and
4. Signature of party against whom enforcement is sought.

MORTGAGES

The purchase price is usually secured by the buyer from a third-party lender, which results in a lien on the property in favor of the lender.
1. Foreclosure: If the buyer defaults in repaying the lender, the property may be foreclosed upon and sold to repay the buyer's debts; the lender or one with a senior lien on the property will then be paid first out of the proceeds of the sale.
2. Equity of Redemption: Upon default, the buyer has the right to remedy the default and gain clear title to the land; some states limit the time in which the buyer may redeem after foreclosure.
3. Purchase Money Mortgage: When load funds are used in part to purchase property, the mortgage securing the loan is a purchase money mortgage.

THE REAL ESTATE CLOSING

At closing, seller conveys marketable title in exchange for the buyer's providing the purchase price, and the rights of the parties shift from sale contract to deed.
1. Marketable Title: All defects and encumbrances must be removed by the time of closing; any defect, including those that do not appear in the chain of title, may make the title unmarketable.
2. Equitable Conversion:
   a. Once buyer and seller have signed an enforceable contract (prior to closing, they enter into the contract for the sale of land) equity converts:
      i. Buyer's interest into interest in realty
      ii. Seller's interest into interest in personalty (the purchase price)
   b. Death of party: If buyer or seller dies before closing, converted rights pass to estate of either.
   c. Risk of loss: If property is destroyed, under the general rule buyer is now the owner of the property and will bear the loss.
3. Breach:
   a. Buyer's Remedies: Upon seller's failure to provide marketable title, buyer can demand specific performance, receive damages, or rescind contract.
   b. Seller's Remedies: Upon buyer's failure to pay the purchase price, seller can demand specific performance, receive damages, or rescind contract.

THE DEED

After closing, the duties of the buyer and seller are contained in the deed.
1. Formalities:
   a. Statute of Frauds:
      i. Must be in writing and signed by the grantor, and
      ii. Must describe property.
   b. Delivery of the Deed:
      i. Delivery is presumed where deed is in possession of grantee at time the issue arises; deed is recorded by grantor.
      i. If grantor retains deed in his possession and dies, no legal delivery.
      iii. Deposit with third party: Delivery effective if grantor intended to vest title in grantee and surrendered control to third party; delivery with conditions (no delivery unless); condition is certain to occur and is within control of the grantee.

EMINENT DOMAIN / TAKINGS

1. *Definitions:* A taking of private property for public use without just compensation, can be either direct or indirect (property is merely burdened); if government pays just compensation, taking is constitutional and therefore permissible.
2. "Public Use": Must be rationally related to accomplishing a public purpose or use results in a public benefit. *Hawaii Housing Authority v. Midkiff*, 467 U.S. 229 (1984).
3. "Just Compensation": Fair market value, valued at highest and best use, special value to owner is not relevant. *United States v. Fuller*, 409 U.S. 488 (1973).
4. Sovereign may not use its eminent domain power to take property of one private party for sole purpose of transferring it to another private party, even if first party is paid just compensation [*Kelo v. City of New London, Conn.*, 125 S.Ct. 2655 (2005)]. However, state may use its eminent domain power to transfer property from one private party to another if purpose of taking is future use by public, hence a city's exercise of eminent domain power in furtherance of economic development plan satisfied constitutional "public use" requirement [*Kelo v. City of New London, Conn.*, 125 S.Ct. 2655 (2005)].

RECORDATION

Grantee who can show that she received her interest in a deed executed earlier than a competing claimant will be recognized as the true owner. Exception: if subsequent purchase is a bona fide purchase (BFP).
1. Types of Recording Statutes:
   a. Pure Race: Whoever records first.
   b. Notice: Unrecorded conveyance is invalid against a BFP who has no notice, regardless of who records first.
   c. Race-Notice: Whoever records first, unless that person has notice of a prior grant.
2. Chain of Title: A title search can give notice of prior interests in the property at issue.
   a. Title Examination:
      i. Grantor/grantee index: Title is traced back through the seller in grantor's indices, and forward to each buyer through grantee indices.
      ii. Marketable title acts: Limits the title examiner's search by providing that chain of title need only be established within a certain range of years.

REAL COVENANTS

1. Types of Real Covenants: Restrictive Covenants and Affirmative Covenants
2. Creation of Real Covenants:
   a. Intent: Promisors intend to bind their successors in interest, or covenant will only be enforced against original parties. *Moseley v. Bishop*, 470 N.E.2d 773 (Ind. App. 1984).
   b. Touch and Concern: Successor to burden will only be bound where the covenant has a connection to her use and enjoyment of the land. *Neponsit Property Owners' Assn. v. Emigrant Industrial Savings Bank*, 278 N.Y. 248, 15 N.E.2d 793 (1938).
   c. Privity of Estate:
      i. Horizontal (for burden to run): between original promisor and promisee.
      ii. Vertical (for benefit to run): between original parties and their assigns or successors.
   d. Must also comply with Statute of Frauds.
3. Scope of Real Covenants: Benefit to dominant estate and burden to servient estate.
4. Termination of Real Covenants: Not really termination, but burden or benefit will not run once horizontal/vertical privity is gone.

EASEMENTS

SCOPE OF EASEMENTS

1. Any change in use beyond the intent of the parties that created the easement is beyond the scope of the easement and not allowed.
2. Intent of parties is guiding principle.
3. Increases in frequency or intensity of use are generally permissible.
4. Scope may be determined from duration of easement, location of easement, or reasonable expectation of parties.

TRANSFER OF EASEMENTS

1. In Gross:
   a. Burden: Always transfers with land.
   b. Benefit: Generally transferable unless use as transferred creates unreasonable burden on servient estate.
2. Appurtenant:
   Note: No separate document is required to effectuate transfer, nor is notice of either required.
   a. Burden: Always transfers with land.
   b. Benefit: Always transfers with land.

TERMINATION OF EASEMENTS

Termination of easements can be made by:
- By Terms.
- Merger of Dominant and Servient Estates.
- Prescription.
- Forfeiture.
- Changed Conditions.
- Frustration of Purpose.
- Abandonment—requires intent and clear act.

CREATION OF EASEMENTS

1. Express Grant: Usually contained in a deed.
2. Deed: Owner of land may convey entire estate and reserve an easement for her own use, or to the benefit of a third party.
3. Donative Transfer: Created by gift deed or will; consideration not necessary unless intent is not clear.
4. Contract: Reciprocal easements are adequate consideration.
5. Estoppel: Easement is asserted in equity when land owner who permits certain use attempts to revoke that use at a later time.
6. Implication: In the absence of express agreement, intent of parties to create an easement can be implied from:
   a. Prior use requires that
      i. Dominant/servient estates were originally a single estate;
      ii. Prior use is permanent or long term, and not temporary;
      iii. Prior use is apparent and not concealed [*Romanchuk v. Plotkin*, 215 Minn. 156, 9 N.W.2d 421 (1943)]; and
      iv. Prior use is reasonably necessary to enjoy the property.
   b. Necessity requires either of the following:
      i. Unity of title followed by a severance;
      ii. Strict necessity, e.g., parcel is landlocked.
7. Prescription: Like adverse possession, use must be:
   a. Adverse—inconsistent with owner's use;
   b. Open/notorious—sufficient to put owner on notice;
   c. Continuous; and
   d. Uninterrupted for duration of statutory period.

TYPES OF EASEMENTS

1. Easement in Gross: Not attached to the land, will not transfer unless the owner of the land so intends.
2. Easement Appurtenant: Attached to the land, rights transfer to any new purchaser of the land.
   a. Dominant estate: Estate benefited, appurtenant easement transfers automatically when dominant estate is transferred.
   b. Servient estate: Estate burdened, need not be adjoining to dominant estate.
3. Negative Easements: Owner of easement has right to demand that the owner of the servient estate refrain from using land in a certain way.

FUTURE INTERESTS

TYPES OF FUTURE INTERESTS

1. In Grantor:
   a. Reversion.
   b. Possibility of reverter.
   c. Right of entry.
2. In Grantee:
   a. Executory Interest:
      i. Springing interest; shifting interest.
   b. Remainders:
      i. Vested:
         1. Indefeasibly,
         2. Subject to Open/Partial Divestment—class gifts.
      ii. Contingent:
         1. Subject to Condition Precedent,
         2. Unborn or Unascertained person.

RULE IN SHELLEY'S CASE

Example: Life estate in A, and remainder in "A's heirs" or the "heirs of A's body"

Effect: If the two estates are either both legal or both equitable, remainder is deemed to be in A, not A's heirs or the heirs of A's body

Doctrine of Merger: Where A has life estate and next vested estate, they merge to form a fee simple.

DOCTRINE OF WORTHIER TITLE

Example: O gives life estate in A, remainder in O's heirs; (future interest must be limited to heirs of grantor, and not issue or devise).

Effect: A will get a life estate and O has a reversion; O's heirs get nothing unless O dies within A's lifetime, at which point they get O's reversion.

RULE AGAINST PERPETUTITIES (RAP)

No interest is good unless it must vest, if at all, no later than 21 years (plus a period of gestation) after some life in being at interest creation.

1. Affected Interests: Contingent remainders, executory interests, vested remainders limited in favor of class of persons.
2. "Life in Being": Any life in existence at the time of the creation of the interest that is in any way connected to the interest.

Examples: Parent of class members, person named in instrument of conveyance, life tenant whose death creates interest.

3. "Within 21 Years": Satisfied if it can be shown that the interest vests during the measuring "life in being" plus 21 years (plus any period of gestation for the measuring life); time of death of measuring life is therefore relevant. *Lucas v. Hamm*, 56 Cal.2d 583, 364 P.2d 685 (1961).
4. Special RAP Cases:
   a. Unborn widow:
      i. Gift to issue is invalid.

Examples: O conveys property to son for life, then to son's widow for life, then to issue. Son could remarry a woman not yet born, and pre-decease her before she gives birth to other members of the class.

   b. Fertile octogenarian: *Jee v. Audley*, 29 Eng. Rep. 1186 (Ch. 1787).
      i. Gift to children is invalid

Example: T gives property to A for life, then to A's children "who attain the age of 25."

Example: A could have a child when he is 80 years old, and then die; the youngest child will not reach age 25 within 21 years of the death of A and the gift cannot vest to the entire class of children.

   c. Charitable transfers: RAP is wholly inapplicable to charitable transfers.

CONCURRENT ESTATES

RIGHTS OF CO-TENANTS BETWEEN THEMSELVES

1. Possession: Co-tenants are equally entitled to possession of the property and cannot exclude other co-tenants.
2. Contribution for expenses: Co-tenants in rightful possession of property bear the cost of maintenance and upkeep such as taxes, insurance, and ordinary repairs. *Barrow v. Barrow*, 527 So. 2d 1373 (Fla. 1988).
3. Right to lease property: A co-tenant may lease the property without the consent of the other co-tenants, but lessee takes subject to the rights of the nonconsenting co-tenants. *Carr v. Deking*, 52 Wash. App. 880, 765 P.2d 40 (1988).
4. Accounting: Co-tenant in possession is responsible for accounting of all rents and profits from third party lessees. *Georgen v. Maar*, 2 A.D.2d 276 [3d Dept. 1956], 153 N.Y.S.2d 826 (1956).
5. Ouster/Partition: Co-tenant takes affirmative actions to take sole possession and exclusive use of the property; co-tenant may file action for partition in court to divide property into individual tenancies, unless all co-tenants voluntarily agree to divide. *Penfield v. Jarvis*, 175 Conn. 463, 399 A.2d 1280 (1978).
6. Effect of will: Since a co-tenant's interest ceases at death, the co-tenant has no interest that can pass by will. *Huff v. Metz*, 676 So. 2d 264 (Miss. 1996).

DOCTRINE OF WASTE (TENANT'S DUTY TO REPAIR)

A tenant who is not the owner of land, or possesses the same interest in property at the same time as one or more co-tenants, is responsible to her co-tenants for any decrease in the value of the property through waste. *Kimbrough v. Reed*, 943 P.2d 1232 (Idaho 1997).

1. Permissive Waste: Tenant allows land to fall into disrepair; must preserve land and structures to a reasonable degree.
2. Voluntary (Affirmative) Waste: Tenant cannot use natural resources on land; use is permissible only for repair and maintenance, where permission is expressly given, or where land is only suitable for such use.
3. Ameliorative Waste: Tenant's use substantially changes the value of property, but the use increases the value of the land; may do it where the market value of future interests is not impaired, and change in character of neighborhood deprives the property of value in its current form.

COMMUNITY PROPERTY

1. *Example:* A husband and wife form a community, which is a separate entity that owns property for the benefit of the husband and wife; all property acquired during marriage is generally characterized as community property.

Separate Property: Property acquired by gift, bequest, or devise during the marriage is characterized as separate property, belonging to the individual spouse who receives it.
2. Division of the Community:
   a. At Death: Community dissolves at death of one spouse; each spouse owns half an interest in each community asset.
   b. At Divorce: Community dissolves upon divorce and all community assets are owned by each spouse as tenants in common and may be divided according to settlement.

LICENSES & PROFITS

LICENSE

1. Bare revocable interest to use property for limited purpose and duration.
2. Irrevocable License: Cannot be revoked if consideration is given.

PROFITS

Right to come onto land solely to remove minerals or other value.

TYPES OF PROPERTY INTERESTS

INTERESTS IN THINGS

1. Wild Animals:
   a. Right to possess: Deprive them of natural liberty [*Pierson v. Post*, 3 Cai. R. 175 (N.Y. Sup. 1805).]:
      i. Actual physical possession.
      ii. Mortally wounding/continued pursuit.
      iii. Capture/netting.
2. Natural Gas and Oil:
   a. Right to possess: Whoever extracts first regardless of where.
3. Lost Property:
   a. *Definition*:
      i. Lost: Possessor can no longer find it.
      ii. Mislaid: Possessor voluntarily leaves it, but forgets where.

iii. Abandoned: Possessor voluntarily relinquishes possession; ordinarily belongs to finder.
   iv. Treasure trove: Property hidden and found, owner unknown.
   b. General Rule: Prior possessor has superior rights to finder. *Armory v. Delamirie*, 1 Strange 525, 93 Eng. Rep. 664 (1722).
   c. Owner of Land (*Locus in Quo*): Owner of land where lost property is found has superior rights to finder who is trespasser. *Favorite v. Miller*, 407 A.2d 974 (Conn. 1978).
4. Bailments/Borrowed Property:
   a. *Definition of Bailment*: Owner (bailor) entrusts goods to possession of another (bailee), who is in lawful possession of goods and has title against wrongdoers.
   b. Legal Relationship: Bailee is liable to bailor for negligent damage to goods, or conversion.

OTHER INTERESTS IN LAND

1. Easements: A nonpossessory interest entitling holder to some type of use or enjoyment of another person's land.
2. Covenants/Equitable Servitudes: A covenant is a type of servitude created by deed or contract and whose benefits or burdens "run with the land" to bind successors in interest. When the rules regarding real covenants are not met, the agreement may be enforced in equity as an equitable servitude.
3. Licenses: Owner grants permission to another to use the land.
4. Profits: An easement entitling holder to come onto the land in order to take something off it.

MISCELLANEOUS PROPERTY INTERESTS

1. Bona Fide Purchaser (BFP):
   a. *Definition*: One who takes possession:
      i. In good faith,
      ii. For valuable consideration, and
      iii. Without notice of any wrongful possession.

Types of Property Interests continues on page 2

LEGAL CONSIDERATIONS ARISING FROM LEASE

	SUBLET		ASSIGNMENT	
	Tenant (T1) transfers less than the entire remaining estate to transferee (T2)			
	Privity of Estate	**Privity of Contract**	**Privity of Estate**	**Privity of Contract**
T2 to Landlord (L) Unless	NO	NO	YES	NO
	1. T2 agrees with T1 to assume all lease provisions 2. T2 enters into separate agreement with L			
T1 to L	YES	YES	NO	YES
T2 to T1	T1 can be reimbursed by T2 for any rent paid to L under sublease		T1 can be reimbursed by T2 for any rent paid to L under assignment	

INTEREST OWNED	UNIQUE FEATURES	HOW TERMINATED
...state in perpetuity, lasts forever	Highest estate recognized by law	Never terminated; perpetual
...state in perpetuity, lasts forever	Terminates automatically on occurrence of an event; otherwise lasts forever	Occurrence or nonoccurrence of condition sometime in future, as set out in governing instrument
...state in perpetuity, lasts forever	Doesn't terminate automatically; unless condition occurs, lasts forever	Grantor elects to terminate due to occurrence of condition
...state for duration of owner's life	Assures that lands stay within a family from generation to generation by passing to owner's heirs	Owner's death
...state with duration measured by life of another	Measuring life can be either land holder or another party	Measuring life ends
...esent and future interests can be concurrent.		
...qual right of possession of the whole by each ...o-tenant, regardless of the actual share owned; ...ay be freely conveyed	Modern Law: Any conveyance to two or more people creates a presumption of a tenancy in common	Partitioned through mutual agreement of co-tenants or judicial decree
...qual right of possession of the whole by each ...o-tenant, regardless of the actual share owned; ...owever, cannot be freely conveyed (Right of ...urvivorship: once a co-tenant dies, remain-...g co-tenants take property free and clear of ...eceased co-tenant's interest)	1. Common Law: Any conveyance to two or more people creates a presumption of a joint tenancy 2. Conveyance: If any co-tenant conveys interest, transferee takes as a tenant-in-common, while remaining co-tenants continue to hold in joint tenancy	Partitioned through mutual agreement of co-tenants or judicial decree
...qual right of possession of the whole by each ...o-tenant, regardless of the actual share owned; ...ay be freely conveyed	Any conveyance to two or more people creates a presumption of a tenancy in common	Partitioned through mutual agreement of co-tenants or judicial decree
...e form of duties owed between a landlord and the renter of the land.		
...ight to occupy tenancy for fixed period (year, ...onth, week, or day)	Automatically renews for a like period at the end of the preceding period	Notice must be given by either landlord or tenant a minimum of one whole period before last day of current period; death does not terminate
...ight to occupy tenancy beginning on a fixed ...ate and ending on a fixed date	Can also last for a period measured by the happening of an event or condition	Fixed end date arrives, or ending event takes place; no notice required
...ight to occupy tenancy "at will" as long as both ...e landlord and tenant so desire	Law disfavors; some states have statutes requiring notice to terminate	May be terminated by either party without notice; death of either party can also terminate
...oldover tenant is treated as trespasser and ...victed, or new periodic tenancy is imposed	Landlord has the right to elect either eviction or creation of new tenancy	If landlord chooses to evict, tenancy ends
...metime in the future.		
...alance of estate left after grantor transfers less ...an she has	May or may not become possessory in future; freely alienable, devisable, and descendible	Interest does not become possessory if prior estate given by grantor does not end
...alance of estate in fee simple absolute, left after ...rantor originally transfers less than she has	Landlord has the right to elect either eviction or creation of new tenancy	If landlord chooses to evict, prior tenancy ends
...alance of estate in fee simple absolute, left after ...rantor originally transfers less than she has	Does not go to grantor automatically; grantor must elect to enforce interest	If condition occurs and landlord chooses to enforce interest, prior tenancy ends
...alance of estate in fee simple absolute, left after ...rantor originally transfers less than she has	1. Springing interest: Becomes possessory upon occurrence of a condition, if no present possessory estate exists in another transferee 2. Shifting interest: Becomes possessory after divesting a present possessory freehold	If condition occurs, prior tenancy ends unless property is currently possessed and interest is springing (and therefore cannot divest an existing possessor)

...n interest limited by the existence of a ...urrently possessory estate created at the ...ame time	1. Vested Remainders: Not subject to RAP, possessory right is certain
	  a. Indefeasibly Vested: Born, ascertainable person
	  b. Subject to Open/Partial Divestment: Class of persons, with at least one living member; interests divest in part as new class members are born; class closes when:
	    i. Person who produces class members dies; or
	    ii. Rule of Convenience: When any class member is entitled to demand possession of entitled shares; no outstanding present possessory estates/conditions precedent for any class member
	2. Contingent remainders: Subject to RAP, right to take is uncertain
	  a. Subject to Condition Precedent: Words condition a person's right to take
	  b. Unborn, unascertained persons
		Remainder interest may never become possessory if outstanding, presently possessory estate continues to exist

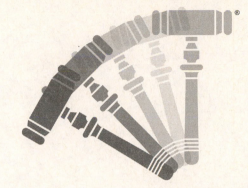

Casenote® Legal Briefs

PROPERTY

Keyed to Courses Using

Singer, Berger, Davidson, and Peñalver's
Property Law: Rules, Policies, and Practices

Sixth Edition

Wolters Kluwer
Law & Business

Copyright © 2014 CCH Incorporated. All Rights Reserved.

Published by Wolters Kluwer Law & Business in New York.

Wolters Kluwer Law & Business serves customers worldwide with CCH, Aspen Publishers, and Kluwer Law International products. (www.wolterskluwerlb.com)

No part of this publication may be reproduced or transmitted in any form or by any means, electronic or mechanical, including photocopy, recording, or utilized by any information storage and retrieval system, without written permission from the publisher. For information about permissions or to request permission online, visit us at wolterskluwerlb.com or a written request may be faxed to our permissions department at 212-771-0803.

To contact Customer Service, e-mail customer.service@wolterskluwer.com, call 1-800-234-1660, fax 1-800-901-9075, or mail correspondence to:

Wolters Kluwer Law & Business
Attn: Order Department
P.O. Box 990
Frederick, MD 21705

Printed in the United States of America.

1 2 3 4 5 6 7 8 9 0

ISBN 978-1-4548-4794-6

About Wolters Kluwer Law & Business

Wolters Kluwer Law & Business is a leading global provider of intelligent information and digital solutions for legal and business professionals in key specialty areas, and respected educational resources for professors and law students. Wolters Kluwer Law & Business connects legal and business professionals as well as those in the education market with timely, specialized authoritative content and information-enabled solutions to support success through productivity, accuracy and mobility.

Serving customers worldwide, Wolters Kluwer Law & Business products include those under the Aspen Publishers, CCH, Kluwer Law International, Loislaw, ftwilliam.com and MediRegs family of products.

CCH products have been a trusted resource since 1913, and are highly regarded resources for legal, securities, antitrust and trade regulation, government contracting, banking, pension, payroll, employment and labor, and healthcare reimbursement and compliance professionals.

Aspen Publishers products provide essential information to attorneys, business professionals and law students. Written by preeminent authorities, the product line offers analytical and practical information in a range of specialty practice areas from securities law and intellectual property to mergers and acquisitions and pension/benefits. Aspen's trusted legal education resources provide professors and students with high-quality, up-to-date and effective resources for successful instruction and study in all areas of the law.

Kluwer Law International products provide the global business community with reliable international legal information in English. Legal practitioners, corporate counsel and business executives around the world rely on Kluwer Law journals, looseleafs, books, and electronic products for comprehensive information in many areas of international legal practice.

Loislaw is a comprehensive online legal research product providing legal content to law firm practitioners of various specializations. Loislaw provides attorneys with the ability to quickly and efficiently find the necessary legal information they need, when and where they need it, by facilitating access to primary law as well as state-specific law, records, forms and treatises.

ftwilliam.com offers employee benefits professionals the highest quality plan documents (retirement, welfare and non-qualified) and government forms (5500/PBGC, 1099 and IRS) software at highly competitive prices.

MediRegs products provide integrated health care compliance content and software solutions for professionals in healthcare, higher education and life sciences, including professionals in accounting, law and consulting.

Wolters Kluwer Law & Business, a division of Wolters Kluwer, is headquartered in New York. Wolters Kluwer is a market-leading global information services company focused on professionals.

Format for the Casenote® Legal Brief

Nature of Case: This section identifies the form of action (e.g., breach of contract, negligence, battery), the type of proceeding (e.g., demurrer, appeal from trial court's jury instructions), or the relief sought (e.g., damages, injunction, criminal sanctions).

Fact Summary: This is included to refresh your memory and can be used as a quick reminder of the facts.

Rule of Law: Summarizes the general principle of law that the case illustrates. It may be used for instant recall of the court's holding and for classroom discussion or home review.

Facts: This section contains all relevant facts of the case, including the contentions of the parties and the lower court holdings. It is written in a logical order to give the student a clear understanding of the case. The plaintiff and defendant are identified by their proper names throughout and are always labeled with a (P) or (D).

Palsgraf v. Long Island R.R. Co.

Injured bystander (P) v. Railroad company (D)

N.Y. Ct. App., 248 N.Y. 339, 162 N.E. 99 (1928).

Party ID: Quick identification of the relationship between the parties.

NATURE OF CASE: Appeal from judgment affirming verdict for plaintiff seeking damages for personal injury.

FACT SUMMARY: Helen Palsgraf (P) was injured on R.R.'s (D) train platform when R.R.'s (D) guard helped a passenger aboard a moving train, causing his package to fall on the tracks. The package contained fireworks which exploded, creating a shock that tipped a scale onto Palsgraf (P).

🏛 RULE OF LAW
The risk reasonably to be perceived defines the duty to be obeyed.

FACTS: Helen Palsgraf (P) purchased a ticket to Rockaway Beach from R.R. (D) and was waiting on the train platform. As she waited, two men ran to catch a train that was pulling out from the platform. The first man jumped aboard, but the second man, who appeared as if he might fall, was helped aboard by the guard on the train who had kept the door open so they could jump aboard. A guard on the platform also helped by pushing him onto the train. The man was carrying a package wrapped in newspaper. In the process, the man dropped his package, which fell on the tracks. The package contained fireworks and exploded. The shock of the explosion was apparently of great enough strength to tip over some scales at the other end of the platform, which fell on Palsgraf (P) and injured her. A jury awarded her damages, and R.R. (D) appealed.

ISSUE: Does the risk reasonably to be perceived define the duty to be obeyed?

HOLDING AND DECISION: (Cardozo, C.J.) Yes. The risk reasonably to be perceived defines the duty to be obeyed. If there is no foreseeable hazard to the injured party as the result of a seemingly innocent act, the act does not become a tort because it happened to be a wrong as to another. If the wrong was not willful, the plaintiff must show that the act as to her had such great and apparent possibilities of danger as to entitle her to protection. Negligence in the abstract is not enough upon which to base liability. Negligence is a relative concept, evolving out of the common law doctrine of trespass on the case. To establish liability, the defendant must owe a legal duty of reasonable care to the injured party. A cause of action in tort will lie where harm,

though unintended, could have been averted or avoided by observance of such a duty. The scope of the duty is limited by the range of danger that a reasonable person could foresee. In this case, there was nothing to suggest from the appearance of the parcel or otherwise that the parcel contained fireworks. The guard could not reasonably have had any warning of a threat to Palsgraf (P), and R.R. (D) therefore cannot be held liable. Judgment is reversed in favor of R.R. (D).

DISSENT: (Andrews, J.) The concept that there is no negligence unless R.R. (D) owes a legal duty to take care as to Palsgraf (P) herself is too narrow. Everyone owes to the world at large the duty of refraining from those acts that may unreasonably threaten the safety of others. If the guard's action was negligent as to those nearby, it was also negligent as to those outside what might be termed the "danger zone." For Palsgraf (P) to recover, R.R.'s (D) negligence must have been the proximate cause of her injury, a question of fact for the jury.

▶ ANALYSIS

The majority defined the limit of the defendant's liability in terms of the danger that a reasonable person in defendant's situation would have perceived. The dissent argued that the limitation should not be placed on liability, but rather on damages. Judge Andrews suggested that only injuries that would not have happened but for R.R.'s (D) negligence should be compensable. Both the majority and dissent recognized the policy-driven need to limit liability for negligent acts, seeking, in the words of Judge Andrews, to define a framework "that will be practical and in keeping with the general understanding of mankind." The Restatement (Second) of Torts has accepted Judge Cardozo's view.

▬

Quicknotes

FORESEEABILITY A reasonable expectation that change is the probable result of certain acts or omissions.

NEGLIGENCE Conduct falling below the standard of care that a reasonable person would demonstrate under similar conditions.

PROXIMATE CAUSE The natural sequence of events without which an injury would not have been sustained.

▬

Concurrence/Dissent: All concurrences and dissents are briefed whenever they are included by the casebook editor.

Analysis: This last paragraph gives you a broad understanding of where the case "fits in" with other cases in the section of the book and with the entire course. It is a hornbook-style discussion indicating whether the case is a majority or minority opinion and comparing the principal case with other cases in the casebook. It may also provide analysis from restatements, uniform codes, and law review articles. The analysis will prove to be invaluable to classroom discussion.

Issue: The issue is a concise question that brings out the essence of the opinion as it relates to the section of the casebook in which the case appears. Both substantive and procedural issues are included if relevant to the decision.

Holding and Decision: This section offers a clear and in-depth discussion of the rule of the case and the court's rationale. It is written in easy-to-understand language and answers the issue presented by applying the law to the facts of the case. When relevant, it includes a thorough discussion of the exceptions to the case as listed by the court, any major cites to the other cases on point, and the names of the judges who wrote the decisions.

Quicknotes: Conveniently defines legal terms found in the case and summarizes the nature of any statutes, codes, or rules referred to in the text.

Wolters Kluwer Law & Business is proud to offer *Casenote® Legal Briefs*—continuing thirty years of publishing America's best-selling legal briefs.

Casenote® Legal Briefs are designed to help you save time when briefing assigned cases. Organized under convenient headings, they show you how to abstract the basic facts and holdings from the text of the actual opinions handed down by the courts. Used as part of a rigorous study regimen, they can help you spend more time analyzing and critiquing points of law than on copying bits and pieces of judicial opinions into your notebook or outline.

Casenote® Legal Briefs should never be used as a substitute for assigned casebook readings. They work best when read as a follow-up to reviewing the underlying opinions themselves. Students who try to avoid reading and digesting the judicial opinions in their casebooks or online sources will end up shortchanging themselves in the long run. The ability to absorb, critique, and restate the dynamic and complex elements of case law decisions is crucial to your success in law school and beyond. It cannot be developed vicariously.

Casenote® Legal Briefs represents but one of the many offerings in Legal Education's Study Aid Timeline, which includes:

- *Casenote® Legal Briefs*
- *Emanuel® Law Outlines*
- Emanuel® *Law in a Flash* Flash Cards
- Emanuel® *CrunchTime®* Series
- *Siegel's Essay and Multiple-Choice Questions and Answers Series*

Each of these series is designed to provide you with easy-to-understand explanations of complex points of law. Each volume offers guidance on the principles of legal analysis and, consulted regularly, will hone your ability to spot relevant issues. We have titles that will help you prepare for class, prepare for your exams, and enhance your general comprehension of the law along the way.

To find out more about Wolters Kluwer Law & Business' study aid publications, visit us online at *www.wolterskluwerlb.com* or email us at *legaledu@wolterskluwer.com*. We'll be happy to assist you.

A. Decide on a Format and Stick to It

Structure is essential to a good brief. It enables you to arrange systematically the related parts that are scattered throughout most cases, thus making manageable and understandable what might otherwise seem to be an endless and unfathomable sea of information. There are, of course, an unlimited number of formats that can be utilized. However, it is best to find one that suits your needs and stick to it. Consistency breeds both efficiency and the security that when called upon you will know where to look in your brief for the information you are asked to give.

Any format, as long as it presents the essential elements of a case in an organized fashion, can be used. Experience, however, has led *Casenote® Legal Briefs* to develop and utilize the following format because of its logical flow and universal applicability.

NATURE OF CASE: This is a brief statement of the legal character and procedural status of the case (e.g., "Appeal of a burglary conviction").

There are many different alternatives open to a litigant dissatisfied with a court ruling. The key to determining which one has been used is to discover *who is asking this court for what.*

This first entry in the brief should be kept as *short as possible.* Use the court's terminology if you understand it. But since jurisdictions vary as to the titles of pleadings, the best entry is the one that addresses who wants what in this proceeding, not the one that sounds most like the court's language.

RULE OF LAW: A statement of the general principle of law that the case illustrates (e.g., "An acceptance that varies any term of the offer is considered a rejection and counteroffer").

Determining the rule of law of a case is a procedure similar to determining the issue of the case. Avoid being fooled by red herrings; there may be a few rules of law mentioned in the case excerpt, but usually only one is *the* rule with which the casebook editor is concerned. The techniques used to locate the issue, described below, may also be utilized to find the rule of law. Generally, your best guide is simply the chapter heading. It is a clue to the point the casebook editor seeks to make and should be kept in mind when reading every case in the respective section.

FACTS: A synopsis of only the essential facts of the case, i.e., those bearing upon or leading up to the issue.

The facts entry should be a short statement of the events and transactions that led one party to initiate legal proceedings against another in the first place. While some cases conveniently state the salient facts at the beginning of the decision, in other instances they will have to be culled from hiding places throughout the text, even from concurring and dissenting opinions. Some of the "facts" will often be in dispute and should be so noted. Conflicting evidence may be briefly pointed up. "Hard" facts must be included. Both must be *relevant* in order to be listed in the facts entry. It is impossible to tell what is relevant until the entire case is read, as the ultimate determination of the rights and liabilities of the parties may turn on something buried deep in the opinion.

Generally, the facts entry should not be longer than three to five *short* sentences.

It is often helpful to identify the role played by a party in a given context. For example, in a construction contract case the identification of a party as the "contractor" or "builder" alleviates the need to tell that that party was the one who was supposed to have built the house.

It is always helpful, and a good general practice, to identify the "plaintiff" and the "defendant." This may seem elementary and uncomplicated, but, especially in view of the creative editing practiced by some casebook editors, it is sometimes a difficult or even impossible task. Bear in mind that the *party presently* seeking something from this court may not be the plaintiff, and that sometimes only the cross-claim of a defendant is treated in the excerpt. Confusing or misaligning the parties can ruin your analysis and understanding of the case.

ISSUE: A statement of the general legal question answered by or illustrated in the case. For clarity, the issue is best put in the form of a question capable of a "yes" or "no" answer. In reality, the issue is simply the Rule of Law put in the form of a question (e.g., "May an offer be accepted by performance?").

The major problem presented in discerning what is *the* issue in the case is that an opinion usually purports to raise and answer several questions. However, except for rare cases, only one such question is really the issue in the case. Collateral issues not necessary to the resolution of the matter in controversy are handled by the court by language known as *"obiter dictum"* or merely *"dictum."* While dicta may be included later in the brief, they have no place under the issue heading.

To find the issue, ask *who wants what* and then go on to ask *why did that party succeed or fail in getting it.* Once this is determined, the "why" should be turned into a question.

The complexity of the issues in the cases will vary, but in all cases a single-sentence question should sum up the issue. *In a few cases,* there will be two, or even more rarely, three issues of equal importance to the resolution of the case. Each should be expressed in a single-sentence question.

Since many issues are resolved by a court in coming to a final disposition of a case, the casebook editor will reproduce the portion of the opinion containing the issue or issues most relevant to the area of law under scrutiny. A noted law professor gave this advice: "Close the book; look at the title on the cover." Chances are, if it is Property, you need not concern yourself with whether, for example, the federal government's treatment of the plaintiff's land really raises a federal question sufficient to support jurisdiction on this ground in federal court.

The same rule applies to chapter headings designating sub-areas within the subjects. They tip you off as to what the text is designed to teach. The cases are arranged in a casebook to show a progression or development of the law, so that the preceding cases may also help.

It is also most important to remember to *read the notes and questions* at the end of a case to determine what the editors wanted you to have gleaned from it.

HOLDING AND DECISION: This section should succinctly explain the rationale of the court in arriving at its decision. In capsulizing the "reasoning" of the court, it should always include an application of the general rule or rules of law to the specific facts of the case. Hidden justifications come to light in this entry: the reasons for the state of the law, the public policies, the biases and prejudices, those considerations that influence the justices' thinking and, ultimately, the outcome of the case. At the end, there should be a short indication of the disposition or procedural resolution of the case (e.g., "Decision of the trial court for Mr. Smith (P) reversed").

The foregoing format is designed to help you "digest" the reams of case material with which you will be faced in your law school career. Once mastered by practice, it will place at your fingertips the information the authors of your casebooks have sought to impart to you in case-by-case illustration and analysis.

B. Be as Economical as Possible in Briefing Cases

Once armed with a format that encourages succinctness, it is as important to be economical with regard to the time spent on the actual reading of the case as it is to be economical in the writing of the brief itself. This does not mean "skimming" a case. Rather, it means reading the case with an "eye" trained to recognize into which "section" of your brief a particular passage or line fits and having a system for quickly and precisely marking the case so that the passages fitting any one particular part of

the brief can be easily identified and brought together in a concise and accurate manner when the brief is actually written.

It is of no use to simply repeat everything in the opinion of the court; record only enough information to trigger your recollection of what the court said. Nevertheless, an accurate statement of the "law of the case," i.e., the legal principle applied to the facts, is absolutely essential to class preparation and to learning the law under the case method.

To that end, it is important to develop a "shorthand" that you can use to make marginal notations. These notations will tell you at a glance in which section of the brief you will be placing that particular passage or portion of the opinion.

Some students prefer to underline all the salient portions of the opinion (with a pencil or colored underliner marker), making marginal notations as they go along. Others prefer the color-coded method of underlining, utilizing different colors of markers to underline the salient portions of the case, each separate color being used to represent a different section of the brief. For example, blue underlining could be used for passages relating to the rule of law, yellow for those relating to the issue, and green for those relating to the holding and decision, etc. While it has its advocates, the color-coded method can be confusing and time-consuming (all that time spent on changing colored markers). Furthermore, it can interfere with the continuity and concentration many students deem essential to the reading of a case for maximum comprehension. In the end, however, it is a matter of personal preference and style. Just remember, whatever method you use, underlining must be used sparingly or its value is lost.

If you take the marginal notation route, an efficient and easy method is to go along underlining the key portions of the case and placing in the margin alongside them the following "markers" to indicate where a particular passage or line "belongs" in the brief you will write:

N   (NATURE OF CASE)
RL   (RULE OF LAW)
I   (ISSUE)
HL   (HOLDING AND DECISION, relates to
      the RULE OF LAW behind the decision)
HR   (HOLDING AND DECISION, gives the
      RATIONALE or reasoning behind the
      decision)
HA   (HOLDING AND DECISION, applies the
      general principle(s) of law to the facts of
      the case to arrive at the decision)

Remember that a particular passage may well contain information necessary to more than one part of your brief, in which case you simply note that in the margin. If you are using the color-coded underlining method instead of marginal notation, simply make asterisks or checks in the margin next to the passage in question in the colors that indicate the additional sections of the brief where it might be utilized.

The economy of utilizing "shorthand" in marking cases for briefing can be maintained in the actual brief writing process itself by utilizing "law student shorthand" within the brief. There are many commonly used words and phrases for which abbreviations can be substituted in your briefs (and in your class notes also). You can develop abbreviations that are personal to you and which will save you a lot of time. A reference list of briefing abbreviations can be found on page x of this book.

C. Use Both the Briefing Process and the Brief as a Learning Tool

Now that you have a format and the tools for briefing cases efficiently, the most important thing is to make the time spent in briefing profitable to you and to make the most advantageous use of the briefs you create. Of course, the briefs are invaluable for classroom reference when you are called upon to explain or analyze a particular case. However, they are also useful in reviewing for exams. A quick glance at the fact summary should bring the case to mind, and a rereading of the rule of law should enable you to go over the underlying legal concept in your mind, how it was applied in that particular case, and how it might apply in other factual settings.

As to the value to be derived from engaging in the briefing process itself, there is an immediate benefit that arises from being forced to sift through the essential facts and reasoning from the court's opinion and to succinctly express them in your own words in your brief. The process ensures that you understand the case and the point that it illustrates, and that means you will be ready to absorb further analysis and information brought forth in class. It also ensures you will have something to say when called upon in class. The briefing process helps develop a mental agility for getting to the *gist* of a case and for identifying, expounding on, and applying the legal concepts and issues found there. The briefing process is the mental process on which you must rely in taking law school examinations; it is also the mental process upon which a lawyer relies in serving his clients and in making his living.

Abbreviations for Briefs

acceptance	acp
affirmed	aff
answer	ans
assumption of risk	a/r
attorney	atty
beyond a reasonable doubt	b/r/d
bona fide purchaser	BFP
breach of contract	br/k
cause of action	c/a
common law	c/l
Constitution	Con
constitutional	con
contract	K
contributory negligence	c/n
cross	x
cross-complaint	x/c
cross-examination	x/ex
cruel and unusual punishment	c/u/p
defendant	D
dismissed	dis
double jeopardy	d/j
due process	d/p
equal protection	e/p
equity	eq
evidence	ev
exclude	exc
exclusionary rule	exc/r
felony	f/n
freedom of speech	f/s
good faith	g/f
habeas corpus	h/c
hearsay	hr
husband	H
injunction	inj
in loco parentis	ILP
inter vivos	I/v
joint tenancy	j/t
judgment	judgt
jurisdiction	jur
last clear chance	LCC
long-arm statute	LAS
majority view	maj
meeting of minds	MOM
minority view	min
Miranda rule	Mir/r
Miranda warnings	Mir/w
negligence	neg
notice	ntc
nuisance	nus
obligation	ob
obscene	obs

offer	O
offeree	OE
offeror	OR
ordinance	ord
pain and suffering	p/s
parol evidence	p/e
plaintiff	P
prima facie	p/f
probable cause	p/c
proximate cause	px/c
real property	r/p
reasonable doubt	r/d
reasonable man	r/m
rebuttable presumption	rb/p
remanded	rem
res ipsa loquitur	RIL
respondeat superior	r/s
Restatement	RS
reversed	rev
Rule Against Perpetuities	RAP
search and seizure	s/s
search warrant	s/w
self-defense	s/d
specific performance	s/p
statute	S
statute of frauds	S/F
statute of limitations	S/L
summary judgment	s/j
tenancy at will	t/w
tenancy in common	t/c
tenant	t
third party	TP
third party beneficiary	TPB
transferred intent	TI
unconscionable	uncon
unconstitutional	unconst
undue influence	u/e
Uniform Commercial Code	UCC
unilateral	uni
vendee	VE
vendor	VR
versus	v
void for vagueness	VFV
weight of authority	w/a
weight of the evidence	w/e
wife	W
with	w/
within	w/i
without	w/o
without prejudice	w/o/p
wrongful death	wr/d

Table of Cases

Trespass

Quick Reference Rules of Law

State v. Shack

State (P) v. Attorney for migrant farmworkers (D)

N.J. Sup. Ct., 277 A.2d 369 (1971).

NATURE OF CASE: Appeal from a conviction of trespassing.

FACT SUMMARY: Tejeras (D) and Shack (D) entered upon private property, against the orders of the owner of that property, to aid migrant farmworkers employed and housed there.

🏛 RULE OF LAW
Real property rights are not absolute; and "necessity, private or public, may justify entry upon the lands of another."

FACTS: Tejeras (D) and Shack (D) worked with migrant farmworkers. Tejeras (D) was a field worker for the Farm Workers Division of the Southwest Citizens Organization for Poverty Elimination (SCOPE), a nonprofit corporation funded by the Office of Economic Opportunity that provided for the "health services of the migrant farm worker." Shack (D) was a staff attorney with the Farm Workers Division of Camden Regional Legal Services, Inc. (CRLS), also a nonprofit corporation funded by the Office of Economic Opportunity that provided (along with other services) legal advice for, and representation of, migrant farmworkers. Tejeras (D) and Shack (D), pursuant to their roles in SCOPE and CRLS, entered upon private property to aid migrant workers employed and housed there. When both Tejeras (D) and Shack (D) refused to leave the property at the owner's request, they were charged with trespassing under a New Jersey statute which provides that "any person who trespasses on any lands . . . after being forbidden so to trespass by the owner . . . is a disorderly person and shall be punished by a fine of not more than $50." After conviction for trespassing, Tejeras (D) and Shack (D) brought this appeal.

ISSUE: Does an owner of real property have the absolute right to exclude all others from that property?

HOLDING AND DECISION: (Weintraub, C.J.) No. Real property rights are not absolute; and "necessity, private or public, may justify entry upon the lands of another." This rule is based upon the basic rationale that "property rights serve human values. They are recognized to that end and are limited by it." Here, a central concern is the welfare of the migrant farmworkers—a highly disadvantaged segment of society. Migrant farmworkers, in general, are "outside of the mainstream of the communities in which they are housed and are unaware of their rights and opportunities, and of the services available to them." As such, here, the "necessity" of effective communication of legal rights and of providing medical services for the migrant farmworkers justifies entry upon the private property. Of course, the owner of such property has the right to pursue his farming activities without interference, but, here, there is no legitimate need for the owner to exclude those attempting to assist the migrant farmworkers. Furthermore, the migrant farmworker must be allowed to receive visitors of his choice, so long as there is no behavior harmful to others, and members of the press may not be denied access to any farmworker who wishes to see them. In any of these situations, since no possessory right of the farmer-employer-landowner has been invaded (i.e., since he has no right to exclude such persons), there can be no trespassing. Reversed and remanded.

▶ ANALYSIS

Generally, the right to exclusive possession is considered "the oldest, most widely recognized right of private property in land." This case, though, illustrates the central limitation on the right to possession or use of private property, i.e., it may not be used to harm others. Here, the exclusion of Tejeras (D) and Shack (D) was, therefore, invalid because it would harm a very disadvantaged segment of society (the farmworkers). Note, that under this principle, an owner of property, also, has no right to maintain a nuisance, to violate a building code, or to violate any "police power" laws (i.e., laws for the general public welfare).

Quicknotes

TRESPASS Unlawful interference with, or damage to, the real or personal property of another.

Desnick v. American Broadcasting Companies, Inc.

Doctor (P) v. Broadcasting company (D)

44 F.3d 1345 (7th Cir. 1995).

NATURE OF CASE: Appeal from dismissal of suit for trespass, defamation, and other torts.

FACT SUMMARY: Dr. Desnick (P) sued American Broadcasting Companies, Inc. (D) for trespass, defamation, and other torts as the result of a broadcast depicting his ophthalmology centers in a derogatory light.

🏛 RULE OF LAW
To enter upon another's land without consent is a trespass.

FACTS: Entine, a producer for American Broadcasting Companies, Inc. (D) Primetime Live show, telephoned Dr. Desnick (P) regarding doing a local segment on cataract practices. Unbeknownst to Desnick (P), Entine dispatched persons equipped with concealed cameras to several of his offices. Employees were secretly videotaped examining the test patients. The broadcast aired, referring to Desnick (P) as a "big cutter," and otherwise portrayed him in a derogatory light. Desnick (P) brought suit claiming trespass and invasion of privacy, fraud, and violation of state and federal law by using electronic surveillance. The trial court dismissed the suit and Desnick (P) appealed.

ISSUE: Is it a trespass to enter upon another's land without consent?

HOLDING AND DECISION: (Posner, C.J.) Yes. To enter upon another's land without consent is a trespass. Consent to an entry is often given legal effect, however, even though the entrant has intentions that if known to the property owner would cause him to understandably revoke his consent. Here, there was no invasion of any of the specific interests that the tort of trespass was designed to protect. The facts do not evidence an interference with the ownership or possession of land. There was no invasion of anyone's private space. Also, American Broadcasting (D) did not reveal the details of Desnick's (P) or anyone else's personal life. Affirmed.

▶ ANALYSIS

Note the fine line between fraud and a misleading omission here. The court uses for an example the case of a restaurant critic, who would not receive the same treatment had he revealed his identity. The law in many areas gives legal effect to consent procured through such types of fraud.

Quicknotes

DEFAMATION An intentional false publication, communicated publicly in either oral or written form, subjecting a person to scorn, hatred, or ridicule, or injuring him or her in relation to his or her occupation or business.

FRAUD A false representation of facts with the intent that another will rely on the misrepresentation to his detriment.

INVASION OF PRIVACY The violation of an individual's right to be protected against unwarranted interference in his personal affairs, falling into one of four categories: (1) appropriating the individual's likeness or name for commercial benefit; (2) intrusion into the individual's seclusion; (3) public disclosure of private facts regarding the individual; and (4) disclosure of facts placing the individual in a false light.

TORT A legal wrong resulting in a breach of duty, which is intentionally or purposefully committed by the wrongdoer.

TRESPASS Unlawful interference with, or damage to, the real or personal property of another.

Uston v. Resorts International Hotel, Inc.

Card counter (P) v. Hotel (D)

N.J. Sup. Ct., 445 A.2d 370 (1982).

NATURE OF CASE: Appeal from lower court decision in favor of plaintiff.

FACT SUMMARY: Uston (P) was well known for his ability to count cards. Resorts International Hotel, Inc. (D) excluded Uston (P) from its casino because his ability increased his chances of winning.

🏛 RULE OF LAW
Owners of property open to the public do not have the right to unreasonably exclude particular members of the public.

FACTS: Uston (P) developed a system of counting cards that allowed him to win at blackjack. Uston (P) was well known for this practice and for teaching the system to others. Because of his ability to increase the chances of his winning, under the Gambling Commission's rules, Resorts International Hotel, Inc. (Resorts) (D) excluded Uston (P) from its casino. Uston (P) brought suit for access. A lower court ruled for Uston (P) and Resorts (D) appealed.

ISSUE: Do owners of property open to the public have the right to unreasonably exclude particular members of the public?

HOLDING AND DECISION: (Pashman, J.) No. Owners of property open to the public do not have the right to unreasonably exclude particular members of the public. The old common law rule gave owners of private property the absolute right to exclude members of the public from the property regardless of the nature of their use of the property. The civil rights amendments and statutes subsequently prevented owners of public facilities from excluding others based on race. To the extent that a property caters to the public, it must also take into account the rights of that public. Uston (P) did not come to the casino to disrupt the activities going on there, nor was he a security risk. Resorts (D) had no legitimate interest in excluding Uston (P) from a place to which the public was invited. Affirmed.

▌ ANALYSIS

The current majority American rule disregards the right of reasonable access applied in the above case. Instead it grants to proprietors of amusement places an absolute right to arbitrarily eject or exclude any person consistent with state and federal civil rights laws. The majority rule may have originated in response to anti-segregation measures taken by the federal government.

■=■

Quicknotes

COMMON LAW A body of law developed through the judicial decisions of the courts as opposed to the legislative process.

STATUTE A law enacted pursuant to the legislature's power and consistent with specified procedure so that it regulates a particular activity.

■=■

Glavin v. Eckman

Neighbor (P) v. Neighbor (D)

Mass. App. Ct., 881 N.E.2d 820 (2008).

NATURE OF CASE: Appeal from jury's verdict in favor of plaintiff.

FACT SUMMARY: Eckman (D) cut down ten large oak trees on Glavin's (P) property without Glavin's (P) permission.

RULE OF LAW
Restoration costs are an appropriate measure of damages for loss of trees when the typical measures such as diminution in value of property or value of the cut timber fail to provide a fair and adequate measure of the plaintiff's damages.

FACTS: Glavin (P) and Eckman (D) owned property near each other on Martha's Vineyard, Massachusetts. In order to improve his view of the ocean, Eckman (D) sought to cut down a number of trees on adjoining property as well as trees on Glavin's (P) property. Eckman (D) asked Glavin's (P) permission to cut down ten oak trees on Glavin's (P) property. Glavin (P) denied the request. Eckman (D) subsequently hired an independent contractor to cut down the trees. The contractor cut down trees on the adjoining land owner's property, with permission, but also cut down the ten oak trees on Glavin's (P) property without any permission. Glavin (P) brought suit under G.L. c. 242 § 7 for wrongful cutting of trees on his property. A jury found for Glavin (P), and awarded him $30,000 in restoration costs based on evidence presented at trial. The trial judge then, pursuant to the statute, trebled the damages due to Eckman's (D) intentional cutting down of the trees. Eckman (D) appealed on the grounds the restoration costs are impermissible under the statute. Eckman (D) also argues that he is not liable for the actions of the independent contractor who actually cut down the trees.

ISSUE: Are restoration costs an appropriate measure of damages for loss of trees when the typical measures such as diminution in value of property or value of the cut timber fail to provide a fair and adequate measure of the plaintiff's damages?

HOLDING AND DECISION: (Grasso, J.) Yes. Restoration costs are an appropriate measure of damages for loss of trees when the typical measures such as diminution in value of property or value of the cut timber fail to provide a fair and adequate measure of the plaintiff's damages. First, it is true that normally, diminution in value of property or cut timber are used as measures of damages. Nothing in the statute, however, limits the measure of damages to those two methods. The trial judge has the discretion to allow any fair and adequate measure of damages. For restoration costs, a test of reasonableness is employed. Here, the cutting down of ten trees was significant, and was carried out willfully. The jury heard expert evidence regarding the restoration of the costs, and their award cannot be said to be unreasonable. Regarding Eckman's (D) argument that he is not liable for the actions of the independent contractor, we disagree. While the contractor had control over the means of the tree removal, Eckman (D) retained control over the scope of the project. Lastly, the judge's trebling of the damages was allowed by statute, and we are not inclined to disagree with a legislative determination that such trebling is appropriate. Affirmed.

ANALYSIS

The significant portion of this decision is its allowance of the restoration damages for tree cutting. As noted in the decision, more traditional measures of damages are most often employed for wrongful cutting of trees. Here, plaintiffs gained a valuable new tool to recover damages for similar factual scenarios.

Quicknotes

DAMAGES Monetary compensation that may be awarded by the court to a party who has sustained injury or loss to his person, property, or rights due to another party's unlawful act, omission, or negligence.

INDEPENDENT CONTRACTOR A party undertaking a particular assignment for another who retains control over the manner in which it is executed.

TREBLE DAMAGES An award of damages triple of the amount awarded by the jury, provided for by statute for violation of certain offenses.

Jacque v. Steenberg Homes, Inc.

Property owner (P) v. Company (D)

Wis. Sup. Ct., 563 N.W.2d 154 (1997).

NATURE OF CASE: Appeal from decision that vacated jury's punitive damages award.

FACT SUMMARY: The Jacques (P) brought suit against Steenberg Homes, Inc. (Steenberg) (D) claiming intentional trespass to their land when Steenberg (D) plowed a path across their field, over their protests, in order to deliver a mobile home.

🏛 **RULE OF LAW**
When nominal damages are awarded for an intentional trespass to land, punitive damages may also be awarded at the jury's discretion.

FACTS: Steenberg Homes, Inc. (Steenberg) (D) was delivering a mobile home. It found the easiest route of delivery was through the Jacques' (P) land. Despite the Jacques' (P) protests, Steenberg (D) plowed a path through the Jacques' (P) field. The Jacques (P) sued Steenberg (D) for intentional trespass. At trial, Steenberg (D) conceded intentional trespass but argued that punitive damages could not be awarded since no compensatory damages had been awarded. Though the jury awarded $1 in nominal damages and $100,000 in punitive damages, the circuit court set aside the punitive damages award. The court of appeals affirmed and the Jacques (P) appealed.

ISSUE: When nominal damages are awarded for an intentional trespass to land, may punitive damages also be awarded at the jury's discretion?

HOLDING AND DECISION: (Bablitch, J.) Yes. When nominal damages are awarded for an intentional trespass to land, punitive damages may also be awarded at the jury's discretion. Steenberg (D) argued that punitive damages could not be awarded by the jury without an award of compensatory damages as a matter of law. The Jacques (P) argued that the rationale supporting the compensatory damage award requirement is not applicable when the wrongful act is an intentional trespass to land. This court agrees. The rationale for the requirement is that if the individual cannot show actual harm, society has little interest in having the unlawful, but harmless, conduct deterred and punitive damages are inappropriate. The issue of whether nominal damages can support a punitive damage award in intentional trespass to land cases is one of first impression. This court has recognized that in certain circumstances of trespass, the actual harm is not the damage to the land, but the loss of the individual's right to exclude others from his property, and has implied that the loss of this right may be punished by a large damage award despite the lack of measurable harm. Thus, the compensa-

tory damages requirement should not apply when the tort supporting the award is intentional trespass to land. Next, we consider whether the $100,000 damage award was excessive. The court must consider three factors in determining whether a punitive damage award violates the Due Process Clause: (1) the degree of reprehensibility of the conduct; (2) the disparity between the harm suffered and the award; and (3) the difference between this remedy and the penalties authorized or imposed in comparable cases. Here the $100,000 award was not excessive. Steenberg's (D) intentional trespass demonstrated an indifference and reckless disregard for the law and for the rights of others. Moreover, such an award is necessary to deter similar conduct in the future. Reversed and remanded.

▶ **ANALYSIS**

The Supreme Court has recognized the interest of a landowner in the right to exclude others from his land as one of the essential property rights. The law recognizes that harm occurs in every trespass to land by the nominal damage award, whether or not actual damages are sustained. The potential harm resulting from intentional trespass to land, which if repeated might ripen into prescription or adverse possession, may result in the owner's loss of property rights. Moreover, society's interest in deterring wrongdoing supports the conclusion in this case as well.

■■■

Quicknotes

COMPENSATORY DAMAGES Measure of damages necessary to compensate victim for actual injuries suffered.

PUNITIVE DAMAGES Damages exceeding the actual injury suffered for the purposes of punishment of the defendant, deterrence of the wrongful behavior, or comfort to the plaintiff.

TRESPASS TO LAND Physical invasion of the plaintiff's property that is intended and caused by the defendant's conduct.

■■■

Lloyd Corporation Ltd. v. Tanner

Property owner (D) v. Protestors (P)

407 U.S. 551 (1972).

NATURE OF CASE: Appeal from federal Circuit Court of Appeals decision holding that protestors (P) had a first amendment right to pass out handbills protesting the Vietnam War within a private shopping mall.

FACT SUMMARY: Tanner (P) and others passed out handbills protesting the Vietnam War within a shopping center owned privately by Lloyd Corporation, Ltd. (D). Security guards from Lloyd (D) removed them from the premises.

RULE OF LAW
An invited member of the public does not have general rights of free speech on privately owned property.

FACTS: Lloyd Corporation, Ltd. (D) owns and operates a large shopping center in Portland, Oregon. All of the stores are located in a large, multi-level building complex. The stores are accessed via the interior of the mall. There are no public streets or sidewalks within the mall. Lloyd (D) has a strict policy banning the distribution of handbills by any person or entity within the mall. Lloyd (D) does allow charitable groups such as the Boy Scouts and the American Legion to use an auditorium within the mall. Lloyd (D) also allows the Salvation Army and similar entities to solicit funds from patrons in the mall. Presidential candidates have also used the auditorium to give campaign speeches. Tanner (P) and others passed out handbills on one occasion protesting the Vietnam War. One customer of the mall complained. Lloyd's (D) security guards removed the protestors from the mall. Tanner (p) brought this suit for a declaratory judgment on the grounds his right to free speech was violated. The lower U.S. District Court (D. Oregon) and the Ninth Circuit Court of Appeals found in favor of Tanner (P). Both courts essentially held the mall was the functional equivalent of a public business district within a municipality. Accordingly, first amendment rights existed within the mall. The United States Supreme Court granted Lloyd's (D) petition for further review.

ISSUE: Does an invited member of the public have general rights of free speech on privately owned property?

HOLDING AND DECISION: (Powell, J.) No. An invited member of the public does not have general rights of free speech on privately owned property. The First and Fourteenth Amendment protect the rights of free speech and assembly against state action, not against of the owner of private property. In a prior case, this Court held that when a corporation owns an entire town and hires the local police to protect the residents, free speech rights do exist in such an entity. In that situation, the private corporation assumed all of the attributes of a municipality. That is not the case here. The mall is completely privately owned and does not provide any municipal services. The public's use of the mall is for private purposes, from shopping to dentist appointments. The sheer size of the mall also is not dispositive. One could not reasonably argue that a small retail store, open to the public, must allow handbilling on or in its premises. The same theory applies to the mall. Reversed.

DISSENT: (Marshall, J.) Lloyd's (D) mall constitutes a public business district where First Amendment rights should be protected. Lloyd (D) invites charitable organizations and presidential candidates to speak at the auditorium within the mall. Lloyd (D) also allows the Salvation Army and similar entities to solicit funds from patrons in the mall. The mall allows the public to shop, to see a dentist, and even lawyers. For many Portland residents, they will be able to receive all of their required services within the mall. If free speech is going to reach these residents, it must do so within the confines of the mall. Although some patrons may be annoyed by protestors passing out handbills, that one factor pales in comparison to the significance of First Amendment rights. As more municipalities allow these types of malls, restricting free speech rights within them will make it harder for citizens to communicate their issues with members of their community.

ANALYSIS

The essential holding of this case remains good law. The First and Fourteenth Amendments protect against only state action, not private action. However, various state supreme courts and legislatures have expanded their state constitutional rights to free speech to include large, quasi-public land, such as shopping malls.

Quicknotes

DECLARATORY JUDGMENT A judgment of the court establishing the rights of the parties.

FIRST AMENDMENT Prohibits Congress from enacting any law respecting an establishment of religion, prohibiting the free exercise of religion, abridging freedom of speech or the press, the right of peaceful assembly and the right to petition for a redress of grievances.

Matthews v. Bay Head Improvement Association

Private citizen (P) v. Homeowner's association (D)

N.J. Sup. Ct., 471 A.2d 355 (1984).

NATURE OF CASE: Action under the public trust doctrine.

FACT SUMMARY: Bay Head Improvement Association (D) permitted only members to use its beach area between 10:00 a.m. and 5:30 p.m. in the summer.

🏛 RULE OF LAW
The public's right to enjoy tidal lands includes a right of access over privately held dry sand lands.

FACTS: Bay Head Improvement Association (the Association) (D) was incorporated as a nonprofit organization to regulate and protect the privately held beaches of the Borough of Bay Head. The Association (D) owned title to 6 of the 26 beachfront lots of land and leased other properties from residents. It operated these lots as a private beach for the benefit of the community, providing lifeguards, beach cleaners, and membership police. The Association (D) limited public access to the dry sand area during certain hours of the day and times of the year. The public could access the foreshore area during low tide from the adjacent boroughs. Matthews (P) brought suit claiming that the public had the right to gain access to the tidal land across the property owned by the Association (D).

ISSUE: Does the public's right to enjoy tidal lands include a right of access over privately held dry sand lands?

HOLDING AND DECISION: (Schreiber, J.) Yes. The public's right to enjoy tidal lands includes a right of access over privately held dry sand lands. Tidal areas and the foreshore are held in the public trust to insure the public's right to use and enjoy such areas. The right to enjoy such areas is meaningless without proper access. The doctrine of public trust also requires that the public has use of the dry sand area so they may fully enjoy their right in the tidal area. Because the Association (D) is a quasi-public institution, it cannot deny the public membership to its beaches. Furthermore, the public right to enjoyment is severely limited by the fact that there are no public beaches in the borough. The public must be given access to the Association's (D) land.

▶ ANALYSIS

The court refrained from stating that the public's interest amounted to a prescriptive easement over privately held beach land. Public use does not readily lend itself to prescription due to the difficulties involved in proving continuous use and taking. In the alternatives, courts have relied on custom and implied dedication to confer access rights.

∎▤∎

Quicknotes

PRESCRIPTION The acquisition of an easement in or on another's property as a result of continuous use for the statutory period.

PUBLIC TRUST DOCTRINE The government holds lands that are submerged beneath the water, or that are capable of being submerged, in trust for the public's benefit.

STATE ACTION Actions brought pursuant to the Fourteenth Amendment claiming that the government violated the plaintiff's civil rights.

∎▤∎

Competing Justifications for Property

Quick Reference Rules of Law

Johnson v. M'Intosh

Landowner (P) v. Landowner (D)

21 U.S. 543 (1823).

NATURE OF CASE: Appeal from action of ejectment.

FACT SUMMARY: Johnson (P) claimed title to a parcel of land through a grant from Native Americans, while M'Intosh (D) claimed the land based on a grant from the newly formed United States government.

🏛 RULE OF LAW
The act of discovery gives the discovering sovereign the power to extinguish the native title of occupancy.

FACTS: In 1763 the King of Britain proclaimed that no British subject could purchase or acquire the land reserved to Native Americans. In 1775, the Tabac Indians conveyed a tract of land in Virginia to Louis Vivant. Thomas Jefferson succeeded to a portion of the lands acquired by Louis Vivant and willed it to his heir Johnson (P) upon his death. In 1776, the colony of Virginia declared its independence from British rule and subsequently acceded to the United States. Fourteen years later, the United States government sold the land in question to M'Intosh (D), who then took possession of the land. Johnson (P) brought an action for ejectment against M'Intosh (D) based on his prior claim. The trial court ruled against Johnson (P), and he appealed.

ISSUE: Does the act of discovery give the discovering sovereign the power to extinguish the native title of occupancy?

HOLDING AND DECISION: (Marshall, C.J.) Yes. The act of discovery gives the discovering sovereign the power to extinguish the native title of occupancy. Although the British government acknowledged Indian possession of the land by the act of discovery, they retained the right to terminate that possession at any time. The Tabac Indians, at most, had the right to convey possession. The discovering country held title to the land. The United States took over Great Britain's claim to title by treaty and, thus, was the party with the authority to transfer the title. Therefore, Johnson (P) was not granted valid title. Affirmed.

▶ ANALYSIS

The Court claims to be applying a kinder rule than that of conquest because it is admitting the existence of a Native American right to occupy the land. However, the Court then states that right to possession is only valid so long as the Native Americans were peaceful inhabitants, thereby immediately negating their rights. Moreover, since absolute title cannot exist at the same time in different governments over the same land, the Court reasons that it would be inconsistent to vest absolute title to the Native Americans as a distinct nation and country.

■=■

Quicknotes

DEED A signed writing transferring title to real property from one person to another.

EJECTMENT An action to oust someone in possession of real property unlawfully and to restore possession to the party lawfully entitled to it.

TENANTS-IN-COMMON Two or more people holding an interest in property, each with equal right to its use and possession; interests may be partitioned, sold, conveyed, or devised.

■=■

International News Service v. Associated Press

Wire service (D) v. Wire service (P)

248 U.S. 215 (1918).

NATURE OF CASE: Appeal from granting of injunctive relief.

FACT SUMMARY: Associated Press (AP) (P) sued to enjoin International News Service (D) from publishing as its own news stories obtained from early editions of AP (P) publications.

🏛 RULE OF LAW
Publication for profit of news obtained from other news-gathering enterprises is a misappropriation of a property right.

FACTS: Associated Press (AP) (P) sued International News Service (INS) (D) for the latter's admitted use of AP (P) news stories in INS (D) publications. INS (D) would obtain advance publication of AP (P) news and would then use such in its newspapers. AP (P) contended it had a proprietary right to all news it gathered through the efforts of its contributors. INS (D) contended any such right terminated upon its first publication. The court of appeals issued AP (P) an injunction, and the United States Supreme Court granted a hearing.

ISSUE: Is the publication for profit of news obtained from other news-gathering enterprises a misappropriation of a property right?

HOLDING AND DECISION: (Pitney, J.) Yes. Publication for profit of news obtained from other news-gathering enterprises is a misappropriation of a property right. News itself is a collection of observable facts that obviously cannot be owned vis-à-vis the public at large. The nonprofit communication of news, regardless of source, is endemic in a free society and involves no property right. However, when two competing news organizations are involved, each gaining their livelihood from beating the other's deadline, the use of such news, for profit, is a misappropriation of the other's product. As a result, injunctive relief is properly issued. Affirmed.

DISSENT: (Holmes, J.) There is no general property right held in the combination of words or the thoughts and facts expressed by those words. Even if it took some labor and genius to produce that combination another person is not excluded from using those same words. However, another ground supporting AP (P) in this instance is that of unfair trade. If its words are repeated in such a way by any competitor, including INS (D), that produces a misrepresentation that materially injures it, then that type of appropriation is actionable. If a competing news service capitalizes upon its competitor's enterprise and expense and releases a contemporaneous story implying that it is the original source, then that amounts to being a fraud. It is a question of how strong an infusion of fraud is necessary to turn a flavor into a poison. The dose seems strong enough here to need a remedy from the law. Having not given proper attribution to the true source of the news reported, INS (D) should be enjoined from publishing news obtained from AP (P) for a number of hours following its publication unless it gives the proper attribution to the true sources of the reporting.

DISSENT: (Brandeis, J.) The issue is whether INS (D) was enjoined in this case because AP (P) gathered the news first or because INS (D) did not reveal the source of the stories it had taken from AP (P) editions. AP (P) contends its news stories are the product of its time and labor, and therefore constitutes property deserving of legal protection. However, the law protects only certain creations of the mind, such as literary efforts, the arts, and inventions. These are all properly protected by copyright statutes. The knowledge and property AP (P) seeks to protect has never been held to deserve protection in the past. Also, INS's (D) manner of using the stories does not constitute unfair commercial practice. There is no breach of contract or fraud involved in INS's (D) manner of purchasing AP (P) newspapers on the open market. Lastly, INS's (D) failure to cite AP (P) as its source does not run afoul of any current copyright laws. Courts are not the proper place for a determination of whether AP (P) has a claim here. The legislature could review such matters and determine that AP's (P) arguments here deserve some measure of protection.

▌ANALYSIS

Some commentators suggest this case as a prime example of the "first in time–first in right" principle of ownership. Some go so far as to argue it provides authority for the proposition that all things created, either tangible or intangible, belong to the creator. This expands the reach of this case beyond news gathering and into any area wherein exclusivity of design or idea is important. This would include everything from clothing design to computer programming.

■▄■

Quicknotes

COPYRIGHT Refers to the exclusive rights granted to an artist pursuant to Article I, section 8, clause 8 of the United States Constitution over the reproduction, display,

Continued on next page.

performance, distribution, and adaptation of his work for a period prescribed by statute.

INJUNCTION A court order requiring a person to do or prohibiting that person from doing a specific act.

MISAPPROPRIATION The unlawful use of another's property or funds.

■▬■

Bayliss v. Bayliss

Ex-wife (P) v. Ex-husband (D)

Ala. Sup. Ct., 550 So. 2d 986 (1989).

NATURE OF CASE: Appeal from decision regarding payment of college expenses.

FACT SUMMARY: Cherry Bayliss (P) sought to have her ex-husband (D) contribute to their son's college costs.

🏛 RULE OF LAW
Alabama trial courts may order divorcing parents to provide for the college educations of their children.

FACTS: Cherry Bayliss (P) and John Bayliss (D) were divorced when their son Patrick was 12 years old. Six years later, Cherry (P) filed a petition to modify the divorce judgment to require that John (D) help pay for Patrick's college costs. Cherry (P) asserted that John (D) had refused to pay although he had ample financial resources. [The lower court ruled that John Bayliss need not contribute to the college expenses. Cherry Bayliss appealed.]

ISSUE: May Alabama trial courts order divorcing parents to provide for the college educations of their children?

HOLDING AND DECISION: (Houston, J.) Yes. Alabama trial courts may order divorcing parents to provide for the college educations of their children. Alabama law provides that the courts may give custody and education to either parent upon granting a divorce. Since 1926, state courts have increasingly determined that college education is a legally necessary expense. Since 1983, Alabama courts have acknowledged that certain necessary support may be required for children who have reached 18 years of age, the age of majority. It is a reasonable interpretation of "children" to include offspring over the age of majority. In the present case, the trial court may order John Bayliss (D) to pay Patrick's college costs if it appears that he probably would assist if there had been no divorce. Therefore, the case is remanded to make this determination. Reversed and remanded.

▶ ANALYSIS

States are split on this issue. At least 19 states agree with Alabama's position. On the other hand, some courts have ruled that when children reach the age of majority, all support duties are ended. See, e.g., *Dowling v. Dowling*, 679 P.2d 480 (Alaska 1984).

■—■

Quicknotes

NONCUSTODIAL PARENT A parent who is not awarded the primary care and control of a child by the court in a dissolution or separation proceeding.

STARE DECISIS Doctrine whereby courts follow legal precedent unless there is good cause for departure.

■—■

Pierson v. Post

Hunter (D) v. Hunter (P)

N.Y. Sup. Ct. of Judicature, 2 Am. Dec. 264 (1805).

NATURE OF CASE: Action of trespass on the case.

FACT SUMMARY: Post (P) was hunting a fox. Pierson (D), knowing this, killed the fox and carried it off.

🏛 RULE OF LAW
Property in wild animals is acquired only by occupancy, and pursuit alone does not constitute occupancy or vest any right in the pursuer.

FACTS: Post (P) found a fox upon certain wild, uninhabited, unpossessed wasteland. He and his dogs began hunting and pursuing the fox. Knowing that the fox was being hunted by Post (P) and within Post's (P) view, Pierson (D) killed the fox and carried it off.

ISSUE: Where property in wild animals is only acquired by occupancy, does pursuit alone constitute occupancy or vest a right in the pursuer?

HOLDING AND DECISION: (Tompkins, J.) No. Property in wild animals is acquired only by occupancy, and pursuit alone does not constitute occupancy or vest any right in the pursuer. One authority holds that actual bodily seizure is not always necessary to constitute possession of wild animals. The mortal wounding of an animal or the trapping or intercepting of animals so as to deprive them of their natural liberty will constitute occupancy. However, here, Post (P) only showed pursuit. Hence, there was no occupancy or legal right vested in Post (P), and the fox became Pierson's (D) property when he killed and carried it off. The purpose of this rule is that if the pursuit of animals without wounding them or restricting their liberty were held to constitute a basis for an action against others for intercepting and killing the animals, "it would prove a fertile source of quarrels and litigation." Reversed.

DISSENT: (Livingston, J.) A new rule should be adopted—that property in wild animals may be acquired without bodily touch, provided the pursuer be in reach or have a reasonable prospect of taking the animals.

▶ ANALYSIS

The ownership of wild animals is in the state for the benefit of all its people. A private person cannot acquire exclusive rights to a wild animal except by taking and reducing it to actual possession in a lawful manner or by a grant from the government. After the animal has been lawfully subjected to control, the ownership becomes absolute as long as the restraint lasts. Mere ownership of the land that an animal happens to be on does not constitute such a re-duction of possession as to give the landowner a property right in the animal, except as against a mere trespasser who goes on such land for the purpose of taking the animal.

◼▬◼

Quicknotes

OCCUPANCY Period of time during which a party possesses and uses real property.

TRESPASS Unlawful interference with, or damage to, the real or personal property of another.

◼▬◼

Popov v. Hayashi

Baseball fan (P) v. Baseball fan (D)

Cal. Super. Ct., WL 31833731 (2002).

NATURE OF CASE: Action for conversion, trespass to chattels, injunctive relief and constructive trust.

FACT SUMMARY: Both Popov (P) and Hayashi (D) intended to establish and maintain control over a baseball that gave Barry Bonds his 73rd home run in 2001, but just as Popov (P) was getting it in his glove, a crowd engulfed him, and brought him to the ground. Hayashi (D), who was near Popov (P) and who also was brought to the ground by the crowd, found the ball and pocketed it. Popov (P) claimed he had established sufficient possession of the ball to gain title to it and brought suit to compel Hayashi (D) to return the ball to him.

RULE OF LAW

Where an actor undertakes significant but incomplete steps to achieve possession of a piece of abandoned personal property and the effort is interrupted by the unlawful acts of others, the actor has a legally cognizable pre-possessory interest in the property sufficient to support a claim of conversion.

FACTS: Barry Bonds, a professional baseball player, hit a record-setting 73rd home run on October 7, 2001. On that day, Popov (P) and Hayashi (D) and many others had positioned themselves in an area of the stadium where Bonds hit the greatest number of home runs in the hopes of catching a record-setting ball (so they brought their baseball gloves with them). The ball hit by Bonds initially landed in Popov's (P) glove, but it was not clear whether the ball was secure there, as Popov (P) may have lost his balance while reaching for the ball. However, even as the ball was going into his glove, a crowd engulfed him and he was tackled and brought to the ground, with people hitting and grabbing him. Hayashi (D), who had been near Popov (P), was also forced by the crowd to the ground, where he saw the ball. He pocketed it and revealed it only when a camera was trained on him, presumably because he wanted proof that he was the owner of the ball. Popov (P), seeing the ball, grabbed for it, believing it to be his, but Hayashi (D) refused to give it to him. Popov (P) then brought suit for conversion, trespass to chattels, injunctive relief, and constructive trust.

ISSUE: Where an actor undertakes significant but incomplete steps to achieve possession of a piece of abandoned personal property and the effort is interrupted by the unlawful acts of others, does the actor have a legally cognizable pre-possessory interest in the property sufficient to support a claim of conversion?

HOLDING AND DECISION: (McCarthy, J.) Yes. Where an actor undertakes significant but incomplete steps to achieve possession of a piece of abandoned personal property and the effort is interrupted by the unlawful acts of others, the actor has a legally cognizable pre-possessory interest in the property sufficient to support a claim of conversion. As an initial matter, there was no trespass to chattels—which requires injury to the chattel—because the ball itself was not damaged and because Popov (P) did not claim that Hayashi (D) interfered with his use and enjoyment of the ball. If there was a wrong at all, it was conversion, which is the wrongful exercise of dominion over the personal property of another. One who has neither title nor possession nor any right to possession may not assert a conversion claim. The key issue, therefore, is whether Popov (P) achieved possession or the right to it. "Possession," however, does not have one meaning; the meaning varies depending on the context in which it is used. Some guidelines, however, do exist, *e.g.*, that possession requires both physical control over an item and an intent to control it and exclude others from it. Here, Popov (P) clearly had the requisite intent, so the issue is whether he had exclusive dominion and control over the ball. Possession in this context is based on custom and what is physically possible. Here, "not only is it physically possible for a person to acquire unequivocal dominion and control of an abandoned baseball, but fans generally expect a claimant to have accomplished as much." Because Popov (P) did not establish by a preponderance of the evidence that he would have retained control of the ball after all momentum ceased and after any incidental contact with other people or objects, he did not achieve full possession. This conclusion does not resolve the case, however, because Popov (P) was attacked illegally by the crowd, and because, therefore, it is unknown whether he would have retained control over the ball absent the crowd's actions. Because Popov (P) has a legally protected pre-possessory interest in the ball, he may advance a legitimate claim to the ball. Hayashi (D), too, was a victim of the crowd's illegal activity, but was able to extricate himself from the crowd. Although Hayashi (D) exercised complete dominion and control over the ball, the ball was encumbered by the qualified pre-possessory interest of Popov (P). Thus, awarding the ball to either of the two parties is unfair to the other. Both have a superior claim to the ball as against all the world, but not against each other; they are equally entitled to the ball. Because the court sits in equity, it may devise an equitable solution to this problem. Here, that solution is equitable division, whereby both Popov (P)

Continued on next page.

and Hayashi (D) have an equal and undivided interest in the ball. Accordingly, Popov's (P) conversion claim is sustained only as to his equal and undivided interest.

▶ *ANALYSIS*

The parties agreed that before Bonds hit the ball, it belonged to Major League Baseball, but that at the time it was hit, it became intentionally abandoned property. Also, to effectuate its decision, the court ordered the sale of the ball, with the proceeds being equally split between the two men. The ball ultimately sold for $450,000—Hayashi (D) estimated that his share would only cover his legal fees.

■━■

Quicknotes

CONSTRUCTIVE TRUST A trust that arises by operation of law whereby the court imposes a trust upon property lawfully held by one party for the benefit of another, as a result of some wrongdoing by the party in possession so as to avoid unjust enrichment.

CONVERSION The act of depriving an owner of his property without permission or justification.

INJUNCTIVE RELIEF A court order issued as a remedy, requiring a person to do, or prohibiting that person from doing, a specific act.

POSSESSORY INTEREST The right to possess particular real property to the exclusion of others.

TRESPASS TO CHATTELS Action for damages sustained as a result of defendant's unlawful interference with plaintiff's personal property.

■━■

Elliff v. Texon Drilling Co.

Landowner (P) v. Oil company (D)

Tex. Sup. Ct., 210 S.W.2d 558 (1948).

NATURE OF CASE: Appeal from reversal of award of damages in negligence action.

FACT SUMMARY: Texon Drilling Co. (D) argued that it should not be liable to the Elliffs (D) after it caused severe damage to the Elliffs' oil drilling operations.

🏛 RULE OF LAW
The law of capture does not insulate a landowner from damages caused by the wrongful drainage of gas and distillate from beneath the land of another.

FACTS: Texon Drilling Co. (Texon) (D) was drilling for oil on land adjacent to the Elliffs' (P) land. The Elliffs (P) owned the surface of their land, as well as an interest in the oil and gas underlying it. They too were involved in drilling on their own land. Texon's (D) well blew out, cratered, and caught fire. The Elliffs' (P) well was destroyed as a result of this blowout, as was the surface of their land, some of their cattle, and a great portion of the underlying mineral reservoir. The Elliffs (P) brought suit for damages, claiming that the blowout was caused by Texon's (D) negligent failure to use the proper drilling mud. The trial court awarded damages. The court of appeals reversed and remanded, stating that the Elliffs (P) could not receive damages for the loss of the mineral estate based on the law of capture since they had no rights in the gas once it migrated from their land. The Elliffs (P) appealed.

ISSUE: Does the law of capture insulate a landowner from damages caused by the wrongful drainage of gas and distillate from beneath the land of another?

HOLDING AND DECISION: (Folley, J.) No. The law of capture does not insulate an adjacent landowner from damages caused by the wrongful drainage of gas and distillate from beneath the land of another. The law of capture states that minerals belong to the party that actually produces them, although part of the minerals, if they are oil or gas, may have migrated from adjoining lands. In other words, there is no liability for reasonable and legitimate drainage from the common pool. However, this does not give any owner the right to waste the gas. In this case, the waste and destruction of the Elliffs' (P) gas was not a legitimate drainage or a lawful appropriation of it. Therefore the Elliffs (P) did not lose their right or title to the gas under the law of capture. Moreover, Texon (D) had a common law duty to exercise due care to avoid injury to the property of others. Since it breached this duty, it should be held liable. Reversed.

▌ ANALYSIS

The court's holding takes into account that advancing technology permits the determination of the approximate amount of oil and gas located in a common pool. However, the rule of capture no longer comes into play vis-à-vis "fugitive" minerals. Instead, oil and natural gas mining is highly regulated by state and federal law.

■━■

Quicknotes

LAW OF CAPTURE The taking or seizing of property by one military force from another.

NEGLIGENCE Conduct falling below the standard of care that a reasonable person would demonstrate under similar conditions.

■━■

Willcox v. Stroup

Possessor of property (P) v. State (D)

467 F.3d 409 (4th Cir. 2006).

NATURE OF CASE: Appeal from lower court decision regarding plaintiff's motion for declaratory judgment.

FACT SUMMARY: Willcox (P), the possessor of Civil War era documents worth $2.4 million, sought a declaratory judgment against South Carolina's Department of Archives (D) that he was the rightful owner of the documents.

🏛 RULE OF LAW
A rebuttable presumption exists that those in possession of property are rightly in possession, absent evidence of superior title in another.

FACTS: Willcox (P) found 444 documents in a closet in his late stepmother's home. The documents contained letters, military reports and telegrams from the Civil War and were valued at $2.4 million. Stroup, the director of South Carolina's Department of Archives and History (D), obtained a temporary restraining order to prevent Willcox (P) from selling the documents. In response, Willcox (P) filed this lawsuit seeking a declaratory judgment that he was the rightful owner. Regarding the chain of title, it appears the documents came to the Wilcox family though a great, great uncle of Wilcox (P). There are certain breaks in the chain and there is no evidence of how Wilcox's (P) late stepmother came into possession of the documents. However, there is no evidence that the documents ever left the Willcox family for the last 140 years. The family did allow the papers to be microfilmed. [The bankruptcy court originally ruled for the state, but the district court found in favor of Willcox (P). Stroup appealed on behalf of the state (D).]

ISSUE: Does a rebuttable presumption exist that those in possession of property are rightly in possession, absent evidence of superior title in another?

HOLDING AND DECISION: (Wilkinson III, J.) Yes. A rebuttable presumption exists that those in possession of property are rightly in possession, absent evidence of superior title in another. Because there is no evidence of a clear chain of title for these papers, common law principles of property take precedence. South Carolina employs the well known rule that one in possession of property enjoys a presumption of ownership. Only clear and convincing evidence of superior title in another will overcome the presumption. The presumption exists to resolve cases such as this where direct evidence of ownership is lacking. In addition, the presumption in favor of possessors promotes stability in society. Lastly, the public will not be harmed by this decision as the family has allowed the documents to be microfilmed for public access. Affirmed.

▶ ANALYSIS

The decision noted at its conclusion that ownership of most state or presidential papers are covered now by statute. Prior to the twentieth century, many politicians retained personal ownership of their own papers. There was no evidence in the record of any South Carolina law that would have granted ownership of the documents in question to the state. Therefore, the case presents a fine example of the rule that possession, absent evidence of title in another, constitutes ownership.

■=■

Quicknotes

POSSESSION The holding of property with the right of disposition.

REBUTTABLE PRESUMPTION A rule of law, inferred from the existence of a particular set of facts, that is conclusive in the absence of contrary evidence.

■=■

Armory v. Delamirie

Jewel finder (P) v. Goldsmith (D)

King's Bench, 1 Strange 505 (1722).

NATURE OF CASE: Action in trover to recover the value of personal property.

FACT SUMMARY: Armory (P) found a jewel. He took the jewel to Delamirie (D), a goldsmith, for appraisal. Delamirie's (D) apprentice removed the stones, which Delamirie (D) refused to return.

> ## RULE OF LAW
> A finder of chattel has title superior to all but the rightful owner upon which he may maintain an action at law or in equity.

FACTS: Armory (P), a chimneysweeper's boy, found a jewel, which he took to Delamirie's (D) goldsmith shop to learn what it was. Delamirie's (D) apprentice, under the pretense of weighing the jewel, removed the stones from the setting and told his master the value. Delamirie (D) offered Armory (P) three halfpence for the stones, but he refused. Delamirie (D) returned the setting without the stones.

ISSUE: Could Armory (P), who lacked legal title to the chattel, maintain an action to recover its value?

HOLDING AND DECISION: [Judge not stated in casebook excerpt.] Yes. The finder of lost property, although he does not acquire absolute ownership, does acquire title superior to everyone else except the rightful owner. Such title is a sufficient property interest in the finder upon which he may maintain an action against anyone (except the rightful owner) who violates that interest. Additionally, Delamirie (D) was liable as he was responsible for the actions of his apprentice. As for the measure of damages, if Delamirie (D) did not show the stones were not of the finest value, their value would be so determined.

▶ ANALYSIS

As to ownership, the finder is in a position similar to that of a bailee. The finder does not obtain absolute ownership, but does have the right of ownership against everybody except the true owner. Here, the chattel, the jewel, was subsequently converted against the finder. Yet the finder, if he should subsequently lose the chattel, may reclaim it from a subsequent finder. The finder has a choice of remedies. He may recover the chattel in specie if it is still in the converter's possession, or he may recover full value from the wrongdoer. Notice that an action in trover, which is an action at law, is to recover the value of the chattel. If it is desired to have the item returned, an action in replevin must be brought in equity.

Quicknotes

BAILEE Person holding property in trust for another party.

Charrier v. Bell

Archaeologist (P) v. Landowner (D)

La. Ct. App., 496 So. 2d 601 (1986).

NATURE OF CASE: Appeal from denial of compensatory and declaratory relief confirming ownership.

FACT SUMMARY: After Charrier (P) uncovered Tunica Indian artifacts while excavating property without the property owner's (D) permission, descendants of the Tunica tribe claimed ownership of the artifacts.

 RULE OF LAW
Ownership in burial artifacts cannot be transferred to another under the theory of abandonment.

FACTS: Charrier (P), an amateur archaeologist, located a Tunica Indian burial site on a privately held plantation. Charrier (P) received permission to excavate from the caretaker but not from the owner. He spent three years uncovering a great number of Tunica artifacts. When he tried to sell the artifacts to a museum, he found he could not do so without proving ownership. Charrier (P) brought suit against Bell (D) and the other landowners to quiet title to the artifacts. The State (D) bought the plantation and took over defense of the suit in favor of the descendants of the Tunica Indians. The trial court found the Tunica-Biloxi Indians to be the owners of the artifacts, and Charrier (P) appealed.

ISSUE: Can ownership in burial artifacts be transferred to another under the theory of abandonment?

HOLDING AND DECISION: (Ponder, J.) No. Ownership in burial artifacts cannot be transferred to another under the theory of abandonment. Charrier's (P) claim to the artifact is based on the theory that the Tunica Indians abandoned them, and he became the owner by finding them. Abandonment requires intent to abandon. Traditionally burial goods do not fall under the classification of treasures to be found. Otherwise burial grounds would be subject to despoilment. When a society buries goods with the deceased person, it is for religious, spiritual or moral reasons, not with the intent that the next person to come along should uncover them. The artifacts were buried with the intent that they would remain there for all eternity. There is thus no intent to abandon connected with burial goods, and finding them cannot transfer them away from the rightful owners. Affirmed.

▶ **ANALYSIS**

Lost property is personal property that has been parted from its rightful owner involuntarily or unintentionally left somewhere and forgotten. Abandoned property has been intentionally relinquished. As a practical matter, however, most states do not make these common law distinctions

any longer; by law, the finder is permitted to claim ownership after depositing the property with the police for a certain amount of time.

■=■

Quicknotes

COMPENSATORY RELIEF Measure of damages necessary to compensate victim for actual injuries suffered.

DECLARATORY RELIEF A judgment of the court establishing the rights of the parties.

OWNERSHIP BY OCCUPANCY Means of acquiring ownership of property by taking possession of property not owned by anyone with the intent to own it.

POSSESSION The holding of property with the right of disposition.

RES DERELICTAE Property that is relinquished by its owner so that the first person to find or occupy the property acquires ownership thereof.

RES NULLIUS The rule that the first person to find property that is not owned by anyone acquires ownership of that property.

UNJUST ENRICHMENT The unlawful acquisition of money or property of another for which both law and equity require restitution to be made.

■=■

Christy v. Scott

Landowner (P) v. Trepasser (D)

55 U.S. 282 (1852).

NATURE OF CASE: Appeal from lower court decision finding that an ejected landowner had no rights to the land at issue against a defendant-trespasser.

FACT SUMMARY: Christy (P) was in actual possession of a tract of land when Scott (D), a trespasser with no title to the land, ejected him.

🏛 RULE OF LAW

A person in actual possession of land has strong enough rights to the land to recover it from a mere trespasser who has no right or title to the land.

FACTS: Christy (P) was in actual possession to a tract of land. Scott (D) ejected him from the land, claiming that the title given to Christy (P) was null and void. Scott (D), a trespasser, had no right or title to the land and was never in possession of it before ejecting Christy (P). Christy (P) brought this action seeking recovery of his land. The United States District Court (D. Texas) found in favor of Scott (D), essentially on the grounds that Christy's (P) title was null and void because it was obtained fraudulently from the State of Texas. The United States Supreme Court granted Christy's (P) petition for further review.

ISSUE: Does a person in actual possession of land have strong enough rights to the land to recover it from a mere trespasser who has no right or title to the land?

HOLDING AND DECISION: (Curtis, J.) Yes. A person in actual possession of land has strong enough rights to the land to recover it from a mere trespasser who has no right or title to the land. Scott (D) does not deny that he has no prior right or title to the land in question. Rather, his defense to the action is that Christy's (P) title to the land is null and void. A mere intruder cannot eject one in possession of the land and then argue that title resides with a third party. As between the two parties in this case, Christy (P), as actual possessor of the land, may recover the land against a simple trespasser. The Court does not decide whether Christy (P) has rights to the land as against the State of Texas, which is not a party to this action. Reversed.

▶ ANALYSIS

This case underscores the primacy of actual possession within the complicated layers of property rights. One who is in actual possession will always have more rights to the land than a mere trespasser. The underlying rationale for the rule is the right to peaceable possession. The law protects actual possessors of land against all except those who have proper title to the land. One who obtains land through force will not obtain any rights to the land.

■—■

Quicknotes

ACTUAL POSSESSION Having direct, immediate and physical control over real property. Unless the possessor is a trespasser, one in actual possession will have superior rights to the property over all others except for one with proper, legal title to the property.

POSSESSION The holding of property with the right of disposition.

TITLE The right of possession over property.

TRESPASSERS Persons present on the land of another without the knowledge or express permission of the owner, and to whom only a minimum duty of care is owed for injuries incurred while on the premises.

■—■

Intellectual and Cultural Property

Quick Reference Rules of Law

Qualitex Co. v. Jacobson Products Co.

Dry cleaning product manufacturer (P) v. Competitor (D)

514 U.S. 159 (1995).

NATURE OF CASE: Review of order reversing finding of a trademark violation.

FACT SUMMARY: Qualitex Co. (P) sought to register a trademark on a color.

 RULE OF LAW
Color alone may be registered as a trademark.

FACTS: Qualitex Co. (P) manufactured and sold pads used by dry cleaners on their presses. The pads made by Qualitex Co. (P) were of a distinctive green-gold color. When Qualitex (P) discovered that Jacobson Products Co. (Jacobson) (D) was also selling pads of the same color, it brought an unfair competition action and also sought to register the color as a trademark. The district court held Jacobson (D) to be in violation of Qualitex's (P) trademark. The Ninth Circuit reversed, holding that color alone could not be registered as a trademark. The United States Supreme Court accepted review.

ISSUE: May color alone be registered as a trademark?

HOLDING AND DECISION: (Breyer, J.) Yes. Color alone may be registered as a trademark. The Lanham Act, which establishes federal trademark law, is quite liberal with respect to the universe of things that can be trademarked. Any symbol that carries a secondary meaning linking it with a particular product may be trademarked. There seems to be no reason why a color cannot fall within this definition. Jacobson's (D) arguments to the contrary are mostly based on pre-Lanham Act common law. Jacobson (D) also argues that since the number of colors is finite, color should not be trademarked. It is not necessary to establish a blanket prohibition for a rare problem. Reversed.

▶ *ANALYSIS*

Numerous things of tenuous tangibility have become trademarks: a bottle shape (Coca-Cola) and sound (NBC Broadcasting Co.). Given this, allowing color to be the subject of a trademark is not unusual.

■■■■

Quicknotes

LANHAM ACT Name of the Trademark Act of 1946 that governs federal law regarding trademarks.

■■■■

Feist Publications, Inc. v. Rural Telephone Service Co.

Publishing company (D) v. Phone book publisher (P)

499 U.S. 340 (1991).

NATURE OF CASE: Appeal from grant of summary judgment to plaintiff in suit for copyright infringement.

FACT SUMMARY: After Feist Publications, Inc. (Feist) (D) took 1,309 listings from Rural Telephone Service Co.'s (Rural's) (P) white pages when compiling Feist's (D) own white pages, Rural (P) filed suit for copyright infringement.

RULE OF LAW

To be copyrightable, a work must be original and possess at least some minimal degree of creativity.

FACTS: As a certified telephone service provided in northwest Kansas, Rural Telephone Service Co. (Rural) (P) published a typical telephone directory as a condition of its monopoly franchise. The white pages alphabetically listed the names, towns, and telephone numbers of Rural's (P) subscribers. Feist Publications, Inc. (Feist) (D) was a publishing company specializing in area-wide telephone directories. The Feist (D) directory that was the subject of this litigation contained 46,878 white pages listings, compared to Rural's (P) approximately 7,700 listings. Feist (D) approached the 11 northwest Kansas telephone companies and offered to pay for the right to use their respective white pages listings. When only Rural (P) refused to license its listings, Feist (D) used them without Rural's (P) consent. A typical Feist (D) listing included each individual's street address, while most of Rural's (P) did not. Of the 46,878 listings in Feist's (D) 1983 directory, 1,309 of those listings were identical to listings in Rural's (P) white pages. Rural (P) sued for copyright infringement. The district court granted summary judgment to Rural (P), and the court of appeals affirmed. Feist (D) appealed.

ISSUE: To be copyrightable, must a work be original and possess at least some minimal degree of creativity?

HOLDING AND DECISION: (O'Connor, J.) Yes. To be copyrightable, a work must be original and possess at least some minimal degree of creativity. This case concerns the interaction of two well-established propositions. The first is that facts are not copyrightable; the other, that compilations of facts generally are. There is an undeniable tension between these two propositions. The key to resolving the tension lies in understanding why facts are not copyrightable. No one may claim originality as to facts because facts do not owe their origin to an act of authorship. Factual compilations, on the other hand, may possess the requisite originality. Compilations were expressly mentioned in the Copyright Acts of 1909 and 1976. Even a directory that contains absolutely no protectable written expression, only facts, meets the constitutional minimum for copyright protection if it features an original selection or arrangement. If the selection and arrangement are original, these elements of the work are eligible for copyright protection. No matter how original the format, though, the facts themselves do not become original through association. There is no doubt that Feist (D) took from the white pages of Rural's (P) directory a substantial amount of factual information. The question that remains is whether Rural (P) selected, coordinated, or arranged these uncopyrightable facts in an original way. It did not. Rural (P) simply took the data provided by its subscribers and listed it alphabetically by surname. There is nothing remotely creative about arranging names alphabetically in a white pages directory. Rural (P) expended sufficient effort to make the white pages directory useful, but insufficient creativity to make it original. Thus, because Rural's (P) white pages lack the requisite originality, Feist's (D) use of the listings cannot constitute infringement. Copyright rewards originality, not effort. Reversed.

ANALYSIS

In the words of the Court, copyright assures authors the right to their original expression, but encourages others to build freely upon the ideas and information conveyed by a work. This principle, known as the idea/expression or fact/expression dichotomy, applies to all works of authorship. As applied to a factual compilation, assuming the absence of original written expression, only the compiler's selection and arrangement may be protected; the raw facts may be copied at will. This is the means by which copyright advances the progress of science and art by encouraging creativity with the reward of exclusive rights for the original creation.

Quicknotes

COPYRIGHT INFRINGEMENT A violation of one of the exclusive rights granted to an artist pursuant to Article I, Section 8, clause 8 of the United States Constitution over the reproduction, display, performance, distribution, and adaptation of his work for a period prescribed by statute.

SunTrust Bank v. Houghton Mifflin Co.

Copyright trustee (P) v. Publisher (D)

268 F.3d 1257 (11th Cir. 2001).

NATURE OF CASE: Appeal from grant of preliminary injunction in copyright infringement action.

FACT SUMMARY: Houghton Mifflin Co. (D) published *The Wind Done Gone* (*TWDG*), a fictional work admittedly based on *Gone With the Wind* (*GWTW*). SunTrust Bank (P), the trustee of the trust that holds the copyright in *GWTW*, alleged copyright violations and sought to enjoin publication of *TWDG*.

🏛 RULE OF LAW
A preliminary injunction of a publication claimed to infringe the copyright of another publication is not proper where there is a likelihood that a fair-use defense will prevail in protecting the allegedly infringing publication and where it has not been shown that the infringing publication will cause irreparable injury to the copyrighted work.

FACTS: The book, *Gone With the Wind* (*GWTW*), written by Margaret Mitchell, has been one of the best-selling books in the world. SunTrust Bank (SunTrust) (P) is the trustee of the Mitchell Trust, which holds the copyright in *GWTW*. Alice Randall authored *The Wind Done Gone* (*TWDG*), a fictional work admittedly based on *GWTW*, which she claimed was supposed to be a critique of *GWTW*'s depiction of slavery and the Civil War era American South. Houghton Mifflin Co. (D) published *TWDG*, and continued to do so despite SunTrust's (P) request that it stop publication. SunTrust (P) brought suit to enjoin publication of *TWDG*, alleging that *TWDG* explicitly referred to *GWTW* in its foreword; copied core characters, character traits, and relationships from *GWTW*; copied and summarized famous scenes and other plot elements from *GWTW*; and copied verbatim dialogues and descriptions from *GWTW*. Houghton Mifflin (D) did not contest the first three claims, but nonetheless argued that there was no substantial similarity between the two works or, in the alternative, that the doctrine of fair use protected *TWDG* because it is primarily a parody of *GWTW*. The district court granted a preliminary injunction, and the court of appeals granted review.

ISSUE: Is a preliminary injunction of a publication claimed to infringe the copyright of another publication proper where there is a likelihood that a fair-use defense will prevail in protecting the allegedly infringing publication and where there has not been a showing that the infringing publication will cause irreparable injury to the copyrighted work?

HOLDING AND DECISION: (Birch, J.) No. A preliminary injunction of a publication claimed to infringe the copyright of another publication is not proper where there is a likelihood that a fair-use defense will prevail in protecting the allegedly infringing publication and where there has not been a showing that the infringing publication will cause irreparable injury to the copyrighted work. The Copyright Clause of the Constitution, based on the English Statute of Anne, was intended by the Framers of the United States Constitution to promote learning, to protect the public domain, and to grant an exclusive right to the author of a work. In the United States, learning is promoted by guarding against censorship and ensuring the public has access to knowledge. The Copyright Act ensures such access by providing an economic incentive for authors to publish books and disseminate ideas to the public. The Copyright Act protects an author's right in derivative works—to prevent imitation—and also only requires that a work be "fixed in any tangible medium of expression" to obtain copyright protection. A copyright is limited in time, so that eventually the work enters the public domain. Finally, an author obtains a limited exclusive right, or monopoly, in order to encourage the creation of original works. The author's ownership is in the copyright, never in the work itself. To balance the goals of the First Amendment (freedom of speech) and the Copyright Clause (limited monopoly by authors), the idea/expression dichotomy and the doctrine of fair use developed. Under the idea/expression dichotomy, copyright cannot protect an idea, but only the expression of that idea. Thus, copyright protects an author's original expression, but encourages others to build freely on the ideas and information conveyed by the work. This supports the First Amendment's goal of open debate and the free exchange of ideas. The Copyright Act also codifies the doctrine of fair use, which contains exceptions to the proscription on copying for such purposes as criticism, comment, news reporting, teaching, scholarship, or research. These exceptions allow later authors to use a previous author's copyright to introduce new ideas or concepts to the public. The issue here is largely whether a preliminary injunction was properly granted against an alleged infringer who, relying on the fair use doctrine, made use of another's copyright for comment and criticism. The answer to this question becomes an analysis of the fair use factors.

The framework for this analysis is the standard test governing the issuance of preliminary injunctions. To prevail, SunTrust (P) must prove four elements: (1) substantial likelihood of success on the merits; (2) substantial threat of irreparable injury if the injunction is not granted; (3) that the threatened injury to the plaintiff outweighs the

Continued on next page.

harm an injunction may cause to the defendant; and (4) a grant of the injunction will not be adverse to the public interest. As to the first of these elements, the initial step in evaluating the likelihood that SunTrust (P) will succeed on the merits is to determine whether it has established a *prima facie* case of copyright infringement. This, in turn, has two elements: (1) SunTrust owns a valid copyright in *GWTW* (this element is not disputed); and (2) that Randall copied original elements of *GWTW* in *TWDG*. This requires a determination of the extent that Randall copied original expression—not ideas. However, there is no bright line that separates original expression from nonprotectable ideas. Stock scenes and hackneyed characters, also known as *scenes a faire*, are considered ideas. As plots and characters become more detailed and idiosyncratic, they become original expression. A review of the two works here reveals that *TWDG* made substantial use of *GWTW*, appropriating numerous characters, settings, plot twists, and relationships from *GWTW*. Particularly in its first half, *TWDG* is largely an encapsulation of *GWTW* that exploits its copyrighted elements. Thus, a *prima facie* case has been established.

Fair Use
Nonetheless, Randall's appropriation of elements of *GWTW* in *TWDG* may not constitute infringement of SunTrust's (P) copyright if the taking is protected as a "fair use." The factors for determining fair use are (1) the purpose and character of the use, including whether such use is commercial or is for nonprofit educational purposes; (2) the nature of the copyrighted work; (3) the amount and substantiality of the portion used in relation to the copyrighted work as a whole; and (4) the effect of the use upon the potential market for or value of the copyrighted work. Houghton Mifflin (D) argues that *TWDG* is entitled to fair-use protection as a parody of *GWTW*. Parody is a form of comment and criticism that may constitute fair use of the work being parodied, and is directed at a particular literary or artistic work. Thus, parody needs to mimic an original to make its point—it must borrow elements from the work being parodied. However, not every parody is a fair use, and every claimed parody must be evaluated in terms of all the elements set forth in the Copyright Act and the constitutional purposes of copyright law. *TWDG* is clearly a parody because it is a specific criticism and rejoinder to the depiction of slavery and the relationships between blacks and whites in *GWTW* that is effected through the appropriation of elements of the original work in creating a new artistic work. Given that *TWDG* meets the definition of a parody of *GWTW*, it must be assessed under the four fair-use factors.

i. Purpose and Character of the Work
First, *TWDG* is undoubtedly a commercial product, as it was published for profit. However, *TWDG*'s for-profit status is strongly outweighed by its highly transformative use of *GWTW*'s copyrighted elements. A work's transformative value is of special importance where a parody is involved, since a parody's aim is, by definition, to transform an earlier work. Here, the degree of transformation is a double-edged sword: on the one hand, *TWDG* adds new expression, meaning, and message to *GWTW*, but on the other, to succeed as a work of fiction, it must draw heavily on copyrighted elements taken from *GWTW*. Thematically, the new work provides a significantly different viewpoint of the antebellum world, and the new work inverts the original by the way it is told and through the words that it uses to tell the new story. Additionally, the last half of *TWDG* tells a completely new story that, although involving characters based on *GWTW* characters, features plot elements found nowhere in *GWTW*. For example, in *TWDG*, nearly every black character is given some redeeming quality that their *GWTW* analogues lacked. In light of this, it is difficult to conclude that Randall simply was lazy and wanted to avoid the hard work of creating something new. Randall has, instead, used the conscripted elements of the original to make war against it. Therefore, *TWDG* reflects transformative value because it can "provide social benefit, by shedding light on an earlier work, and, in the process, creating a new one." Consideration of this factor militates in favor of finding fair use.

ii. Nature of the Copyrighted Work
Although *GWTW* is entitled to the greatest degree of copyright protection as an original work of fiction, this factor is given little weight in a parody case because parodies almost invariably copy publicly known, expressive works.

iii. Amount and Substantiality of the Portion Used
This factor presents particular difficulty in the context of a parody. Parody must take enough of an original to conjure up the original to make the object of its critical wit recognizable. Once enough has been taken to "conjure up" the original, however, any further taking must specifically serve the new work's parodic aims. SunTrust (P) argues that because *GWTW* is so popular and well known, very little reference is required to conjure up *GWTW*. Houghton Mifflin (D) counters that *TWDG* takes nothing from *GWTW* that does not serve a parodic purpose. There are numerous minor details that Randall takes from *GWTW* that arguably do not serve a parodic purpose, and numerous elements that clearly are transformative. However, in determining fair use, it must be kept in mind that literary relevance is a highly subjective analysis ill-suited for judicial inquiry. The law is clear that parodists need not take only a bare minimum amount of copyrighted material necessary to conjure up the original, as parody needs to be more than a fleeting evocation of an original to make its humorous point. Even more extensive use than necessary to conjure up the original may still be fair use, provided the parody builds on the original. How much more is reasonable depends on the extent to which the work's overriding purpose is to parody the original (here, that is *TWDG*'s *raison d'etre*), or, in contrast, the likelihood that the parody

Continued on next page.

may serve as a market substitute for the original (here, based on the record at this juncture, it is not possible to conclude with certainty whether the quantity and value of the materials used are reasonable in relation to the purpose of the copying).

iv. Effect on the Market Value of the Original
This factor requires a consideration of the effect that the publication of *TWDG* will have on the market for or value of SunTrust's (P) copyright in *GWTW*, including the potential harm it may cause to the market for derivative works based on *GWTW*—in particular the harm of market substitution. Although SunTrust (P) offered evidence that its copyright in *GWTW* and several authorized derivative works has a very high value, it fails to present evidence or argument that *TWDG* would supplant demand for Sun-Trust's (P) licensed derivatives. Particularly in cases of parody, evidence of harm to the potential market for or value of the original copyright is crucial to a fair use determination. In contrast, the evidence offered by Houghton Mifflin (D) focuses on market substitution and demonstrates why *TWDG* is unlikely to displace sales of *GWTW*. Accordingly, this factor weighs in favor of *TWDG*. In light of the weight given to these factors, *TWDG* is entitled to a fair-use defense.

▌ *ANALYSIS*

Under the current Copyright Act, most copyrights for works created after 1978 last for the lifetime of the author plus 70 years. The United States Supreme Court rejected claims that this extension of the copyright term (which had been shorter) violated the Constitution's mandate that copyrights granted to authors be for "limited times." With a work as old as *GWTW*, on which the original copyright may soon expire, creation of a derivative work only serves to protect that which is original to the latter work and does not extend the copyright in the copyrightable elements of the original work (§ 103(b)).

■▬■

Quicknotes

COPYRIGHT ACT   Copyright Act of 1976 extends copyright protection to "original works of authorship fixed in any tangible medium of expression, now known or later developed, from which they can be perceived, reproduced, or otherwise communicated, either directly or with the aid of a machine or device." 17 U.S.C. § 102.

FAIR-USE DEFENSE   An affirmative defense to a claim of copyright infringement providing an exception from the copyright owner's exclusive rights in a work for the purposes of criticism, comment, news reporting, teaching, scholarship or research; the determination of whether a use is fair is made on a case-by-case basis and requires the court to consider: (1) the purpose and character of the use; (2) the nature of the work; (3) the amount and substantiality of the portion used; and (4) the effect of the use on the potential market for, or value of, the work.

■▬■

Association for Molecular Pathology v. Myriad Genetics, Inc.

Challengers to patent (P) v. Patent holder (D)

133 S. Ct. 2107 (2013).

NATURE OF CASE: Appeal from a decision by the United States Court of Appeals for the Federal Circuit holding that Myriad's (D) patent for two human genes was valid.

FACT SUMMARY: Using a widely known process to isolate DNA and human genes, Myriad Genetics, Inc. (D) successfully identified and isolated two specific human genes naturally occurring in the human body. Mutations in these two genes can significantly increase a woman's risk of developing breast and ovarian cancer.

RULE OF LAW
Laws of nature, natural phenomena, and abstract ideas are not patentable because they are tools of scientific and technological work that lay beyond the domain of patent protection.

FACTS: Myriad Genetics, Inc. (Myriad) (D) successfully identified and isolated two specific human genes that exist naturally in the human body. Mutations in these two genes, BRCA1 and BRCA2, can significantly increase a woman's risk of developing breast and ovarian cancer. Myriad (D) discovered the two genes using a widely recognized method of identifying such genes. Many other entities and scientists employed the same method. After discovery of the two genes that related to breast and ovarian cancer, Myriad (D) sought a patent that would give it the exclusive right to perform genetic testing on women by isolating and examining the genes at issue. Myriad (D) also sought a patent to synthetically create the two genes to allow for further research. After Myriad (D) received the patents, a group of advocacy groups, patients, and physicians known as the Association for Molecular Pathology (P) brought suit against Myriad (D), challenging the validity of the patents. A federal District Court found the patents invalid because they involved genes that occurred naturally. The United States Court of Appeals for the Federal Circuit reversed and held that Myriad's (D) patent for the two human genes was valid. The United States Supreme Court vacated that decision and returned the case to the Court of Appeals. That court disagreed over the patentability of the two genes but did find that the creation of synthetic genes was patentable. The United States Supreme Court again granted the petition for further review.

ISSUE: Are laws of nature, natural phenomena, and abstract ideas not patentable because they are tools of scientific and technological work that lay beyond the domain of patent protection?

HOLDING AND DECISION: (Thomas, J.) Yes. Laws of nature, natural phenomena, and abstract ideas are not patentable because they are tools of scientific and technological work that lay beyond the domain of patent protection. 35 U.S.C. § 101 provides that "whoever invents or discovers any new or useful . . . composition of matter, or useful improvement thereof, may obtain a patent therefor." However, laws of nature or natural phenomena are generally not patentable. Granting patents in these cases would tie up research tools and potentially inhibit further innovations. Patent law strikes a balance between creating incentives that lead to inventions and impeding the flow of knowledge and information that assists with such inventions and creations. The issue in this case is: do Myriad's (D) patents relate to "new and useful composition of matter," or naturally occurring phenomena? Regarding the two genes, BRCA1 and BRCA2, Myriad (D) did not create anything. It did discover the two genes, but the act of separating those genes and identifying them is not an act of creation. In addition, the method of identifying genes is well known and widely employed. However, Myriad's (D) creation of the two synthetic genes resembling BRCA1 and BRCA2 is patentable. Synthetic DNA or cDNA is distinct from the naturally occurring DNA from which it is derived. To create the cDNA, a lab technician must isolate only part of a DNA strand as opposed to the entire strand. This portion of a gene is therefore not something that naturally occurs. The lab technician must take steps to add nucleotides to create a synthetic DNA molecule. There is no question the lab technician is creating something new in this situation. Accordingly, Myriad's (D) patent relating to the creation of synthetic BRCA1 and BRCA2 is patentable. Reversed in part and affirmed in part.

ANALYSIS

This unanimous decision from the United States Supreme Court explains the well-known patent exception for things that occur naturally. The case deals with patentability, the first of five requirements an invention must meet before it can be patented. The five requirements are: (1) the subject matter must be a composition of matter or a method of manufacture; (2) the invention must be novel; (3) the invention must be nonobvious; (4) the invention must be useful; and (5) the invention must be particularly described.

Quicknotes

PATENT A limited monopoly conferred on the invention or discovery of any new or useful machine or process that is novel and nonobvious.

Juicy Whip, Inc. v. Orange Bang, Inc.

Patent holder (P) v. Alleged patent infringer (D)

185 F.3d 1364 (Fed. Cir. 1999).

NATURE OF CASE: Appeal from lower court decision finding that the plaintiff's patent was invalid because it lacked the requirement of utility.

FACT SUMMARY: Juicy Whip, Inc. (P), a manufacturer of beverage dispensers, created a dispenser that displayed a previously mixed beverage in an opaque bowl, leading consumers to believe they would receive their drinks directly from that bowl. Instead, when the operator poured the beverage, the dispenser would combine water from one bowl and syrup concentrate from a separate, hidden bowl to create the beverage.

RULE OF LAW
An invention does not lack the utility requirement for patentability simply because it deceives the public through imitation in an effort to increase product sales.

FACTS: Juicy Whip, Inc. (P), a manufacturer of beverage dispensers, created a dispenser that displayed a previously mixed beverage in an opaque bowl, leading consumers to believe they would receive their drinks directly from that bowl. Instead, when the operator poured the beverage, the dispenser would combine water from one bowl and syrup concentrate from a separate, hidden bowl to create the beverage. Juicy Whip (P) received a patent for the post-mix dispenser. The term post-mix derives from the time of the mixing. The mixing only occurs after a consumer has ordered the drink. Juicy Whip (P) brought this infringement suit against Orange Bang (D) after discovering Orange Bang (D) was using similar machines. Orange Bang (D) defended the suit on the grounds Juicy Whip (P) was deceiving its customers by appearing to dispense "pre-mix" beverages when in actuality, the beverages were of the post-mix variety. The lower court granted Orange Bang's (D) motion for summary judgment on the ground Juicy Whip's (P) hidden-bowl, post-mix dispenser lacked utility. The court found Juicy Whip's (P) only purpose was to increase sales by deceiving customers into thinking they were receiving their beverages directly from the opaque, pre-mixed bowl in front of them. Juicy Whip (P) appealed to the United States Court of Appeals for the Federal Circuit.

ISSUE: Does an invention lack the utility requirement for patentability simply because it deceives the public through imitation in an effort to increase product sales?

HOLDING AND DECISION: (Bryson, J.) No. An invention does not lack the utility requirement for patentability simply because it deceives the public through imitation in an effort to increase product sales. 35 U.S.C.

§ 101 provides that whoever invents or discovers any new or useful composition of matter or improvement thereof, may obtain a patent therefor. The threshold for utility or usefulness is low. An invention is useful if it can provide some identifiable benefit. A patent will fail for lack of utility only if it is totally incapable of achieving a useful result. Altering a product to make it imitate another product is itself a specific benefit that satisfies the utility requirement. Cubic zirconium is designed to appear as a diamond and imitation leather is designed to appear real. Laminated wood is designed to mimic the appearance of real wood. All of these have had valid patents. The value of these products is that they appear to be something they are not. Here, Juicy Whip's (P) post-mix dispenser satisfies the utility requirement by embodying the features of a post-mix dispenser while imitating the outward appearance of a pre-mix dispenser. The fact that Juicy Whip (P) is allegedly deceiving its customers does not override the utility of the invention. The federal Patent Office does not serve as arbiter of alleged deceptive trade practices. In addition, Orange Bang (D) has not argued there is anything illegal with the display of a drink that is not actually served to the customers. Accordingly, the district court erred in granting summary judgment to Orange Bang (D). Reversed.

▶ ANALYSIS

The decision highlighted Justice Joseph Story's seminal patent opinion in *Lowell v. Lewis*, 15 F. Cas. 1018 (C.C.D. Mass. 1817). In that case, Justice Story, who went on to become a United States Supreme Court justice, held that inventions that are injurious to the well-being or sound morals of society are not patentable. Over the years, courts have moved away from the rigid, morals-based law regarding patents in favor of the utility test as codified in 35 U.S.C. § 101.

▬▬▬

Quicknotes

PATENT A limited monopoly conferred on the invention or discovery of any new or useful machine or process that is novel and nonobvious.

SUMMARY JUDGMENT Judgment rendered by a court in response to a motion made by one of the parties, claiming that the lack of a question of material fact in respect to an issue warrants disposition of the issue without consideration by the jury.

▬▬▬

eBay Inc. v. MercExchange, L.L.C

Alleged patent infringer (D) v. Patent holder (P)

547 U.S. 388 (2006).

NATURE OF CASE: Appeal from a decision by the United States Court of Appeals for the Federal Circuit to allow patent holder's motion for a permanent injunction against a patent infringer.

FACT SUMMARY: MercExchange, L.L.C. (P) holds a valid business method patent for an electronic, internet-based market used for the sale of goods between private individuals. It brought a patent infringement suit against eBay Inc. (D) and a subsidiary, Half.com (D).

RULE OF LAW
Under the Patent Act, a court has discretion to issue an equitable injunction against a patent infringer only if the patent holder can satisfy the well-established, four-factor test for the issuance of a permanent injunction.

FACTS: MercExchange, L.L.C. (P) holds a valid business method patent for an electronic, internet-based market used for the sale of goods between private individuals. MercExchange (P) sought to license its patent to eBay, Inc. (D) but negotiations failed. MercExchange (P) then brought a patent infringement suit against eBay (D) and a subsidiary, Half.com (D), for using a similar internet-based market to sell goods. A jury in United States District Court for the Eastern District of Virginia found that MercExchange's (P) patent was valid and awarded it damages. MercExchange (P) then filed a motion for a permanent injunction to prohibit eBay (D) from employing its internet-based market. The federal district court denied the motion but the United States Court of Appeals for the Federal Circuit reversed. It held that, as a general rule, courts should issue permanent injunctions against patent infringers. The United States Supreme Court granted eBay's (D) petition for further review.

ISSUE: Under the Patent Act, does a court have discretion to issue an equitable injunction against a patent infringer only if the patent holder can satisfy the well-established, four-factor test for the issuance of a permanent injunction?

HOLDING AND DECISION: (Thomas, J.) Yes. Under the Patent Act, a court has discretion to issue an equitable injunction against a patent infringer only if the patent holder can satisfy the well-established, four-factor test for the issuance of a permanent injunction. A plaintiff must demonstrate: (1) that it has suffered an irreparable injury; (2) that remedies available at law, such as monetary damages, are inadequate to compensate for that injury; (3) that considering the balance of hardships between the

plaintiff and defendant, a remedy in equity is warranted; and (4) that the public interest would not be disserved by a permanent injunction. Accordingly, a finding of a patent infringement does not automatically warrant the issuance of a permanent injunction as the circuit court contends. This Court has similarly held that a copyright infringement does not necessarily lead to a permanent injunction. Traditional equitable considerations remain paramount and each motion for a permanent injunction must be made on a case-by-case basis. Because neither the district court nor the circuit court applied the four-factor test for the issuance of permanent injunctions, the circuit court's decision is vacated. The case is remanded to the district court for a consideration of MercExchange's (P) motion for a permanent injunction based upon traditional equitable principles. Reversed and remanded.

CONCURRENCE: (Roberts, C.J.) The majority is correct that courts should not automatically issue injunctions based on patent infringements. However, since the 19th century, courts in a majority of cases have issued various forms of equitable injunctive relief after finding that a patent has been infringed. While equitable considerations remain paramount, courts should look to prior decisions for guidance when issuing injunctions in patent cases.

CONCURRENCE: (Kennedy, J.) The Patent Act and the principles surrounding the issuance of a permanent injunction recognize that the existence of a right to exclude does not dictate the scope of the remedy for a violation of that right. While a review of historical practice may be beneficial, the economic function of the patent in many current cases is very different from earlier cases. Today, many companies obtain patents for the sole purpose of licensing those patents. Accordingly, once the patent is obtained, the holder then has the ability to threaten an injunction on another potential rival if it refuses to execute a license agreement. In these cases, where a violation is found, monetary damages may be more appropriate than a permanent injunction.

ANALYSIS

Justice Kennedy's concurring opinion relates to the rise of companies that exist solely to purchase patents. These companies then demand licensing fees from other companies that have created an invention, perhaps totally unaware that a patent already exists for the product. Accordingly, even where a patent may technically be

Continued on next page.

infringed, a permanent injunction should be avoided where the patent holder exists solely to obtain license fees.

━━■

Quicknotes

INJUNCTIVE RELIEF A court order issued as a remedy, requiring a person to do, or prohibiting that person from doing, a specific act.

LICENSE A right that is granted to a person allowing him or her to conduct an activity that without such permission he or she could not lawfully do, and which is unassignable and revocable at the will of the licensor.

PERMANENT INJUNCTION A remedy imposed by the court ordering a party to cease the conduct of a specific activity until the final disposition of the cause of action.

━━■

Martin Luther King, Jr. Center for Social Change v. American Heritage Products

Nonprofit organization (P) v. Manufacturer (D)

Ga.Sup. Ct., 296 S.E.2d 697 (1982).

NATURE OF CASE: Certified question from Eleventh Circuit Court of Appeals to Georgia Supreme Court.

FACT SUMMARY: Martin Luther King, Jr. Center for Social Change (P) sued Bolen (D) for the unauthorized development and marketing of a plastic bust of Dr. Martin Luther King, Jr.

RULE OF LAW
Public figures have a right of publicity that survives the death of the figure, and thus is inheritable and devisable, the measure of damages for violation of which is the value of the appropriation to the user.

FACTS: Bolen (D) is the sole proprietor of a business that manufactures and sells plastic products as funeral accessories. He developed the concept of marketing a plastic bust of Martin Luther King, Jr., and formed a company in order to sell them. Although Bolen (D) sought the endorsement of Martin Luther King, Jr. Center for Social Change (the Center) (P), it refused to endorse the product. He nevertheless pursued the idea, hiring persons to prepare the model and taking out advertising. The Center (P) filed suit demanding Bolen (D) cease and desist from further marketing and development of the bust. The Eleventh Circuit Court of Appeals certified the question to this Court of whether a right of publicity exists in the state of Georgia, and whether it is devisable and inheritable.

ISSUE: Do public figures have a right of publicity that survives the death of the figure, and thus is inheritable and devisable, the measure of damages for violation of which is the value of the appropriation to the user?

HOLDING AND DECISION: (Hill, Jr., Presiding J.) Yes. Public figures have a right of publicity that survives the death of the figure, and thus is inheritable and devisable, the measure of damages for violation of which is the value of the appropriation to the user. Similar to the right of privacy in private figures, a public figure has a right in the publicity value of his likeness, the rationale for which is the prevention of unjust enrichment. Private citizens as well as public ones have a right not to have their names and photographs used for financial gain of the user without their consent. Furthermore the right of publicity is inheritable and devisable, and as such furthers the purpose of rewarding and encouraging effort and creativity. There is no requirement that the owner of the right have commercially exploited it before his death for the right to survive.

CONCURRENCE: (Weltner, J.) This new right of publicity jeopardizes the right to freedom of speech.

ANALYSIS

The right of publicity has been extended to also apply to imitations of public figures. Several California cases have held that where a well-known singer's voice is deliberately imitated in order to sell merchandise, misappropriation of the celebrity's likeness has occurred.

Quicknotes

FREEDOM OF SPEECH The right to express oneself without governmental restrictions on the content of that expression.

RIGHT OF PUBLICITY The right of a person to control the commercial exploitation of his name or likeness.

UNJUST ENRICHMENT The unlawful acquisition of money or property of another for which both law and equity require restitution to be made.

United States v. Schultz

Federal government (P) v. Criminal defendant (D)

178 F. Supp. 2d 445 (S.D.N.Y. 2002).

NATURE OF CASE: Federal district court's consideration of defendant's motion to dismiss the criminal indictment against him.

FACT SUMMARY: The Government (P) charged Schultz (D) with conspiracy to steal valuable ancient artifacts from Egypt and sell them in New York City.

🏛 RULE OF LAW
Because Egypt mandated by law that all ancient artifacts and antiquities discovered in Egypt after 1983 constitute state property, a criminal defendant may be guilty of conspiracy by arranging to receive or dispose of any such antiquities that have crossed a state line or a United States boundary.

FACTS: The Government (P) charged Schultz (D) with conspiracy to steal valuable ancient artifacts from Egypt and sell them in New York City. One of the items was the head of Egyptian Pharaoh Amenhotep III. Prior to trial, Schultz (D) moved to dismiss the indictment. He argued principally that even though Egypt Law 117 mandated that all Egyptian antiquities are property of the government of Egypt, that law created instead a licensing scheme for antiquities. Accordingly, a violation of that scheme would not rise to the level appropriating "stolen" goods in violation of § 2315 of Title 18 of the United States Code. This decision is the federal district court's consideration of Schultz's (D) motion to dismiss.

ISSUE: Because Egypt mandated by law that all ancient artifacts and antiquities discovered in Egypt after 1983 constitute state property, may a criminal defendant be guilty of conspiracy by arranging to receive or dispose of any such antiquities that have crossed a state line or a United States boundary?

HOLDING AND DECISION: (Rakoff, J.) Yes. Because Egypt mandated by law that all ancient artifacts and antiquities discovered in Egypt after 1983 constitute state property, a criminal defendant may be guilty of conspiracy by arranging to receive or dispose of any such antiquities that have crossed a state line or a United States boundary. Schultz's (D) argument that Egypt Law 117 creates some type of licensing scheme is incorrect. The law unequivocally asserts state ownership of all antiquities and prohibits, with some exceptions, private ownership of these antiquities. The law also mandates that anyone who finds any new antiquity must notify the Antiquities Authority, which then takes possession of the artifact. Even those antiquities held in private hands at the time Egypt passed Law 117 must be registered with the state. Separately,

Schultz (D) also argues the United States should not recognize these special property interests created by a patrimonial law such as Law 117. However, § 2315 of Title 18 specifically refers to thefts of foreign as well as domestic commerce. The law is purposely designed to deter Americans from receiving and disposing of foreign thefts. At trial, the Government (P) must still prove that Schultz (D) was aware that he was dealing with stolen antiquities. The motion to dismiss is denied.

▶ ANALYSIS

This brief decision highlights the efforts by many countries, including the United States, to protect cultural artifacts. Many new laws and regulations have sprung up over the last quarter century to prevent the import and export of cultural artifacts from various nations. There has been some criticism of such laws on the grounds they inhibit the flow of culture among different nations.

■═■

Quicknotes

CONSPIRACY Concerted action by two or more persons to accomplish some unlawful purpose.

INDICTMENT A formal written accusation made by a prosecutor and issued by a grand jury, charging an individual with a criminal offense.

■═■

Wana the Bear v. Community Construction, Inc.

Miwok Indian (P) v. Developer (D)

Cal. Ct. App., 128 Cal. App. 3d 536, 180 Cal. Rptr. 423 (1982).

NATURE OF CASE: Appeal from judgment in action seeking to enjoin development of an area that included a Native American burial ground.

FACT SUMMARY: Wana the Bear (P) filed suit to enjoin continued development, by Community Construction, Inc. (D), of property containing a burial ground used by the Miwok Indians before they were driven out of the area.

🏛 RULE OF LAW
A burial ground used as a public graveyard prior to the enactment of the cemetery law is not protected under that law as a public cemetery.

FACTS: While excavating property for development of a residential tract, Community Construction, Inc. (D) uncovered human remains on the property. Community Construction (D) continued developing the property, disinterring the remains of over 200 human beings in the process. The burial ground had been used by the Miwok Indians until they were driven out of the area between 1850 and 1870. California's applicable cemetery law was enacted in 1872. Wana the Bear (P), descendant of the Bear People Lodge of the Miwok Indians and related to some or all of the persons whose remains lay there, brought suit to enjoin further excavation and other desecration of the property. The lower court found that the burial ground was not a cemetery entitled to protection under the California cemetery law. Wana the Bear (P) appealed.

ISSUE: Is a burial ground used as a public graveyard prior to the enactment of the cemetery law protected under that law as a public cemetery?

HOLDING AND DECISION: (Blease, J.) No. A burial ground used as a public graveyard prior to the enactment of the cemetery law is not protected under that law as a public cemetery. The 1854 cemetery law applied to burial sites created prior to 1872. However, the 1854 law was not incorporated into the 1872 law. The 1872 law contained a prescriptive use condition, vesting title of the graveyard in the city or village using it only when the land was used as a burial ground continuously, without interruption, for five years. In addition, the new law further declared that no part of the code was retroactive unless expressly so declared. The Miwoks were no longer using the burial ground when the new law replaced the 1854 law. Therefore, the burial ground was not made a cemetery by the operation of the 1872 law. The legislative judgment is binding on this court in the absence of a supervening constitutional right, and none has been claimed. Affirmed.

▶ ANALYSIS

A public cemetery is generally created by one of two methods, dedication or prescriptive use. After the decision in this case, the California legislature enacted legislation providing for the protection of Native American burial sites. Under the new legislation, when property owners find Native American remains on their property, they must notify public officials and meet with representatives of the affected tribes to negotiate for reburial of the remains and any other objects found with them.

Human Beings and Human Bodies

Quick Reference Rules of Law

Dred Scott v. Sanford

Slave (P) v. Slaveowner (D)

60 U.S. 93 (1857).

NATURE OF CASE: Appeal from a judgment dismissing an action by a slave to assert the title of himself and his family to freedom.

FACT SUMMARY: Dred Scott (P) brought this action, asserting that he and his family, who were held as slaves by Sanford (D), were entitled to freedom.

RULE OF LAW

The descendants of Africans who were imported into this country and sold and held as slaves are not citizens of a state within the meaning of the federal Constitution, whether or not they are emancipated.

FACTS: Dred Scott (P) and his family were held as slaves by Sanford (D) in the state of Missouri. Scott (P) brought this action, asserting that he and his family were entitled to freedom. Although Scott (P) and his family were held as slaves in Missouri, Sanford (D) was a resident of the state of New York. Thus, Scott (P) claimed the circuit court had diversity jurisdiction, since the parties were "citizens" of different states. The lower court dismissed the case, and Scott (P) appealed.

ISSUE: Are the descendants of Africans who were imported into this country and sold and held as slaves citizens of a state within the meaning of the federal Constitution, whether or not they are emancipated?

HOLDING AND DECISION: (Taney, C.J.) No. The descendants of Africans who were imported into this country and sold and held as slaves are not citizens of a state within the meaning of the federal Constitution, whether or not they are emancipated. When the Constitution was written, African slaves were considered as an inferior class of beings who had been subjugated by the dominant race and, whether emancipated or not, remained subject to their authority, with no rights or privileges other than the ones those in power chose to grant them. Thus, the words "people of the United States" and "citizens" cannot be held to include persons who are descendants of Africans who were imported into this country to be held and sold as slaves. Since they are not citizens, they are not entitled to all the rights, privileges, and immunities guaranteed by the Constitution. One of those rights is the privilege of suing in a U.S. court. It follows, therefore, that Scott (P) is not a citizen of the state of Missouri within the meaning of the Constitution of the United States, and he is not entitled to sue in its courts. Affirmed.

ANALYSIS

The Court also declared that no state could, by any act or law of its own, introduce a new member into the political community created by the U.S. Constitution. While the language of the Declaration of Independence would seem to embrace the whole human family, the Court found it too clear that the enslaved African race were not intended to be included. For if the language would embrace them, the Court concluded, the conduct of those who framed the Declaration of Independence would have been utterly and flagrantly inconsistent with the principles they asserted, since many of them were themselves slaveowners.

In the Matter of Baby M

Surrogate mother (D) v. Parents (P)

N.J. Sup. Ct., 537 A.2d 1227 (1988).

NATURE OF CASE: Appeal of order determining parentage and child custody.

FACT SUMMARY: Whitehead (D) reneged on an agreement to provide a baby fathered by Stern (P) and give it up to the Sterns (P).

RULE OF LAW

A "surrogacy contract" wherein a woman agrees to have a child and surrender it is void.

FACTS: Elizabeth Stern (P) did not wish to give birth due to a possible genetic defect. Nonetheless, the Sterns (P) wanted a baby. They contracted with Whitehead (D) that she would be artificially inseminated with William Stern's (P) sperm, give up the baby, and receive $10,000. Whitehead (D) had the baby, but did not want to give it up. Following a protracted series of maneuverings, the Sterns (P) obtained custody. They filed a complaint seeking to have the contract enforced and custody permanently awarded to them. The trial court found the contract valid, awarded custody to the Sterns (P), and cut off Whitehead's (D) parental rights entirely. Whitehead (D) appealed.

ISSUE: Is a "surrogacy contract" wherein a woman agrees to have a child and surrender it void?

HOLDING AND DECISION: (Wilentz, C.J.) Yes. A "surrogacy contract" wherein a woman agrees to have a child and surrender it is void. A contract of this nature conflicts with at least three categories of statutes: (1) laws prohibiting the use of money in connection with adoptions; (2) laws requiring proof of parental unfitness prior to termination of parental rights; and (3) laws that make surrender of custody and consent to adoption revocable. Further, contracts of this type conflict with nonstatutory, but nonetheless accepted, policy considerations governing child placement. First and foremost of these is that the paramount consideration in deciding where a child shall be placed be the best interests of the child. A contract such as that in question gives no weight to that consideration. Also, such contracts, by favoring the natural father over the natural mother, conflict with the policy that natural parents shall receive equal considerations. Further, it is impossible not to conclude that such contracts constitute baby selling, which public policy strongly disfavors. For these reasons, contracts such as those at issue here are void. [The court went on to decide custody based on a best-interest-of-the-child test, and awarded custody to Mr. Stern (P), but reinstated Whitehead's (D) parental rights, including visitation.]

ANALYSIS

This was one of the country's most closely watched cases in 1987 and 1988. It was the first major case on the validity of surrogate parenting contracts. What little legislative reaction that had occurred as of the time of this writing tended to codify the court's holding. The court's decision does not prohibit voluntary arrangements performed without consideration (i.e., payment to the natural mother).

Moore v. Regents of the University of California

Patient (P) v. Medical center (D)

Cal. Sup. Ct., 793 P.2d 479 (1990).

NATURE OF CASE: Appeal from action for conversion.

FACT SUMMARY: Moore (P) claimed that Dr. Golde (D) wrongfully used cells from Moore's (P) diseased spleen and other organs for pecuniary advantage.

🏛 RULE OF LAW
A person does not have a property interest in his cell tissue.

FACTS: John Moore (P) went to UCLA Medical Center where he was diagnosed with hairy-cell leukemia. His treating physician, Dr. Golde (D), recommended that he have his spleen removed. Golde (D) was aware that the cells of the diseased spleen were valuable for research and commercial purpose; however, he secured Moore's (P) consent for the operation without disclosing this information. Dr. Golde (D) and his colleagues (D) arranged to preserve the removed cells and, through their own efforts, developed the cells into a lucrative cell line. After the surgery, Moore (P) was required to return to UCLA from his home in Seattle for additional samples of genetic materials. The materials were used for further research on the cell line again without Moore's (P) knowledge or consent. Dr. Golde (D) patented the cell line and received several hundred thousand dollars from pharmaceutical companies for products derived from the cell line. Moore (P) brought suit for conversion.

ISSUE: Does a person have a property interest in his cell tissue?

HOLDING AND DECISION: (Panelli, J.) No. A person does not have a property interest in his cell tissue. Although a person does have a right to his own likeness, the products produced from cells are based on genetic material that is common to all human beings. Thus, Moore (P) had no unique personality interest in the materials taken. California law dictates specifically how removed human tissue must be disposed of. Dr. Golde's (D) use of the tissue was in accordance with statutory requirements. If Moore (P) had desired to dispose of the cells on his own, he would have been barred by law from doing so. Once the cells were removed, he no longer had the right to possess them. Moore (P) cannot be held to have a property interest in the cells. Furthermore, public policy mitigates against a finding that would chill beneficial research. Moore (P) may sue for breach of fiduciary duty or lack of informed consent, but not for conversion.

CONCURRENCE: (Arabian, J.) Moore (P) asks the court to recognize and enforce a right to sell one's own body tissue for profit. Golde's (D) conduct was outrageous, but the legislature is the proper forum for resolution of this problem.

CONCURRENCE AND DISSENT: (Broussard, J.) The court's holding is anomalous; it prevents Moore (P) from selling his body for profit but allows Golde (D) and the Regents (D) to profit from cells wrongfully acquired.

DISSENT: (Mosk, J.) The concept of property refers to a "bundle of rights" that encompasses the right to exclude others from that property or to dispose of it by gift or sale. Certain legal constraints, however, intervene for a variety of policy reasons to limit the exercise of these rights. While these legal restrictions may limit the bundle of rights, what always remains is a protectable property interest. "Every individual has a legally protectable property interest in his own body and its products." This basic principle stems from society's ethical imperative to respect the human body and prohibit economic exploitation of one person by another. Such exploitation is akin to the institution of slavery. Our society also values fundamental fairness when it comes to dealings between people and condemns the unjust enrichment of anyone at the expense of another. Moore's (P) protectable property interest in his own tissue at minimum must match that of the defendants. Moore (P) could have contracted with researchers and pharmaceutical companies to develop the potential of his tissue. It is absurd to allow the defendants to appropriate Moore's (P) tissue saying they have a legal right to his property, while at the same time saying Moore (P) had no such right. It is unethical and immoral not to allow Moore (P) to share in the proceeds attained from his cells, without which defendants would have nothing.

▌ ANALYSIS

Justice Mosk makes two compelling policy arguments in his dissent—one based on equity and the other on ethics. Because, he argues, Moore (P) made a crucial contribution to the cell line developed by Golde (D), he should be permitted to share in the profits. Mosk contends that when research treats the human body as a mere commodity, the dignity and respect due the human body are sacrificed. For more on this debate, see *Danforth, Cells, Sales, and Royalties,* 6 Yale L. and Pol'y Rev. 179 (1988).

⬛▬▬

Quicknotes

CONVERSION The act of depriving an owner of his property without permission or justification.

Continued on next page.

FIDUCIARY DUTY   A legal obligation to act for the benefit of another, including subordinating one's personal interests to that of the other person.

■≡■

Flynn v. Holder

Challengers to statute (P) v. Federal government (D)

684 F.3d 852 (9th Cir. 2012).

NATURE OF CASE: Appeal from lower court decision that dismissed the plaintiffs' constitutional challenge to the National Organ Transplant Act.

FACT SUMMARY: The National Organ Transplant Act bans any compensation for human organs, including bone marrow. The plaintiffs—a group of patients, physicians, and nonprofits—challenged the constitutionally of the ban.

> **🏛 RULE OF LAW**
> While the direct removal of bone marrow is prohibited by the National Organ Transplant Act (NOTA), the removal of immature bone marrow stem cells from the blood, rather than from the marrow itself, is similar to a blood donation and is not prohibited by NOTA.

FACTS: The National Organ Transplant Act (NOTA) bans any compensation for human organs, including bone marrow. The plaintiffs—a group of patients, physicians, and nonprofits—challenged the constitutionally of the ban. The plaintiffs seek to create a program that would offer $3,000 to possible bone marrow donors. Because there are millions of bone marrow cell types, the chances of a donor match are very rare. The plaintiffs seek to offer the $3,000 compensation to incentivize possible donors and increase the match ratio for those suffering from leukemia or other blood-related diseases. The older method of extracting bone marrow involved the use of a long needle that would be inserted directly into the cavity of the larger bones of the donor, such as the hipbone. A newer method is less invasive. Scientists discovered that blood stem cells are born in bone marrow and typically develop into mature blood cells before passing into the blood stream. Significantly, they also discovered that some of the bone marrow stem cells pass into the blood stream before maturing into full blood cells. A process called "apheresis" was developed to remove only the immature bone marrow stems cells from a donor's blood stream. The process involves a needle being inserted into the vein of a donor. The donor then sits for an hour or two while the stems cells are removed from his or her blood. Those immature bone marrow stem cells are then injected into the donee where they grow into healthy, cancer-free blood cells. The plaintiffs argue the ban on bone marrow transplants is a violation of Equal Protection. A federal district court dismissed their complaint. The plaintiffs appealed to the United State Court of Appeals for the Ninth Circuit.

ISSUE: While the direct removal of bone marrow is prohibited by the NOTA, is the removal of immature bone marrow stem cells from the blood, rather than from the marrow itself, similar to a blood donation and therefore not prohibited by NOTA?

HOLDING AND DECISION: (Kleinfeld, J.) Yes. While the direct removal of bone marrow is prohibited by the NOTA, the removal of peripheral bone marrow stem cells from the blood, rather than from the marrow itself, is similar to a blood donation and is not prohibited by NOTA. Turning first to the older method of extracting bone marrow directly, there is no question that NOTA has banned compensation for extracted bone marrow. Congress had rational basis to outlaw the sale of bone marrow as well as all other organs of the body, including subparts thereof. One concern was that rich patients would induce the poor to sell their organs, even if the process was a painful one. Compensation for donors may also degrade the quality of the organs donated if potential donors lie about their medical histories. Accordingly, Congress has a rational basis for banning the sale of organs and it is not for this Court to substitute its own judgment. Separately, however, the process known as "apheresis" is not covered by NOTA. That method only involves the removal of blood from a donor, similar to the process of giving blood. Payments for blood have been common for some time and NOTA does not ban that practice. The Government (D) is incorrect in saying that the bone marrow stem cells are a "subpart" of the bone marrow. Blood contains red cells, white cells, platelets, and stem cells. To ban the removal of the stem cells alone would necessarily include a ban on blood donations themselves. Accordingly, NOTA does not ban compensation to donors for their bone marrow stem cells extracted using the apheresis method. Affirmed in part and reversed in part.

▶ **ANALYSIS**

In fall 2013, the Department of Health and Human Services proposed a rule that would effectively ban the new apheresis method of extracting bone marrow stem cells from blood. If adopted, the rule would moot the Ninth Circuit's decision in this case. As of this printing, a final rule on the issue had yet to be adopted.

■=■

Quicknotes

MOTION TO DISMISS Motion to terminate an action based on the adequacy of the pleadings, improper service or venue, etc.

Continued on next page.

RATIONAL BASIS REVIEW A test employed by the court to determine the validity of a statute in equal protection actions, whereby the court determines whether the challenged statute is rationally related to the achievement of a legitimate state interest.

■━■

CHAPTER 5

Adverse Possession

Quick Reference Rules of Law

Brown v. Gobble

Property owner (P) v. Adjoining property owner (D)

W. Va. Sup. Ct. App., 474 S.E.2d 489 (1996).

NATURE OF CASE: Appeal from judgment in an action to enjoin interference with use of real property.

FACT SUMMARY: The Browns (P) and the Gobbles (D) disputed ownership of a two-foot-wide tract of property on the boundary of their properties.

🏛 RULE OF LAW
The doctrine of tacking allows parties claiming adverse possession to use their predecessors' conduct on the property to meet the time requirements of adverse possession.

FACTS: The Gobbles (D) purchased real property in 1985. At the time, a fence ran along the rear boundary of the property that adjoined property purchased by the Browns (P) in 1989. The Browns (P) discovered, prior to buying, that this fence actually extended two feet past the true boundary. However, the Browns (P) did not claim ownership of this two-foot-wide tract until 1994, when they decided to build a road along that property. The Gobbles (D) sought to prevent the building of the road, and the Browns (P) filed suit to enjoin this interference. The Gobbles (D) counterclaimed that they owned the two-foot-wide tract through adverse possession. The Gobbles (D) presented evidence that both the Blevins and the Fletchers, who owned the Gobbles' (D) property from 1937 through 1985, believed they owned the boundary tract and treated the property as their own. However, the trial court ruled that adverse possession had not been proved and entered judgment for the Browns (P). The Gobbles (D) appealed.

ISSUE: Does the doctrine of tacking allow parties claiming adverse possession to use their predecessors' conduct on the property to meet the time requirements of adverse possession?

HOLDING AND DECISION: (Cleckley, J.) Yes. The doctrine of tacking allows parties claiming adverse possession to use their predecessors' conduct on the property to meet the time requirements of adverse possession. In order to prove adverse possession, a party must prove the following elements: (1) the property has been held adversely; (2) there has been actual possession; (3) possession has been open and notorious; (4) possession has been exclusive; (5) possession has been continuous; and (6) the property has been held under claim or color of title. In the case at hand, the requisite period of time for adverse possession is ten years. The principle of tacking has long been recognized in adverse possession cases. This principle allows different adverse possessions to make up the requi-

site time for holding such possessions, so long as they are connected by privity of title or claim. Thus, although the Gobbles (D) had personally adversely held the property for only nine years, the adverse possession by the prior owners of the property, who are connected to them through the title to their property, helps to satisfy the elements of adverse possession long before the ten-year period. Accordingly, if their adverse possession was tacked onto the Gobbles' own adverse possession, the Gobbles (D) would meet the time requirement. The trial court apparently misunderstood the relationship between tacking and adverse possession. Reversed and remanded.

▶ ANALYSIS

This decision also established the standard of proof for adverse possession claims. The court held that adverse possession must be proved by clear and convincing evidence. Although some jurisdictions require only a preponderance standard, the majority view is in accord with this decision.

■■■

Quicknotes

ADVERSE POSSESSION A means of acquiring title to real property by remaining in actual, open, continuous, exclusive possession of property for the statutory period.

AFFIRMATIVE EASEMENT The right to utilize a portion of another's real property in order to conduct a specific activity thereon.

NEGATIVE EASEMENT Refers to the duty to refrain from conducting a specific lawful activity on the servient estate because it interferes with the use of the dominant estate.

POSSESSION UNDER COLOR OF TITLE A means of acquiring title to real property by remaining in actual, open, continuous, exclusive possession of property for the statutory period.

PRESCRIPTIVE EASEMENT A manner of acquiring an easement in another's property by continuous and uninterrupted use in satisfaction of the statutory requirements of adverse possession.

TACKING The attachment of periods of adverse possession by different adverse possessors in order to fulfill the requirement of continuous possession for the period proscribed by statute.

■■■

Romero v. Garcia

Adverse possessor (P) v. Former owner (D)

N.M. Sup. Ct., 546 P.2d 66 (1976).

NATURE OF CASE: Appeal from suit to quiet title.

FACT SUMMARY: Romero (P) brought suit to quiet title to land she and her deceased husband bought from his parents.

🏛 RULE OF LAW
An indefinite and uncertain description of property in a deed may be clarified by subsequent acts of the parties.

FACTS: Romero (P) and her deceased husband, son of defendants, purchased 13 acres of property from their father-in-law. They entered into possession and built a home on the property, and recorded a deed. Following her husband's death, Romero (P) moved and subsequently remarried. She brought suit to quiet title to the property based on her ten years of possession under color of title and payment of taxes. Judgment was entered for Romero (P) and the Garcias (D) appealed.

ISSUE: May an indefinite and uncertain description of property in a deed be clarified by subsequent acts of the parties?

HOLDING AND DECISION: (Sosa, Jr., J.) Yes. An indefinite and uncertain description of property in a deed may be clarified by subsequent acts of the parties. The evidence here is clear that the subsequent acts of the parties in entering upon and pointing out the boundaries of the property to the surveyor, combined with other extrinsic evidence, aided the surveyor in preparing the plat relied upon here. Affirmed.

▶ ANALYSIS

The main dispute here evolved around the sufficiency of the deed for adverse possession because it failed to adequately describe the particular parcel of property. The court follows the decision of *Richardson v. Duggar*, 525 P.2d 854, 857 (N.M. 1974), which held that a deed is not void for failure to describe the property adequately if a surveyor is able to determine the boundaries by the deed and extrinsic evidence.

Quicknotes

ADVERSE POSSESSION A means of acquiring title to real property by remaining in actual, open, continuous, exclusive possession of property for the statutory period.

DEED A signed writing transferring title to real property from one person to another.

EXTRINSIC EVIDENCE Evidence that is not contained within the text of a document or contract but which is derived from the parties' statements or the circumstances under which the agreement was made.

Nome 2000 v. Fagerstrom

Landowner (P) v. Adverse possessor (D)

Alaska Sup. Ct., 799 P.2d 304 (1990).

NATURE OF CASE: Suit for ejectment and counter-claim to acquire title by adverse possession.

FACT SUMMARY: Charles and Peggy Fagerstrom (D) used a parcel of land owned by Nome 2000 (P) for various purposes from 1944 to 1987 but did not build a house on it until 1978, thereby defeating their adverse possession claim, according to Nome (P).

 RULE OF LAW

A determination of whether a claimant's physical acts upon the land of another are sufficiently continuous, notorious, and exclusive does not necessarily depend on the existence of significant improvements, substantial activity, or absolute exclusivity.

FACTS: Charles Fagerstrom's family (D) used a rural parcel of land owned by Nome 2000 (P) for recreational purposes beginning in 1944. In 1963, Charles and Peggy Fagerstrom married. In the 1970s, Charles and Peggy Fagerstrom (D) and their family began to make more substantial use of the land, adding improvements and spending more time there each year. In 1977, they built a reindeer shelter that occasionally housed reindeer. They also excluded trailers from the land and spent weekends there. In 1987, the Fagerstroms (D) built a cabin on the land and continued to use the land on weekends and vacations for recreational purposes. In 1987, Nome 2000 (P) brought suit to quiet title. The Fagerstroms (D) counterclaimed for title by adverse possession.

ISSUE: Does a determination of whether a claimant's physical acts upon the land of another are sufficiently continuous, notorious, and exclusive necessarily depend on the existence of significant improvements, substantial activity, or absolute exclusivity?

HOLDING AND DECISION: (Matthews, Jr., C. J.) No. A determination of whether a claimant's physical acts upon the land of another are sufficiently continuous, notorious, and exclusive does not necessarily depend on the existence of significant improvements, substantial activity, or absolute exclusivity. Use consistent with the use by any similarly situated owner is sufficient to establish claim by adverse possession. The statute requires continuous, notorious, hostile, and exclusive use of a property for ten years in order to succeed in a claim for adverse possession. Nome (P) claimed that the Fagerstroms' (D) possession only became adverse when they built the cabin in 1978, and thus they did not meet the statutory ten-year period. But the statute does not require actual improve-ments to the land, only sufficient use based on the type of property occupied. The land in question is rural and thus has a lower requirement of use. The Fagerstroms (D) occupied the land sufficiently that their occupation was visible in 1977. The various structures erected and the feeling of the community that the Fagerstroms (D) were the owners of the property meets the statutory requirement of continuous, notorious, exclusive, and hostile possession. Reversed in part and remanded.

ANALYSIS

The court found that what the Fagerstroms (D), as Native Alaskans, believed or intended vis-à-vis the property had nothing to do with whether their possession was hostile. The hostility requirement merely means that the adverse possessor acted toward the land as if he were the owner. But the Fagerstroms (D) claim title to a large portion of the land was only partially granted by the court. The Fagerstroms' (D) use of certain trails for hiking did not constitute dominion and control over the south portion of the land sufficient to demonstrate adverse possession.

Quicknotes

ADVERSE POSSESSION A means of acquiring title to real property by remaining in actual, open, continuous, exclusive possession of property for the statutory period.

EJECTMENT An action to oust someone in possession of real property unlawfully and to restore possession to the party lawfully entitled to it.

PRESCRIPTIVE EASEMENT A manner of acquiring an easement in another's property by continuous and uninterrupted use in satisfaction of the statutory requirements of adverse possession.

Community Feed Store, Inc. v. Northeastern Culvert Corp.

Landowner seeking easement (P) v. Landowner (D)

Vt. Sup. Ct., 559 A.2d 1068 (1989).

NATURE OF CASE: Appeal from rejection of claim of prescriptive easement and judgment for defense of counterclaim of ejectment.

FACT SUMMARY: Community Feed Store, Inc. (P) claimed a prescriptive easement over a portion of a gravel area used by its vehicles but owned by Northeastern Culvert Corp. (D).

🏛 RULE OF LAW
A general outline of consistent use is sufficient to establish a prescriptive easement.

FACTS: Community Feed Store, Inc. (Community) (P) used a parcel of land lying between their building and that of Northeastern Culvert Corp's building as a turning and backing up area for trucks making deliveries to the store. The use was continuous from 1956 to 1984. A survey in 1984 showed that the majority of this area was owned by Northeastern Culvert Corp. (D). Upon this finding, Northeastern Culvert Corp. (D) erected a wall to discontinue Community's (P) use. Community (P) brought suit, claiming a prescriptive easement. The trial court found for Northeastern Culvert Corp. (D) on the basis that the use was not stated with enough specificity to establish a prescriptive easement and that the use was consensual. Community (P) appealed.

ISSUE: Is a general outline of consistent use sufficient to establish a prescriptive easement?

HOLDING AND DECISION: (Gibson, III, J.) Yes. A general outline of consistent use is sufficient to establish a prescriptive easement. A prescriptive easement acquires a non-fee interest in land by adverse possession. The trial court found that Community (P) had not been able to define the easement acquired with enough specificity. The extent of the use need not be absolute. Instead, Community (P) need only show the general outline of consistent pattern of use with certainty. Community (P) introduced more than sufficient evidence of a pattern of use. Reversed.

▶ ANALYSIS

The second basis on which the lower court rejected the claim was that use of the area was made by Community (P) with the permission of Northeastern Culvert Corp. (D). The Vermont Supreme Court applied the general presumption that open and notorious use is adverse to ownership and rejected the consent defense. There is a "public use" exception to the general presumption of adversity, whereby an owner "throws open" his land to general passage, but that exception did not apply in the instant case because Northeastern Culvert Corp. (D) could not show a generalized public use of the loading area.

■=■

Quicknotes

ADVERSE POSSESSION A means of acquiring title to real property by remaining in actual, open, continuous, exclusive possession of property for the statutory period.

EJECTMENT An action to oust someone in possession of real property unlawfully and to restore possession to the party lawfully entitled to it.

PRESCRIPTIVE EASEMENT A manner of acquiring an easement in another's property by continuous and uninterrupted use in satisfaction of the statutory requirements of adverse possession.

■=■

Somerville v. Jacobs

Improver (P) v. Landowner (D)

W. Va. Sup. Ct. App., 170 S.E.2d 805 (1969).

NATURE OF CASE: Appeal from claim for equitable relief.

FACT SUMMARY: The Somervilles (P) built a warehouse on property that they mistakenly believed to be their own.

🏛 RULE OF LAW
An improver who mistakenly improves the land of another is entitled to the value of the improvement that the landowner has benefited from.

FACTS: The Somervilles (P) owned three plots of land. Based on a surveyor's report, they constructed a warehouse on what they believed to be their own land. Jacobs and other owners (D) discovered that the warehouse was in fact built upon their land only after it was completed. The Somervilles (P) brought suit for equitable relief either in the form of sale of the land to them or reimbursement of the value of the improvements.

ISSUE: Is an improver who mistakenly improves the land of another entitled to the value of the improvement that the landowner has benefited from?

HOLDING AND DECISION: (Haymond, Pres.) Yes. An improver who mistakenly improves the land of another is entitled to the value of the improvement that the landowner has benefited from. The Somervilles (P) made a reasonable good-faith mistake of fact in building on Jacobs's (D) land. If Jacobs (D) keeps the improvements to the land without compensating the Somervilles (P), he will be unjustly enriched. Equity allows the type of relief the Somervilles (P) are requesting. Jacobs (D) must either pay for the improvement he received or sell the land back to Somerville (P) in order to avoid unjust enrichment.

DISSENT: (Caplan, J.) Having been entirely without fault, Jacobs (D) should not be forced to purchase the building. That is nothing less than condemnation of private property, a power reserved to government only. He who made the mistake should suffer the hardship.

▎ ANALYSIS

Other jurisdictions hold that a trespasser, no matter how innocent, cannot be compensated for any improvements. However, all courts agree that under the doctrine of annexation, intentional improvements by one who knows he is trespassing belong to the owner of the real estate. In that case, the bad faith of the improver negates the injustice of the enrichment.

Quicknotes

ANNEXATION The attachment or joining of one thing to another; in the property context, refers to the attachment of a chattel to real property thereby becoming a fixture.

EQUITABLE RELIEF A remedy that is based upon principles of fairness as opposed to rules of law.

UNJUST ENRICHMENT The unlawful acquisition of money or property of another for which both law and equity require restitution to be made.

Nuisance

Quick Reference Rules of Law

Dobbs v. Wiggins

Neighbor (P) v. Owner of dog kennel (D)

Ill. App. Ct., 401 Ill. App. 3d 367 (2010).

NATURE OF CASE: Appeal from lower court decision finding that barking from an adjoining dog kennel constituted a private nuisance.

FACT SUMMARY: Dobbs (P) and another landowner brought suit against Wiggins (D), alleging that the loud barking from almost 100 dogs in his adjoining kennel constituted a private nuisance.

🏛 RULE OF LAW
A private nuisance is a substantial invasion of another's interest in the use and enjoyment of his land.

FACTS: Wiggins (D) operated an active dog kennel on his property. He started the kennel in 1995 and by 2007 he had almost 100 dogs on his property. The Dobbses (P) lived on land next to Wiggins' (D) property. The Dobbses (P) and another neighbor began to complain about the barking noise from the dogs in 2007. After Wiggins (D) did not decrease the number of dogs, the Dobbses (P) brought this suit against Wiggins (D) alleging that the chronic barking constituted a private nuisance. At a bench trial, several other neighbors also testified as to the constant barking. The trial court ruled in favor of the Dobbses (P), finding that the barking dogs resulted in an invasion of the Dobbses' (P) interest in the use and enjoyment of their land. The court then ordered Wiggins (D) to reduce the number of dogs from the 69 he kenneled at the time of trial to six. The court also ordered Wiggins (D) to kennel those dogs on the southern portion of his property, away from the Dobbses' (P) property. Wiggins (D) appealed to an intermediate court of appeals.

ISSUE: Is a private nuisance a substantial invasion of another's interest in the use and enjoyment of his land?

HOLDING AND DECISION: (Stewart, J.) Yes. A private nuisance is a substantial invasion of another's interest in the use and enjoyment of his land. The invasion can be intentional or negligent but must be unreasonable. The nuisance must be so physically offensive to the senses that it makes life uncomfortable. Private nuisances can include noise, smoke, and odors produced from one person's land that reaches adjoining lands. Whether some activity constitutes a private nuisance is typically a question of fact for a judge in a bench trial or a jury. In any action to enjoin an alleged nuisance, a reviewing court must balance the harm done to the plaintiffs against the utility of the defendant's business and the suitability of the land for that business. The lower court properly concluded that the barking was substantial. It also properly concluded that

Wiggins (D), by virtue of the large number of dogs he kenneled, knew that the barking was certain to result in the invasion of others' use and enjoyment in their lands. The court then determined that the noise nuisance was unreasonable. It found that even though Wiggins (D) made efforts to control the noise, the barking did not abate. It also gave weight to the Dobbses' (P) longer ownership in the neighborhood. Accordingly, the lower court properly concluded the barking constituted a nuisance. However, the court erred when it ordered Wiggins (D) to reduce the number of dogs from 69 to six. The evidence at trial was insufficient to support a finding that Wiggins (D) must reduce the number of dogs to that amount. The evidence at trial revealed that Wiggins (D) began kenneling dogs on his property in 1995. For roughly ten years, he received no complaints about the kennel. There simply was no sufficient evidence to determine what should be the maximum number of dogs Wiggins (D) could kennel. Accordingly, the matter is remanded to the lower court for a determination as to the proper scope of the injunction against Wiggins (D). Affirmed in part and reversed in part.

▶ ANALYSIS

In any matter involving an injunction, there are always two issues. The first issue is whether the plaintiff has a legal right that the other party has violated. Here, that right was the Dobbses' (P) right to the quiet enjoyment of their land. The second issue to be determined in an injunction case is the scope of remedy. If a right has been violated, a reviewing court will seek to fashion an injunction that protects the plaintiff's right but does so in a manner that is the least restrictive on the defendant's use of his or her own land.

━■━

Quicknotes

PERMANENT INJUNCTION A remedy imposed by the court ordering a party to cease the conduct of a specific activity until the final disposition of the cause of action.

PRIVATE NUISANCE An unlawful use of property interfering with the enjoyment of the private rights of an individual or a small number of persons.

━■━

Page County Appliance Center, Inc. v. Honeywell, Inc.

Appliance retailer (P) v. Neighboring business with computer (D)

Iowa Sup. Ct., 347 N.W.2d 171 (1984).

NATURE OF CASE: Appeal from jury award of damages for claim of nuisance and tortious interference with business relations.

FACT SUMMARY: Honeywell, Inc. (D) placed a computer in a business adjoining Page County Appliance Center (Page) (P) that interfered with Page's (P) business of selling television sets.

> ## 🏛 RULE OF LAW
> Lawful activity constitutes a nuisance if it unreasonably interferes with another's enjoyment of his or her property.

FACTS: Since 1953, Page County Appliance Center (Page) (P) had engaged in the sale of electrical appliances, including television sets, in a store located next to a travel agent. In 1980, Honeywell, Inc. (D) placed a computer in the travel agency, and from that time forward, Page (P) experienced reception problems on his display televisions. The reception problem was traced to a radiation leak in the computer. It took Honeywell (D) over two years to completely resolve the reception problem. Page (P) brought suit for nuisance and tortious interference. The trial court awarded Page (P) compensatory and punitive damages. Honeywell (D) appealed.

ISSUE: Does lawful activity constitute a nuisance if it unreasonably interferes with another's enjoyment of his or her property?

HOLDING AND DECISION: (Reynoldson, C.J.) Yes. Lawful activity constitutes a nuisance if it unreasonably interferes with another's enjoyment of his or her property. A litigant need not show negligence in an action for nuisance; he only need show that the activity was unreasonable in the context in which it took place. Honeywell (D) contends that placement of the computer in a business area was reasonable and Page's (P) use of the property was unreasonably sensitive. However, it is unlikely that the presence of a television set constitutes a hypersensitive use. However, the trial court did not sufficiently instruct the jury on the standard of reasonableness. Reversed and remanded for a new trial consistent with the finding of this court.

▶ ANALYSIS

Courts often rely on the nuisance analysis stated in the Restatement (Second) of Torts. It balances the social utility of the harmful conduct against its effect on the plaintiff. If the gravity of the harm outweighs the utility of the actor's conduct, in view of all the surrounding circumstances, then the use will be held to be unreasonable.

■=■

Quicknotes

INDEMNIFICATION Reimbursement for losses sustained or security against anticipated loss or damages.

NUISANCE An unlawful use of property that interferes with the lawful use of another's property.

TORTIOUS INTERFERENCE WITH BUSINESS RELATIONS An intentional tort whereby a defendant intentionally elicits the breach of a valid contract resulting in damages.

■=■

Boomer v. Atlantic Cement Company

Landowners (P) v. Cement plant (D)

N.Y. Ct. App., 26 N.Y.2d 219, 257 N.E.2d 870 (1970).

NATURE OF CASE: Action to enjoin maintenance of nuisance and for damages.

FACT SUMMARY: A trial court refused to issue an injunction that would close down a neighboring cement plant but awarded permanent damages instead.

🏛 RULE OF LAW
Although the rule in New York is that a nuisance will be enjoined even when there is a marked disparity shown in economic consequence between the effect of the injunction and the effect of the nuisance, an injunction should not be applied if the result is to close down a plant. Permanent damages may be awarded as an alternative.

FACTS: A group of landowners (P), complaining of injury to their property from dirt, smoke, and vibration emanating from a neighboring cement plant (D), brought an action to enjoin the continued operation of the plant and for damages. The trial court held that the plant constituted a nuisance, found substantial damage but, because an injunction would shut down the plant's operation, refused to issue one. Permanent damages of $185,000 were awarded the group of landowners (P) instead.

ISSUE: Where the issuance of an injunction to enjoin the maintenance of a business would shut down a business, may permanent damages be issued as an alternative?

HOLDING AND DECISION: (Bergan, J.) Yes. Damages may be awarded as an alternative to an injunction in nuisance cases. Another alternative would be to grant the injunction but postpone its effect to a specified future date to give opportunity for technical advances to permit the company (D) to eliminate the nuisance. However, there is no assurance that any significant technical improvement would occur. Moreover, the problem is universal and can only be solved by an industry-wide effort. Permanent damages would themselves be a spur to conduct more research. Future owners of this land would not be able to recover additional damages, since the award is to the land. Reversed and remanded.

DISSENT: (Jasen, J.) The majority approach is licensing a continuing wrong. Furthermore, permanent damages alleviate the need for more research and decrease incentive.

▶ ANALYSIS

The reasoning advanced here has been carried one step further by other courts. In *Pennsylvania Coal Co. v. Sanderson*, 113 Pa. St. 126, 6 A. 453 (1886), a suit for damages was frowned upon by the Supreme Court which said, "To encourage the development of the great natural resources of a country, trifling inconveniences to particular persons must sometimes give way to the necessities of a great community."

Quicknotes

INJUNCTION A court order requiring a person to do or prohibiting that person from doing a specific act.

NUISANCE An unlawful use of property that interferes with the lawful use of another's property.

TEMPORARY DAMAGES Monetary compensation awarded by the court to a party for injuries sustained as the result of another party's occasional wrongful actions.

Johnson v. Paynesville Farmers Union Cooperative Oil Co.

Organic farmer (P) v. Nonorganic farmers (D)

Minn. Sup. Ct., 817 N.W.2d 693 (2012).

NATURE OF CASE: Appeal from intermediate appellate court's decision that reinstated the plaintiff's nuisance, negligence, and trespass claims against a nonorganic farmer located next to the plaintiff's organic farm.

FACT SUMMARY: Johnson (P), owner of an organic farm, alleged that on several occasions, the Paynesville Farmers Union Cooperative Oil Co. (Cooperative) (D) sprayed pesticides onto its fields that allegedly drifted over and onto Johnson's (P) fields.

> ## RULE OF LAW
> (1) A trespass is the wrongful and unlawful entry upon the plaintiff's property by a defendant and the plaintiff need not prove actual damages.
> (2) Disruption and inconvenience caused by a private nuisance are actionable damages for which a property owner may recover.

FACTS: Johnson (P), owner of an organic farm, alleged that on several occasions, the Paynesville Farmers Union Cooperative Oil Co. (Cooperative) (D) sprayed pesticides onto its fields that allegedly drifted over and onto Johnson's (P) fields. Under the Organic Foods Production Act and the National Organic Program, an organic farmer cannot market its products as "organic" unless the farmer's fields have not had any prohibited substances applied to them in the prior three years. After Cooperative (D) sprayed pesticides that drifted onto Johnson's (P) soybean fields, Johnson (P) was compelled to notify the Minnesota Department of Agriculture (the Department). The Department tested the soybean fields and found that while pesticides were present in the soybeans, they were within acceptable levels. However, the Department still ordered Johnson (P) to clear ten acres of his soybean field and not to sell anything from that area for another three years. Another occurrence led to the presence of pesticides on Johnson's (P) alfalfa fields. Johnson (P) had to clear those fields and not sell products from those fields for another three years. Johnson (P) brought claims of trespass, nuisance, and negligence against Cooperative (D). The trial court granted summary judgment to Cooperative (D) on the ground Johnson (P) did not prove he suffered any actual damages. An intermediate appellate court reversed and reinstated Johnson's (P) claims. The Minnesota Supreme Court granted Cooperative's (D) petition for further review.

ISSUE:
(1) Is a trespass the wrongful and unlawful entry upon the plaintiff's property by a defendant and does the plaintiff not need to prove actual damages?

(2) Are disruption and inconvenience caused by a private nuisance actionable damages for which a property owner may recover?

HOLDING AND DECISION: (Gildea, J.)
(1) Yes. A trespass is the wrongful and unlawful entry upon the plaintiff's property by a defendant and the plaintiff need not prove actual damages. Johnson (P) petitions this court to adopt other states' expansion of the tort of trespass. Other states have held that a trespass claim may be based on particulate matter entering onto the plaintiff's property. Those states also include a necessary showing of actual damages caused by the unwelcome particulate matter. This is inconsistent with the law in Minnesota, as well as the law of most other states. A property owner need not prove actual damages as a result of a trespass. In addition, a trespass typically results from a person intentionally entering upon the land of another. The trespass must include some physical or tangible act. Invasions by particulates in the air may affect the owner's right to use and enjoy his land, but they do not require the landowner to share his land with a trespasser or some physical, trespassing object. Accordingly, the trial court was correct to dismiss Johnson's (P) claim of trespass.

(2) Yes. Disruption and inconvenience caused by a private nuisance are actionable damages for which a property owner may recover. The trial court properly dismissed the nuisance claims as they related to Johnson's (P) claims that he was forced to take several of his fields out of production. The Department of Agriculture improperly ordered Johnson (P) to destroy those crops. While pesticides were present, they were under the minimal threshold and Johnson (P) still would have been able to sell those products as organic. Accordingly, his claims should have been against the state of Minnesota and not the Cooperative (D). However, Johnson (P) also claimed the pesticide sprays actually spurred weed growth around his crops. This forced him to take extra measures to prevent weed growth in the years following the occurrences. Johnson (P) himself complained that the pesticide spray caused him to suffer cotton mouth, swollen throat, and headaches. These types of disruptions and inconveniences are actionable under nuisance law. Accordingly, Johnson's (P) claim for nuisance may continue and the trial court should not have granted full summary judgment to the Cooperative (D). Affirmed in part and reversed in part.

Continued on next page.

▶ *ANALYSIS*

The Minnesota Supreme Court sought in this decision to retain the distinction between a trespass claim and a private nuisance claim. A trespass is more of an intentional tort that includes a physical entry upon the land, causing the landowner to share his land with someone or something tangible. A nuisance claim deals more with indirect or intangible interference with the landowner's use and enjoyment of his land.

■━■

Quicknotes

PRIVATE NUISANCE An unlawful use of property interfering with the enjoyment of the private rights of an individual or a small number of persons.

TRESPASS Unlawful interference with, or damage to, the real or personal property of another.

■━■

Fontainebleau Hotel Corp. v. Forty-Five Twenty-Five, Inc.

Hotel (P) v. Neighbor hotel (D)

Fla. Dist. Ct. App., 114 So. 2d 357 (1959).

NATURE OF CASE: Interlocutory appeal from issuance of an injunction.

FACT SUMMARY: Forty-Five Twenty-Five, Inc. (Forty-Five) (P) sought to enjoin the Fontainebleau Hotel's (D) construction of an addition that would block all sunshine from Forty-Five's (P) hotel.

🏛 RULE OF LAW
There is no legal right to the free flow of light or air from an adjoining parcel of land.

FACTS: Forty-Five Twenty-Five, Inc. (Forty-Five) (P) owned the Eden Roc Hotel (Eden Roc) (P), which was subsequently built next to the Fontainebleau (D). Fontainebleau Hotel Corp. (Fontainebleau) (D) commenced construction on an addition which, when completed, would be 14 stories tall and completely block all light from Eden Roc's (P) swimming pool area. Forty-Five (P) sought an injunction to halt construction on the tower, claiming it would interfere with their pre-existing light and air easement. The lower court issued an injunction, and Fontainebleau (D) appealed.

ISSUE: Is there a legal right to the free flow of light or air from an adjoining parcel of land?

HOLDING AND DECISION: (Per curiam) No. There is no legal right to the free flow of light or air from an adjoining parcel of land. Forty-Five (P) claims the right to an injunction based on the law of nuisance. However, nuisance law states that one property holder cannot use his property right to harm the lawful rights of an adjacent landholder. No court has ever found that a property owner has a legal right to air or sunlight. Absent a legal right to the light, Forty-Five (P) has not made a claim in nuisance. Order granting injunction reversed.

▶ ANALYSIS

Should the fact that the Fontainebleau (D) apparently erected the addition where it did out of spite and malice have any effect on the court's decision? To enjoin the addition as a so-called "spite fence," Forty-Five (P) would have to prove that the addition's sole purpose was to irritate; in other words, that the addition had no social utility whatsoever. In mixed motive cases, however, courts will almost certainly deny the injunction.

Quicknotes

EASEMENT The right to utilize a portion of another's real property for a specific use.

INJUNCTION A remedy imposed by the court ordering a party to cease the conduct of a specific activity.

NUISANCE An unlawful use of property that interferes with the lawful use of another's property.

Prah v. Maretti

Homeowner (P) v. Neighbor (D)

Wis. Sup. Ct., 321 N.W.2d 182 (1982).

NATURE OF CASE: Appeal from summary judgment denying relief from a proposed obstruction of sunlight.

FACT SUMMARY: Prah (P) sued to enjoin Maretti (D) from building on his land so as to block the flow of sunlight to Prah's (P) solar heated house.

RULE OF LAW
The doctrine of prior appropriation applies to the use of sunlight as a protectable resource.

FACTS: In 1978, Prah (P) built a house that was equipped to use solar energy. Subsequently, Maretti (D) proposed to build a house that would have obstructed the free flow of sunlight onto Prah's (P) land and therefore interfered with his solar energy system. He sued to enjoin the construction contending he had begun using sunlight as a resource prior to Maretti's (D) plans and therefore under the doctrine of prior appropriation he had a protectable right in the sunlight. He then asserted that Maretti's (D) construction constituted a private nuisance. The trial court granted Maretti's (D) motion for a summary judgment holding that prior appropriation doctrine did not apply and no easement in light and air could be recognized. Prah (P) appealed.

ISSUE: Does the doctrine of prior appropriation apply to the use of sunlight as a protectable resource?

HOLDING AND DECISION: (Abrahamson, J.) Yes. The doctrine of prior appropriation applies to the use of sunlight as a protectable resource. Because of the development of technology allowing the practical use of solar energy, sunlight has taken on an enhanced value. At early American common law, sunlight was valued for the aesthetic purposes only, and it was left that an adjacent landowner's ability to use his land as he wished outweighed this aesthetic value, and no easement of light and air was recognized. However, given this new technology, sunlight must be regarded as a valuable resource and the doctrine of prior appropriation applies to protect those who first exploit the resource. Consequently, Prah (P) could maintain an action for nuisance. A factual question is presented whether Prah's (P) use was reasonable, therefore summary judgment should not have been granted. Reversed.

DISSENT: (Callow, J.) The facts of the present case do not give rise to a cause of action for private nuisance. The majority has failed to establish the obsolescence of the policies behind the restrictions in protecting a landowner's access to sunlight in spite fence cases. The majority's policy arguments are more properly directed to a case involving a public, not a private nuisance. This court should not intrude on an area of legislative responsibility. A private nuisance involves an "invasion," and the obstruction involved in the present case does not appear to fall within the definition of invasion. Maretti's (D) actions were lawful and should not be considered intentional and unreasonable. The "sensitive use" of the property by Prah (P) should not convert this otherwise lawful use into a public private nuisance, especially where Prah (P) has taken no efforts to protect his investment. The prospective application of its decision is also troubling.

ANALYSIS

Some states, such as New Mexico, have enacted statutes that create property rights in access to solar energy. Local governments are given the power under which statutes to enact zoning regulations concerning solar rights. The New Mexico statute provides regulations protecting access in the absence of local regulations. Also, in order to be protected, solar rights as other property rights must be recorded.

Quicknotes

EASEMENT OF "LIGHTS" An interest in land granted for the unobstructed passage of light and air, from English common law.

NUISANCE An unlawful use of property that interferes with the lawful use of another's property.

Armstrong v. Francis Corp.

Landowner (P) v. Land developer (D)

N.J. Sup. Ct., 120 A.2d 4 (1956).

NATURE OF CASE: Appeal from decision enjoining landowner from artificially discharging waste waters from his land.

FACT SUMMARY: Francis Corp. (D) drained off excess water from its land by means of culverts and pipes, thereby causing severe injury to its neighbor's (P) property.

🏛 RULE OF LAW
A possessor of land is not privileged to discharge upon adjoining land, by artificial means, large quantities of surface water in a concentrated flow otherwise than through natural drainways, regardless of the means by which the surface water is collected and discharged.

FACTS: Francis (D) wanted to develop a tract of land for residential subdivision. To drain off excess water, Francis (D) constructed a series of underground pipes and culverts. Water from this system emptied into a natural stream that ran across the lands of Armstrong (P) and Klemp (P). Because of the increased flow of water, the stream often flooded and caused considerable erosion or silting on surrounding banks. In addition, the stream, being polluted by Francis's (D) pipes, became discolored and evil-smelling and lost all fish. Armstrong (P) and Klemp (P) sued to have Francis (D), on its own cost, pipe the rest of its water discharge. The lower court agreed and ordered Francis (D) to pipe the remainder of the discharge. Francis (D) appeals on the grounds he has a right to discharge the water onto adjoining lands.

ISSUE: Is a possessor of land privileged to discharge upon adjoining land, by artificial means, large quantities of surface water in a concentrated flow otherwise than through natural drainways, regardless of the means by which the surface water is collected and discharged?

HOLDING AND DECISION: (Brennan, Jr., J.) No. A possessor of land is not privileged to discharge upon adjoining land, by artificial means, large quantities of surface water in a concentrated flow otherwise than through natural drainways, regardless of the means by which the surface water is collected and discharged. Most states adopt the rule that, since surface water is the "common enemy" of necessary development, the landowner has an absolute right to discharge it upon adjoining land regardless of the harm caused his neighbors by the means he employs. However, no state applies this harsh rule literally. Courts will read in a "reasonable use" approach that has the particular virtue of flexibility. The issue of reasonableness includes such factors as the amount of harm caused, the foreseeability of the harm that results, the purpose or motive with which the possessor acted, and other relevant matter. Affirmed.

▶ ANALYSIS

The competing approach with the "common enemy" rule is the civil law rule, which holds that a possessor has no privilege, under any circumstances, to interfere with the surface water on his land so as to cause it to flow upon adjoining land in a manner or quantity substantially different from its natural flow. Even here, however, courts will read in a "reasonable use" exception to permit minor alterations.

■=■

Quicknotes

CIVIL LAW RULE Rule of law pertaining to an individual's private rights; rule based upon statutory law rather than court decisions.

COMMON ENEMY RULE The right of a landowner to conduct activities on his land so as to ward against the intrusion of surface water without regard to the effect of such activities on other landowners.

■=■

Noone v. Price

Homeowner (P) v. Neighbor (D)

W. Va. Sup. Ct. App., 298 S.E.2d 218 (1982).

NATURE OF CASE: Appeal from grant of summary judgment denying damages for eroding lateral support of land.

FACT SUMMARY: Noone (P) contended Price (D) breached her duty to supply lateral support for Noone's (P) hillside home by allowing a retaining wall to fall into disrepair.

🏛 RULE OF LAW
An adjacent landowner is strictly liable for acts of commission and omission that result in the withdrawal of lateral support to his neighbor's land in its natural state.

FACTS: In 1912, a house was built at the base of a hill, along with a stone and cement wall located at the base of the hillside. In 1928, Union Carbide built a house on the hillside, above the wall. After several years, the wall fell into disrepair. In 1955, Price (D) purchased the house at the base of the hill. She made no repairs to the wall. Noone (P) bought the house above on the hillside in 1960. Subsequently, Noone (P) discovered that his house was slipping down the hillside, and sued Price (D), contending the wall was constructed to supply lateral support to his property, and that its disrepair caused the slippage. Price (D) moved for summary judgment, contending Noone (P) was negligent in failing to protect his own property and estopped from suing because he had purchased his house with knowledge of the wall's deteriorating condition. The trial court agreed and granted summary judgment to Price (D). Noone appealed.

ISSUE: Is an adjacent landowner strictly liable for acts of commission and omission that result in the withdrawal of lateral support to his neighbor's land in its natural state?

HOLDING AND DECISION: (Neely, J.) Yes. An adjacent landowner is strictly liable for acts of commission and omission that result in the withdrawal of lateral support to his neighbor's land in its natural state. However, if as a result of the additional weight of a building so much strain is placed on the lateral support that it will not hold, then in the absence of negligence, the adjacent landowner is not liable for any resulting damages. At the time the retaining wall was built, there were no structures on Noone's (P) land. Therefore, the wall needed to support only the land in its natural state. The builder was not required to provide support sufficient to withstand the erection of any building on the land. Price, as the successor in interest, was not obligated to strengthen the wall to support Noone's (P) house. If Noone (P) is to recover, he must do so by proving that the disrepair of the wall would have inevitably led to the subsidence of his land in its natural condition, without the house upon it. Because this is a factual question, the entry of summary judgment was in error. Reversed and remanded for trial.

▶ ANALYSIS

This case illustrates the scope of the duty to supply lateral support. The duty is absolute as to the land in its natural state, but to recover for damages to a building, negligence must be shown. A negligent withdrawal of support is actionable even if the land would not have slipped but for the presence of the added weight of a building. In determining whether negligence exists, the type of withdrawal, the nature of the soil, and whether notice of the proposed withdrawal was given are all relevant.

Quicknotes

LATERAL SUPPORT The right of a landowner to have his land supported by adjoining property.

NEGLIGENCE Conduct falling below the standard of care that a reasonable person would demonstrate under similar conditions.

STRICT LIABILITY Liability for all injuries proximately caused by a party's conducting of certain inherently dangerous activities without regard to negligence or fault.

Friendswood Development Co. v. Smith-Southwest Industries, Inc.

Landowner (D) v. Landowner (P)

Tex. Sup. Ct., 576 S.W.2d 21 (1978).

NATURE OF CASE: Appeal from summary judgment in class action in tort.

FACT SUMMARY: Friendswood Development Co. (D) pumped a great deal of subsurface water from their land, causing subsidence in adjoining plots of land.

RULE OF LAW
A person is liable for damages caused by drawing water from his own land only to the extent that his activity was negligent.

FACTS: Friendswood Development Co. (Friendswood) (D) pumped water from their land for sale to industrial users. Friendswood (D) pumped vast quantities despite an engineer report stating that withdrawal of such quantities would cause subsidence in the area surrounding the pumping. Southwest Industries (P) filed suit, claiming that Friendswood's (D) negligent withdrawal of excessive quantities of ground water was the cause in fact of severe subsidence on their lands. The appellate court refused to grant Friendswood's (D) request for summary judgment. Friendswood (D) appealed.

ISSUE: Is a person liable for damages caused by drawing water from his own land limited to the extent that his activity was negligent?

HOLDING AND DECISION: (Daniel, J.) Yes. A person is liable for damages caused by drawing water from his own land only to the extent that his activity was negligent. Under the common law, a landowner had absolute right to withdraw the water lying beneath his land. Under this rule, a landowner could not be held liable for any damage to neighboring property that resulted from activity on his own land. However, modern lawmakers have moved away from this harsh rule to hold a landowner liable for the damage to the extent his activity was negligent. Nonetheless, the case law to date has upheld the common law. Thus it would be unjust to apply a new standard to Friendswood (D) at this time. From this day forward, however, landowners will be held liable for damages caused by the negligent, willfully wasteful, or malicious withdrawal of subterranean waters. Reversed and remanded.

DISSENT: (Pope, J.) The principal opinion incorrectly applies the common law in regard to water rights and then declares that stare decisis dictates their conclusion. Smith-Southwest (P) raised absolutely no claim, and sought no damages, in relation to Friendswood's (D) capture and sale of the ground water. The complaint is that Friendswood's (D) action caused the subsidence of their land, and a landowner's right to lateral support for his adjacent land is an absolute right. Our prior holdings involving mining and oil now stand in contradiction to the present holding. A landowner may assert a cause of action against one destroying the lateral support to maintain his land in its natural state when the destruction is knowingly caused, or when the landowner can prove negligence or nuisance.

ANALYSIS

Restatement (Second) of Torts § 818 gives landowners absolute right to subadjacent support. This strict liability approach, however, is the rule in only a few states such as Washington. See *Muskatell v. City of Seattle*, 116 P.2d 363 (1941).

Quicknotes

NEGLIGENCE Conduct falling below the standard of care that a reasonable person would demonstrate under similar conditions.

NUISANCE An unlawful use of property that interferes with the lawful use of another's property.

STARE DECISIS Doctrine whereby courts follow legal precedent unless there is good cause for departure.

Land Use and Natural Resources Regulation

Quick Reference Rules of Law

Village of Euclid v. Ambler Realty Co.

Municipal corporation (D) v. Tract owner (P)

272 U.S. 365 (1926).

NATURE OF CASE: Action to enjoin enforcement of a zoning ordinance.

FACT SUMMARY: Euclid (D) zoned property of Ambler Realty (P) in a manner which materially reduced its potential value.

RULE OF LAW

A zoning ordinance, as a valid exercise of the police power, will only be declared unconstitutional where its provisions are clearly arbitrary and unreasonable, having no substantial relation to the public health, safety, morals, or general welfare.

FACTS: Ambler Realty (P) was the owner of 68 acres in the village of Euclid (D). The 68 acres is surrounded primarily by residential neighborhoods, but a major thoroughfare abuts it to the south and a railroad abuts it to the north. Euclid (D) instituted zoning ordinances placing use, height, and area restrictions. Restrictions were placed on Ambler Realty's (P) property prohibiting (1) apartment houses, hotels, churches, schools, or any other public or semi-public buildings for the first 620 feet from Euclid Avenue, the above-described major thoroughfare, and (2) industry, theatres, banks, shops, etc., for the next 130 feet after that. As a result of this zoning, the value of Ambler Realty's (P) property has declined from $10,000 per acre to $2,500 per acre. Ambler Realty (P) brought an action to enjoin Euclid (D) from enforcing the ordinance on the ground that it constitutes a violation of Fourteenth Amendment due process. From a decree in favor of Ambler Realty (P), Euclid (D) appeals, contending that the ordinance was a valid exercise of the police power of the state.

ISSUE: Is a zoning ordinance unconstitutional as a deprivation of property without due process because it results in a diminution of value in the property zoned?

HOLDING AND DECISION: (Sutherland, J.) No. A zoning ordinance, as a valid exercise of the police power, will only be declared unconstitutional where its provisions are clearly arbitrary and unreasonable, having no substantial relation to the public health, safety, morals, or general welfare. Zoning ordinances, and all similar laws and regulations, must find their justification in some aspect of the police power, asserted for the public welfare. Until recent years, urban life was comparatively simple; but with the great increase and concentration of population, problems have developed which require new restrictions on the use and occupation of private lands in urban communities. There is no serious difference of opinion on the state power to avoid the nuisances which industry may cause in a residential area. As for residential regulation, many considerations point toward their validity. Segregation of residential business and industrial buildings makes it easier to provide appropriate fire apparatus, for example. Further, it is often observed that the construction of one type of building destroys an area for other types. In light of these considerations, the court is not prepared to say that the end of public welfare here is not sufficient to justify the imposition of this ordinance. It clearly cannot be said that it "... passes the bounds of reason and assumes the character of a merely arbitrary fiat." The decree must be reversed.

ANALYSIS

Village of Euclid v. Ambler Realty is the landmark United States Supreme Court decision on zoning ordinances as valid exercises of the police power. Essentially, any zoning ordinance which is tied to public health, safety, morals, or welfare will be upheld unless clearly arbitrary and unreasonable. So-called *Euclidian* Zoning, which resulted from this decision, usually consists in the division of areas into zones, in which building use, height, and area are regulated in a manner designed to guarantee homogeneity of building patterns. All too often, however, zoning operates not so much to protect the public interest as to protect the vested interests in a community. Building restrictions may all too easily be used as an economic sanction by which social segregation is perpetuated. (Barring low-cost housing keeps out economically deprived segment of the population.) Note, however, that *Euclid* did not foreclose the possibility that government land-use regulations may constitute a "taking" which requires compensation. In *Pennsylvania Coal Co. v. Mahon*, 260 U.S. 393 (1922), the United States Supreme Court held that an anti-mining restriction, which totally destroyed the interest of the party who owned only the mineral rights, constituted a taking as to that person for which compensation had to be paid. In the *Mahon* case, the diminution in value of the party's property was total, and was thus clearly a "taking."

Quicknotes

INJUNCTION A court order requiring a person to do or prohibiting that person from doing a specific act.

POLICE POWER The power of a government to impose restrictions on the rights of private persons, as long as those restrictions are reasonably related to the promotion

Continued on next page.

and protection of public health, safety, morals, and the general welfare.

PUBLIC WELFARE The well-being of the general community.

TAKING A governmental action that substantially deprives an owner of the use and enjoyment of his or her property, requiring compensation.

ZONING ORDINANCE A statute that divides land into defined areas and which regulates the form and use of buildings and structures within those areas.

■▬■

Town of Belleville v. Parrillo's, Inc.

City (P) v. Discotheque (D)

N.J. Sup. Ct., 416 A.2d 388 (1980).

NATURE OF CASE: Appeal from the reversal of a conviction for continued operation of a nonconforming business whose usage underwent a change.

FACT SUMMARY: When Parrillo's, Inc. (D) changed its existing nonconforming use from a restaurant to a discotheque, the Town of Belleville (P) filed charges that led to a conviction of Parrillo's (D) owners. However, the appellate division reversed the conviction, prompting this appeal.

RULE OF LAW

An existing nonconforming use may continue only where it is a continuance of substantially the same kind of use as that to which the premises were devoted when the zoning ordinance was passed.

FACTS: Parrillo's, Inc. (D) already operated as a restaurant when the Town of Belleville (the Town) (P) enacted a zoning ordinance designating the area in which Parrillo's (D) was located as a residence zone. Parrillo's (D) owners later made certain renovations to the premises, and then opened as a discotheque. Shortly after opening under the new format, Parrillo's (D) owners applied for a discotheque license as required by the Town's (P) ordinance regulating dance halls. Although the application was denied, Parrillo's (D) continued business as usual. The Town (P) filed charges that culminated in a conviction and a court-imposed fine. On a trial de novo after appeal, Parrillo's (D) was again found guilty. The court concluded that there had been a prohibited change in the use of the premises. The appellate division reversed. The Town (P) appealed.

ISSUE: May an existing nonconforming use continue only where it is a continuance of substantially the same kind of use as that to which the premises were devoted when the zoning ordinance was passed?

HOLDING AND DECISION: (Clifford, J.) Yes. An existing nonconforming use may continue only where it is a continuance of substantially the same kind of use as that to which the premises were devoted when the zoning ordinance was passed. Parrillo's (D) conversion of the premises from a restaurant to a discotheque resulted in a substantial, and therefore impermissible, change. The entire character of the business has been altered. What was once a restaurant is now a dance hall. Measured by the zoning ordinance, the general welfare of the neighborhood has been demonstrably affected adversely by the conversion of Parrillo's (D) business. Reversed.

ANALYSIS

Because nonconforming uses are inconsistent with the objectives of uniform zoning, the courts have required that consistent with the property rights of those affected and with substantial justice, they should be reduced to conformity as quickly as is compatible with justice. In that regard, the courts have permitted municipalities to impose limitations upon nonconforming uses. The method generally used to limit nonconforming uses is to prevent any increase or change in the nonconformity.

Quicknotes

NONCONFORMING USE The use of a structure that is rendered unlawful by the promulgation or revision of a zoning ordinance.

ZONING ORDINANCE A statute that divides land into defined areas and that regulates the form and use of buildings and structures within those areas.

Stone v. City of Wilton

Landowner (P) v. City (D)

Iowa Sup. Ct., 331 N.W.2d 398 (1983).

NATURE OF CASE: Appeal from the dismissal of a petition for declaratory judgment, injunctive relief, and damages in an action involving rezoning.

FACT SUMMARY: When the City of Wilton (D) considered a rezoning recommendation that would affect Stone's (P) property and his plan to construct a multi-family housing project, he filed a petition with the court, contending he had a vested right in developing his land.

🏛 RULE OF LAW
The validity of a police power enactment, such as zoning, depends on its reasonableness.

FACTS: Stone (P) purchased land to develop a low-income, federally subsidized housing project consisting of several multi-family units. About one-fourth of the land was zoned single-family residential, while the remainder was zoned multi-family residential. After purchasing the land, Stone (P) incurred expenses for an architect and an engineer. Stone (P) also secured a Farmers' Home Administration (FHA) loan commitment for construction of the project. Later, the planning and zoning commission recommended rezoning part of the city to single-family residential due to alleged inadequacies of sewer, water, and electrical services. The rezoning recommendation affected all of Stone's (P) property. When the City of Wilton (D) denied Stone's (P) application for a building permit due to the pending rezoning recommendation, he filed a petition with the court. Stone (P) also contended that he had a vested right in developing his property. This appeal followed the trial court's ruling.

ISSUE: Does the validity of a police power enactment, such as zoning, depend on its reasonableness?

HOLDING AND DECISION: (McGiverin, J.) Yes. The validity of a police power enactment, such as zoning, depends on its reasonableness. A city's comprehensive plan is always subject to reasonable revisions designed to meet the ever-changing needs and conditions of a community. Here, the city council (D) rationally decided to rezone this section of the city to further the public welfare in accordance with a comprehensive plan. In addition, Stone's (P) efforts and expenditures prior to rezoning were not so substantial as to create vested rights in the completion of the housing project. Finally, the rezoning only deprived Stone (P) of the land's most beneficial use, which does not render it an unconstitutional taking. This court cannot substitute its view of reasonableness for that of the city council (D). Thus, the ordinance is valid and applicable to Stone's (P) land and project. Affirmed.

▶ ANALYSIS

The Wilton (D) city council was faced with a number of competing concerns in regard to the proper zoning of the area where Stone's (P) land was situated. Because legislative bodies are faced with balancing such competing concerns, courts refrain from reviewing the merits of their decisions if at least a debatable question exists as to the reasonableness of their action. However, where a discriminatory purpose is a motivating factor in the decision, such judicial deference is no longer justified.

Quicknotes

DECLARATORY JUDGMENT A judgment of the rights between opposing parties that is binding, but does not award coercive relief (i.e., damages).

POLICE POWERS The power of a state or local government to regulate private conduct for the health, safety, and welfare of the general public.

ZONING ORDINANCE A statute that divides land into defined areas and that regulates the form and use of buildings and structures within those areas.

Durand v. IDC Bellingham, L.L.C.

Town Residents (P) v. Power Plant Owner (D)

Mass. Sup. Jud. Ct., 793 N.E.2d 359 (2003).

NATURE OF CASE: Appeal from lower court decision in favor of town residents.

FACT SUMMARY: After IDC Bellingham, L.L.C. (IDC) (D) offered an $8,000,000 "gift" to the town of Bellingham, Massachusetts, the local town meeting voted to rezone a parcel of land to allow IDC (D) to develop the parcel. Durand (P) and seven other town residents sued, alleging the vote was an improper use of "contract zoning."

🏛 RULE OF LAW
The voluntary offer of public benefits not related to mitigation of the proposed development of property does not, standing alone, invalidate a legislative act of a local town meeting.

FACTS: On two prior occasions, IDC Bellingham, L.L.C. (IDC) (D) had sought unsuccessfully to develop a parcel of land in the town of Bellingham, Massachusetts (the town). Then in 1997, IDC (D) offered the town an $8,000,000 gift if the town voted to rezone the parcel and allow development of a power plant. IDC (D) informed the town it could use the money toward construction of a new high school or for any other municipal purpose. The rezoning article for the parcel in question proceeded through the normal channels, without issue or complaint. The town meeting voted to approve the rezoning of the site. Durand (P) and seven other residents near the site filed suit. Durand (P) alleged the rezoning of the site constituted illegal "contract zoning." The lower court agreed that the town went through the proper zoning procedures to adopt the rezoning article. However, the lower court then held that the $8,000,000 gift was improper because it was not given for the purpose of mitigating the impact of the development of the site. The gift constituted an improper "extraneous consideration." Accordingly, the court invalidated the rezoning article. IDC (D) appealed.

ISSUE: Does the voluntary offer of public benefits not related to mitigation of the proposed development of property, standing alone, invalidate a legislative act of a local town meeting?

HOLDING AND DECISION: (Cordy, J.) No. The voluntary offer of public benefits not related to mitigation of the proposed development of property does not, standing alone, invalidate a legislative act of a local town meeting. First, the enactment of zoning bylaws and articles by a town meeting carries a strong presumption of validity. A court will invalidate a zoning bylaw only where the bylaw is arbitrary or capricious or unrelated to public health, safety, or the general welfare. A reviewing court will nor-

mally not analyze the motivations behind the enactment. There is no dispute the town followed the rezoning procedure properly. Nor is there a claim that the rezoning act regarding IDC's (D) parcel was in any way arbitrary or capricious. There is also no contract zoning present here because the town meeting members were under no obligation to approve the rezoning of the parcel. Lastly, we do not invalidate the legislative act because of the $8,000,000 gift. We defer to the legislative enactments "without regard to motive." We can find no persuasive authority that would invalidate legislative acts because they were encouraged by a voluntary gift. Reversed.

CONCURRENCE AND DISSENT: (Spina, J.) I concur in the judgment because I would find that the plaintiffs do not have standing to bring this claim. The plaintiffs claim no injury to themselves. They are not a party to a contract between IDC (D) and the town. Nor are they authorized to bring this suit in the name of the town. Accordingly, I would grant IDC (D) summary judgment on those grounds. Separately, I dissent from the majority opinion. A prior decision, *Sylvania Elec. Prods. Inc. v. Newton*, 344 Mass. 428 (1962), held that considerations not related to the proposed development may not provide the basis for legislative enactment. Here, IDC's (D) $8,000,000 gift was unrelated to its plan to develop the site and provided an improper basis for the town meeting vote. Moreover, there is no question the town approved the plan because of the gift. Accordingly, I dissent from the majority opinion on this issue.

▌ANALYSIS

This case, a four to three decision, has spawned a sharp debate in Massachusetts. The decision greatly increased real estate developers' ability to make voluntary financial offers, totally unrelated to the proposed project, as methods to obtain municipal approval. The extent of the ruling, however, is in question. Some commentators feel the ruling applies to any type of municipal order, such as the granting of a building permit or a variance. Others feel it only applies to town meeting votes or other similar "legislative enactments."

Quicknotes

ZONING Municipal statutory scheme dividing an area into districts in order to regulate the use or building of structures within those districts.

Continued on next page.

ZONING ORDINANCE A statute that divides land into defined areas and that regulates the form and use of buildings and structures within those areas.

■≡■

Krummenacher v. Minnetonka

Landowner (P) v. Municipality (D)

Minn. Sup. Ct., 783 N.W.2d 721 (2010).

NATURE OF CASE: Appeal from lower court decisions finding that a municipality properly granted a variance to a landowner seeking to add a second story to a garage.

FACT SUMMARY: The City of Minnetonka (D) granted a variance to JoAnne Liebeler (D), allowing her to add a second story to a detached garage. Krummenacher (P), a neighbor of Liebeler's (D), brought suit against Minnetonka (D) and Liebeler (D) on the grounds the variance was granted in violation of current statutory law.

RULE OF LAW

To obtain a use variance, an applicant must demonstrate undue hardship by satisfying the following three factors: (1) the property cannot be put to reasonable use if a variance is not allowed; (2) the landowner's plight is not due to conditions created by the landowner; and (3) the variance, if granted, will not alter the character of the neighborhood.

FACTS: The City of Minnetonka (D) granted a variance to Joanne Liebeler (D), allowing her to add a second story to a detached garage. The detached garage, built in the 1940s, was a permissible, nonconforming use because it was only set back 17 feet from the road. A new zoning ordinance required such structures to be set back 50 feet. Liebeler (S) sought to add a second story that would include a yoga studio and craft room. Krummenacher (P), a neighbor of Liebeler's (D), objected because of the new height of the structure. Minnetonka's (D) Planning Commission and City Council approved the project. Krummenacher (P) brought suit against Minnetonka (D) and Liebeler (D) on the grounds the variance was granted in violation of current statutory law. Krummenacher (P) argued that a municipality can only allow a variance if the property in question cannot be put to any reasonable use without the variance. He argued that Liebeler (D) already had a reasonable use for the garage—as storage for vehicles and bicycles. The trial court and an intermediate appellate court affirmed Minnetonka's (D) approvals. The Minnesota Supreme Court granted Krummenacher's (P) petition for further review.

ISSUE: To obtain a use variance, must an applicant demonstrate undue hardship by satisfying the following three factors: (1) the property cannot be put to reasonable use if a variance is not allowed; (2) the landowner's plight is not due to conditions created by the landowner; and (3) the variance, if granted, will not alter the character of the neighborhood?

HOLDING AND DECISION: (Gildea, J.) Yes. To obtain a use variance, an applicant must demonstrate undue hardship by satisfying the following three factors: (1) the property cannot be put to reasonable use if a variance is not allowed; (2) the landowner's plight is not due to conditions created by the landowner; and (3) the variance, if granted, will not alter the character of the neighborhood. Municipalities have broad discretion to grant or deny variances. Courts review those decisions to determine if jurisdiction was proper and whether the municipality acted arbitrarily or capriciously. Krummenacher (P) argues that a municipality can only allow a variance if the property in question cannot be put to any reasonable use without the variance. A prior appellate court decision required property owners to prove only that the owner will use the property in a reasonable manner currently prohibited by an ordinance. This is known as the "reasonable manner" standard. The statute, however, requires the applicant to show that the property cannot be put to any reasonable use without the variance. Simply allowing the variance if the proposed use is reasonable would water down the statute. Because this decision announces a new standard for variances, the matter is remanded to the trial court to determine if the variance complies with the new, stricter standard. Reversed.

▶ **ANALYSIS**

In this decision, Minnesota sought to rein in municipalities that grant variances without any regard to applicable legal standards. Local municipalities in all states often grant variances simply based on whether the improvements would complement the character of the particular neighborhood. This decision effectively will only allow variances if the structure could not be used in any reasonable manner without the variance.

Quicknotes

VARIANCE Exemption from the application of zoning laws.

Southern Burlington County NAACP v. Township of Mount Laurel

NAACP (P) v. Town (D)

N.J. Sup. Ct., 336 A.2d 713 (1975).

NATURE OF CASE: Appeal from invalidation of zoning ordinance.

FACT SUMMARY: The trial court held that a bona fide attempt by a municipality to provide zoned land for low-cost housing fulfilled its constitutional obligations.

🏛 RULE OF LAW
Municipal land use regulations must provide a realistic opportunity for low- and moderate-income housing.

FACTS: The NAACP (P) sued Mount Laurel (D), contending the municipality's zoning scheme violated the New Jersey constitution by failing to provide for low-income housing outside of depressed areas. The New Jersey Supreme Court invalidated the ordinances and remanded for further proceedings. The trial court held that it was sufficient that Mount Laurel (D) had made a bona fide attempt to comply with the Supreme Court decision and upheld the new ordinance enacted in response. The NAACP (P) appealed, contending a mere attempt to provide such zoning did not discharge Mount Laurel's (D) constitutional obligations.

ISSUE: Must municipal land use regulations provide a realistic opportunity for low- and moderate-income housing?

HOLDING AND DECISION: (Hall, J.) Yes. Municipal land use regulations must provide a realistic opportunity for low- and moderate-income housing. Such obligation extends beyond attempting to provide for such housing. The housing must be in direct proportion to the percentage of lower income residents in the city. To reach this goal, affirmative governmental action may be required. The elimination of some obstacles and the creation of a new zoning scheme may be frustrated by other restrictions that effectively deprive the poor of adequate housing. Therefore, the zoning scheme that merely manifested an intent to abide by the original Supreme Court holding was insufficient to discharge Mount Laurel's (D) constitutional obligations. Reversed and remanded.

▶ ANALYSIS

The rationale behind the *Mount Laurel* case is that the use of all land is controlled by the state. The state has constitutional obligations to all its residents whether rich or poor. Municipalities, as state subjects, must set aside a fair share of its land for lower income housing. They cannot allocate only dilapidated land for the poor and retain valuable land for the rich exclusively. While this rationale appears clear in theory, in execution it has proven very difficult. The main difficulty is in developing an equitable formula for determining "fair share." Until a definitive formula is developed, this will prevent widespread application of this rule.

■=■

Quicknotes

BONA FIDE In good faith.

ZONING ORDINANCE A statute that divides land into defined areas and that regulates the form and use of buildings and structures within those areas.

■=■

Anderson v. City of Issaquah

Developer (P) v. Municipality (D)

Wash. Ct. App., 70 Wash. App. 64, 851 P.2d 744 (1993).

NATURE OF CASE: Appeal from denial of building permit.

FACT SUMMARY: The building code of the City of Issaquah, Washington (D) included criteria with respect to building design that were strictly subjective in nature.

🏛 RULE OF LAW
A building code cannot consist of design criteria that are strictly subjective in nature.

FACTS: The City of Issaquah, Washington (the City) (D) included, as part of its municipal building code, certain design criteria to be followed in new building developments. The code mandated, inter alia, that buildings be "harmonious" with surrounding architecture and that building proportions be "appropriate." Anderson (P), intending to develop certain commercial property, submitted his building design to the Development Commission. During several hearings, the members expressed dissatisfaction with the design, although the members themselves did not seem to agree on what could be done to make the design more acceptable. After several revisions, Anderson (P) submitted his final plans, which were not approved. Anderson (P) appealed to the city council, which also denied approval. Anderson (P) filed suit seeking an injunction mandating approval. The trial court dismissed the complaint, and Anderson (P) appealed.

ISSUE: Can a building code consist of design criteria that are strictly subjective in nature?

HOLDING AND DECISION: (Kennedy, J.) No. A building code cannot consist of design criteria that are strictly subjective in nature. A statute that either forbids or requires the doing of an act in terms so vague that persons of common intelligence must necessarily guess at its meaning and differ as to its application violates due process. It is inherent in due process that laws be crafted in such a fashion that a person can reasonably be able to understand them. Terms that are totally subjective cannot meet this standard. The ordinance at issue here is an example of this. It mandates that design be "harmonious" and "appropriate." Obviously, what might or might not meet these standards is strictly in the eye of the beholder. This is borne out by the fact that the individual Commission members seemed to have had differing ideas as to what Anderson (P) had to do to bring his design into compliance, which left him in a totally impossible situation. Since the ordinance was clearly unconstitutionally vague, the City (D) should have issued the building permit. So ordered.

▶ ANALYSIS

Private developments, such as condominium complexes, often have similar design criteria and their own architectural committees. Courts, as a general rule, have been much more deferential to decisions of private developments. Of course, the state constitution applies to state actions only, so the Due Process Clause is generally inapplicable in such situations.

Quicknotes

BUILDING CODE Local ordinances that govern requirements for residential housing.

DUE PROCESS CLAUSE Clauses found in the Fifth and Fourteenth Amendments to the United States Constitution providing that no person shall be deprived of "life, liberty, or property, without due process of law."

INJUNCTION A court order requiring a person to do or prohibiting that person from doing a specific act.

STATE ACTION Actions brought pursuant to the Fourteenth Amendment claiming that the government violated the plaintiff's civil rights.

Westchester Day School v. Village of Mamaroneck

Religious elementary school (P) v. Town (D)

504 F.3d 338 (2d. Cir. 2007).

NATURE OF CASE: Appeal from lower court decision finding that a local town improperly denied a school's application to expand its operations.

FACT SUMMARY: The Westchester Day School (P), an Orthodox Jewish co-educational day school, sought to expand its buildings on its large campus. Mamaroneck's (D) Zoning Board of Appeals rejected the application in its entirety.

☷ RULE OF LAW
While the neutral application of legitimate zoning regulations may not constitute an improper substantial burden placed upon a religious organization, a substantial burden may exist if the municipality imposed the land-use restrictions arbitrarily, capriciously, or unlawfully.

FACTS: The Westchester Day School (WDS) (P), an Orthodox Jewish co-educational day school, sought to expand its buildings on its large campus. The project included a $12 million dollar expansion plan that would update current buildings and expand others. All of the classes, regardless of subject, include an aspect of religious and Judaic concepts to reinforce the school's core religious and educational purposes. After a vocal group of residents opposed the plan, Mamaroneck's (D) Zoning Board of appeals rejected the project in its entirety. It also denied WDS (P) the opportunity to propose modifications to the project that would address concerns over increased traffic and parking. WDS (P) brought suit against Mamaroneck (D) on the grounds the permit denial ran afoul of the federal Religious Land Use and Institutionalized Persons Act (RLUIPA). This act prohibits a local government from imposing a zoning regulation that constitutes a substantial burden upon any religious organizations. After a bench trial, a federal district court agreed and ordered Mamaroneck (D) to approve the project. Mamaroneck (D) appealed to the United States Court of Appeals for the Second Circuit.

ISSUE: While the neutral application of legitimate zoning regulations may not constitute an improper substantial burden placed upon a religious organization, may a substantial burden exist if the municipality imposed the land-use restrictions arbitrarily, capriciously, or unlawfully?

HOLDING AND DECISION: (Cardamone, J.) Yes. While the neutral application of legitimate zoning regulations may not constitute an improper substantial burden placed upon a religious organization, a substantial burden may exist if the municipality imposed the land-use restrictions arbitrarily, capriciously, or unlawfully. Specifically,

RLUIPA prohibits governments from imposing a zoning regulation upon a religious organization or entity in a manner that constitutes a substantial burden, unless the government meets two conditions. First, the burden must be in furtherance of a compelling government interest and second, the burden must be the least restrictive means of furthering that particular interest. The trial court properly concluded that WDS's (P) improvements to the school involved religious education or practice. The larger issue is whether the Mamaroneck (D) imposed a substantial burden on the school (P). A denial of a religious institution's application to expand may constitute a substantial burden but all facts must be considered. If the denial allows the opportunity to revise the plans in response to public health and safety concerns, that type of denial may not constitute a substantial burden. In addition, there must be a close nexus between the impeded conduct, here, the expansion of the school, and the institution's religious exercise. However, the test is not an "effects test." Municipalities are free to impose neutral zoning regulations upon religious entities in the same manner as other private institutions. The crux is that such applications of zoning laws upon religious entities must not be imposed because of the religious nature of the entity. This type of arbitrary application of the zoning laws may evidence a discriminatory bias against the religious entity. In this case, the district court properly found that Mamaroneck's (D) reasons to deny the project did not bear substantial relation to any public health or safety concerns. The Zoning Board's (D) conclusions relating to the traffic and parking concerns were incorrect and contradicted by their own experts at trial. Accordingly, because the Zoning Board (D) did not have substantial evidence to support its decision, its actions were arbitrary and capricious. This same lack of evidence also reveals the Zoning Board (D) failed to demonstrate that it had a compelling reason to deny the application. Affirmed.

▶ ANALYSIS

The Religious Land Use and Institutionalized Persons Act uses a similar strict scrutiny test employed by courts to review freedom of religion or other First Amendment-based challenges. Any government regulation that infringes freedoms of religion, speech, or the press must further a compelling governmental interest and be narrowly tailored to achieve the intended results. In most cases, once a court determines that strict scrutiny will apply, the governmental regulation at issue will likely be found unconstitutional.

Continued on next page.

Quicknotes

STRICT SCRUTINY Method by which courts determine the constitutionality of a law, when a law affects a fundamental right. Under the test, the legislature must have had a compelling interest to enact the law and measures prescribed by the law must be the least restrictive means possible to accomplish its goal.

■=■

State Department of Ecology v. Grimes

State (D) v. Landowner (P)

Wash. Sup. Ct., 852 P.2d 1044 (1993).

NATURE OF CASE: Appeal from lower trial court decision that affirmed a special master's report and recommendation that provided the Grimeses (P) with lower amounts of a local water supply than the amount they (P) requested.

FACT SUMMARY: For the public's interest, the Washington Department of Ecology (D) petitioned the Superior Court for an adjudication of water rights to a lake. An appointed special master recommended that the Grimeses (P), a local farming couple, receive lower amounts of the water supply than the amount they (P) requested.

> 🏛 **RULE OF LAW**
> A prior appropriated water right is established by a determination of the amount of water put to a beneficial use upon the land.

FACTS: For the public's interest, the Washington Department of Ecology (D) petitioned the Superior Court for an adjudication of water rights to Marshall Lake and the Marshall Creek drainage basin. During the process, Grimeses (P) filed a claim, along with many other local property owners, for the use of the waters for domestic supply, irrigation, and recreational purposes. The Grimeses' (P) rights are pre-1917, having been established 11 years before the state's adoption of the water code in 1917. Grimes (P) sought a flow rate of 3 cubic feet per second for irrigation purposes and a storage right in Marshall Lake of 1,520 acre feet of water for storage purpose. However, the Grimeses (P) did not provide actual use figures. An appointed special master recommended that the Grimeses (P) receive 1.5 cubic square feet for irrigation and a storage right of 183 feet plus 737 acre feet for evaporative loss, for a total storage right of 920 acre feet. The trial court confirmed the recommendations from the special master. The Grimeses (P) appealed. An intermediate appellate court certified this issue of public importance to the Washington Supreme Court.

ISSUE: Is a prior appropriated water right established by a determination of the amount of water put to a beneficial use upon the land?

HOLDING AND DECISION: (Smith, J.) Yes. A prior appropriated water right is established by a determination of the amount of water put to a beneficial use upon the land. The right is appurtenant to the land and operates to the exclusion of later claimants. This matter is a general adjudication of water rights. These adjudications may not be used to lessen, enlarge, or modify existing rights. To confirm existing rights, a special master must determine: (1) the amount of water that has been put to beneficial use; and (2) the priority of water rights relative to other claimants and property owners. This state established the law of prior appropriation in 1873. An appropriated water right is perpetual and excludes any subsequent claims. The key to determining the extent of one's vested right is the concept of beneficial use. Beneficial use refers to the quantity of water used by a landowner. Beneficial use, itself, includes two separate elements of a water right. First, it refers to the manner in which the landowner uses the water. Use of water for irrigation purposes is a beneficial use. Second, the beneficial use determines the actual measure of the landowner's right to the water. In other words, the extent of a landowner's water right is based upon how much he has been using for reasonable purposes. To determine the amount one has been using for beneficial use, courts have developed the principle of reasonable use. In turn, reasonable use is determined by the factors of water duty and waste. Water duty is the measure of water reasonably required to be applied to land to allow for the maximum amount of crops typically grown in the area. The special master relied upon irrigation reports from the State (D) to determine the Grimeses' (P) use of water. His conclusion that the Grimeses (P) required 1.5 cubic feet per second to irrigate their alfalfa farm was reasonable and will not be disturbed by this court. The factor of waste involves a consideration of the efficiency of the irrigation systems at issue. All systems lose water during the process. The special master considered this and still properly determined the amount the Grimeses (P) were entitled to for irrigation purposes. The special master stated that when determining the extent of the Grimeses' (P) overall vested water right, he employed a reasonable efficiency test. However, upon review of his report, it does not appear he actually relied upon this test, which would be inconsistent with this state's law of prior appropriation. In an adjudicatory hearing, the special master can only confirm existing rights. He cannot lower or modify existing rights based upon competing claims from other property owners. Such a test would be contrary to the vested rights of the water uses. Included in those rights are diversion, delivery, and application according to the reasonable customs of the locality. It does appear that the special master properly determined the Grimeses' (P) reasonable use by measuring their beneficial use of the water for their alfalfa fields. The special master granted the Grimeses (P) an amount lower than that requested because the Grimeses (P) were unable to provide sufficient evidence

Continued on next page.

as to their actual use. The special master used the best evidence he had available to him: the irrigation reports from the State (D). Accordingly, this court will not overturn the special master's findings and recommendations that were properly approved by the trial court below. Affirmed.

▌ *ANALYSIS*

In the United States, there are two main doctrines that control rights to surface water such as lakes, streams, and rivers. In most states, the riparian doctrine utilizes a reasonable test that balances the costs and benefits of a claimant's use of water versus any harm to competing uses from other claimants. In the western part of the country, most states employ the prior appropriation doctrine seen in this decision. This doctrine gives precedence to any older beneficial uses of water over later claimants.

■══■

Quicknotes

ADJUDICATORY PROCEEDING A hearing conducted by an administrative agency or court resulting in a final judgment regarding the rights of the parties involved.

RIPARIAN RIGHT The right of an owner of real property to the use of water naturally flowing through his land.

■══■

Servitudes

Quick Reference Rules of Law

Green v. Lupo

Landowner (P) v. Transferee (D)

Wash Ct. App., 647 P.2d 51 (1982).

NATURE OF CASE: Appeal from refusal to enforce an agreement to grant an easement.

FACT SUMMARY: Green (P) granted Lupo (D) a deed release upon the sale of his property on the condition that when Lupo (D) acquired title he would grant Green (P) an easement.

> ## RULE OF LAW
> An easement is not personal if there is anything in the grant to suggest that it was intended to be tied to the land retained or conveyed.

FACTS: Green (P) originally owned an entire parcel of land. Later he transferred a portion of the land to Lupo (D). Lupo (D) asked Green (P) for a deed release he needed in order to obtain financing to build a home. Green (P) granted the release on the condition that Lupo (D) grant him an easement for ingress and egress when he acquired title. Lupo (D) agreed. Green (P) turned his parcel into a mobile home park, and the occupants used the part of the land designated as the easement as a runway for motorcycles. In protest of Green's (P) use, Lupo (D) refused to transfer the easement as promised when he acquired title. Green (P) brought suit to specifically enforce the grant of the easement. The trial court found that the easement was personal and enjoined the motorcycles' use of it. Green (P) appealed.

ISSUE: Is an easement personal if there is anything in the grant to suggest that it was intended to be tied to the land retained or conveyed?

HOLDING AND DECISION: (Petrich, C.J.) No. An easement is not personal if there is anything in the grant to suggest that it was intended to be tied to the land retained or conveyed. There is a presumption against personal easements. The written instrument granting Lupo (D) his easement states the easement would be granted to Green (P) for ingress and egress to their property. Thus the easement was granted to gain access to a particular piece of land and is thus appurtenant, not personal. The lower court erred in ordering the cycles banned. Reversed and remanded.

ANALYSIS

The appeal was actually based on the admissibility of parol evidence. The court found that parol evidence is always admissible to demonstrate intent when the written instrument is unclear.

Quicknotes

APPURTENANT A burden attached to real property that either benefits or burdens the owner's right to utilize that property.

EASEMENT The right to utilize a portion of another's real property for a specific use.

PAROL EVIDENCE Evidence given verbally; extraneous evidence.

Cox v. Glenbrook Co.

Developer (P) v. Easement grantor (D)

Nev. Sup. Ct., 371 P.2d 647 (1962).

NATURE OF CASE: Appeal from request for declaratory judgment.

FACT SUMMARY: Glenbrook Co. (D) owned land subject to an easement for access from Cox's (P) land; the parties contested the extent of the easement.

🏛 RULE OF LAW
Where the grant is unclear, the extent of the easement must be construed as broadly as necessary to carry out the purposes for which it was granted.

FACTS: The Quill property was surrounded on four sides by land owned by others. There was an easement granted through the Glenbrook Co. (D) property to provide ingress and egress to the Quill property. The Quill property changed hands several times before it ended up in the hands of Cox (P). Cox (P) planned to develop the land as resort area. To achieve this goal, Cox (P) would have to expand the existing easement from a one-lane dirt road to a paved, two-way road. Both parties brought suit for declaratory judgment as to the extent of the easement. The trial court found that the easement was limited to those uses necessary for access by a single family. Cox (P) appealed.

ISSUE: Where the grant is unclear, must the extent of the easement be construed as broadly as necessary?

HOLDING AND DECISION: (Thompson, J.) Yes. Where the grant is unclear, the extent of the easement must be construed as broad as necessary to carry out the purposes for which it was granted. The trial court's construction of the limits on the easement erroneously makes the easement personal. As broadly as necessary for family use defines the easement by the person holding it rather than the land it benefits. The grant was intended to give ingress and egress to the land. This intent does not support doubling the size of the road and paving it. The easement is limited to the size and nature at the time of the grant.

▶ ANALYSIS

Another way appurtenant easements are limited is by the nature of the servient estate. An easement cannot cause unwarranted interference or burden on the servient estate. The court found that mere grading of the road in this case would not pose such a burden, but that widening the road would.

■═■

Quicknotes

DOMINANT ESTATE Property whose owners benefit from the use of another's property.

EASEMENT The right to utilize a portion of another's real property for a specific use.

SERVIENT ESTATE Property that is burdened in some aspect for the benefit of a dominant estate.

■═■

Henley v. Continental Cablevision of St. Louis County, Inc.

Landowner (P) v. Telephone company (D)

Mo. Ct. App., 692 S.W.2d 825 (1985).

NATURE OF CASE: Action for injunction and damages.

FACT SUMMARY: Henley (P) granted the telephone company the right to construct and maintain telephone and electrical systems that Continental Cablevision of St. Louis County, Inc. (D) licensed in order to install cable services.

RULE OF LAW
Easements in gross are freely transferable.

FACTS: In 1922, Henley's (P) predecessors granted the telephone company an easement in gross to install and maintain electrical and telephone systems on the back five feet of all the properties in their subdivision. This easement was transferable to other parties to create such systems. In 1981, Continental Cablevision of St. Louis County, Inc. (Continental) (D) acquired licenses from the phone company to install a cable system in the area. Henley (P) filed suit for injunction to prevent and compel removal of Continental's (D) cables, and for damages.

ISSUE: Are easements in gross freely transferable?

HOLDING AND DECISION: (Gaerntner, J.) Yes. Easements in gross are freely transferable. The easement granted by Henley (P) was not tied to a dominant estate and was thus in gross. The easement granted was exclusive to the telephone company, and thus the owners of the servient estate could not affect how the rights are exercised. Because the rights are exclusive they are also alienable, consistent with the use for which the easement was granted. When determining the purpose of the grant, technological advances must be considered. The addition of cable wire falls into the same electrical and telephone wiring and is no more burdensome on the servient estate. The easement should be broadly construed to allow the addition of cable wire. Judgment for Continental (D).

ANALYSIS

A court looks at three factors in determining the scope of an easement: (1) the burden the use causes, (2) the type of use proposed, and (3) whether the easement is alienable. Even if the grantor of the easement contemplates the activities, the easement's scope may be too burdensome if it puts too much stress on the easement. However, most courts will allow the subdivision of a dominant tenement even if the usage of the easement is increased thereby, unless the grantor has specifically forbidden subdivision.

Quicknotes

DOMINANT ESTATE Property whose owners benefit from the use of another's property.

EASEMENT IN GROSS A right to use the land of another that is specific to a particular individual and that expires upon the death of that person.

QUANTUM MERUIT Equitable doctrine allowing recovery for labor and materials provided by one party, even though no contract was entered into, in order to avoid unjust enrichment by the benefited party.

Lobato v. Taylor

Easement holders (P) v. Landowner (D)

Colo. Sup. Ct., 71 P.3d 938 (2002) (*en banc*).

NATURE OF CASE: Appeal from lower court decisions finding that prior easement holders had no rights to a certain large tract of land owned by defendant.

FACT SUMMARY: For more than 100 years, local landowners had been able to use a mountainous tract of land in Colorado to procure water, firewood, and timber. In 1960, Taylor (D) purchased the land and began denying the adjoining landowners their prior rights to the land.

🏛 RULE OF LAW
An implied easement by estoppel may exist when: (1) a landowner permits another to use his land in a manner that would make it foreseeable that the user would substantially rely upon the permission granted; (2) the user substantially changed position in reasonable reliance that the permission would not be revoked; and (3) revocation of the permitted use would create a significant injustice.

FACTS: The history of the easement rights in this case date back to the Mexican-American War of the 1840s. At the conclusion of the war, Mexico ceded significant lands to the United States, including California, Nevada and a portion of Colorado. One of the holders of a large tract of land in Colorado was Charles ("Carlos") Beaubien. He began granting small strips of land to new settlers while also leaving aside common areas of the tract that would be used collectively by the new settlers for grazing and as a source of timber, firewood, fish, and game. In 1863, he executed the Beaubien Document, which attempted to formally establish the settlers' rights in the common areas of the land. Beaubien's heirs eventually sold the property to William Gilpin. That transaction stated that Gilpin took the land subject to the rights of the settlers to use the open, uncultivated and common areas of the tract. In 1960, Jack Taylor (D) purchased the common land known then as the mountainous tract. Taylor's (D) deed specifically stated his land was subject to the claims of the local people to use the land for pasture, firewood, and lumber. Taylor (D) immediately began fencing off the area and stationing guards around the property to deny the locals use of the property. In 1981, a number of local landowners (P) filed this suit, seeking easement rights they had enjoyed on the land prior to Taylor's (D) purchase of the property. The trial court and an intermediate court of appeals denied their claims. The landowners (P) appealed to the Colorado Supreme Court.

ISSUE: May an implied easement by estoppel exist when: (1) a landowner permits another to use his land in a manner that would make it foreseeable that the user

would substantially rely upon the permission granted; (2) the user substantially changed position in reasonable reliance that the permission would not be revoked; and (3) revocation of the permitted use would create a significant injustice?

HOLDING AND DECISION: (Mullarkey, J.) Yes. An implied easement by estoppel may exist when: (1) a landowner permits another to use his land in a manner that would make it foreseeable that the user would substantially rely upon the permission granted; (2) the user substantially changed position in reasonable reliance that the permission would not be revoked; and (3) revocation of the permitted use would create a significant injustice. The landowners have satisfied each of the elements for an easement by estoppel. First, the prior landowners of Taylor's (D) property allowed the settlers to use the land in a manner that made it foreseeable that the settlers would substantially rely upon the permitted usage not being revoked. Their reliance was reasonable because the rights to use the common land were necessary for their survival. There is no dispute settlers were induced to come to this area by the promise they would have access to the common land and everything it could provide for them. The settlers needed wood to heat their homes and the ability to hunt game to feed their families. The second element is also satisfied. The evidence is clear that settlers left their homes in the east and settled in Colorado in reliance upon Beaubien's promise of access. The final element—the creation of an injustice if the rights are revoked—is also present. These rights existed for over 100 years, were properly stated in various real estate transactions, and Taylor (D) was fully aware of these rights. A revocation of these rights would constitute an injustice. The final issue is to establish the extent of the rights. The landowners should continue to have the rights as stated in the original Beaubien Document. These are the rights to firewood, timber, and for grazing of cattle. This court rejects the landowners' rights to hunting, fishing, and recreation. Reversed.

CONCURRENCE AND DISSENT: (Martinez, J.) The majority is correct that the landowners should continue to have the same easement rights to Taylor's (D) land as they existed for over 100 years. However, the rights should be all-encompassing and include the right to fish, hunt, and recreate. The evidence in the record reveals that landowners had these rights as well at least from the mid-1800s.

Continued on next page.

DISSENT: (Kourlis, J.) The adjoining landowners claims should be rejected on the ground the Beaubien Document was not valid. In 1863, Colorado law required any document conveying a real estate interest to include a specific description of the property and the names of the grantees. The document failed to do both. An easement by prescription also did not arise because there was evidence Beaubien intended others to rely upon his promise that he would grant them rights to the common land.

▶ *ANALYSIS*

First, the easements discussed here dealt with easements for *profits à prendre*, i.e., profits from the land such as wood, fish, and game. These were not easement simply for access rights. Most jurisdictions analyze easements for profit and easement for access under the same legal standards. Second, the decision briefly discussed easements created by prior use. An easement from a prior use may be found where the easement exists prior to the partition of the land. The easement must be obvious or apparent and necessary for enjoyment of the land. The court found the adjoining landowners also satisfied the elements for creation of this second type of implied easement.

Quicknotes

EASEMENT BY ESTOPPEL Easement that arises when a landlord imposes a servitude on his property and another person reasonably relies on the existence of such servitude in undertaking, or forbearing from undertaking, a particular act.

EASEMENT BY IMPLICATION An easement that is not expressly stated in a deed, but which is inferred upon conveyance, that a portion of one parcel had been used to benefit the other parcel and that upon sale the buyer of the benefited parcel could reasonably expect such benefits to continue.

Granite Properties Limited Partnership v. Manns

Property seller (P) v. Purchaser (D)

Ill. Sup. Ct., 512 N.E.2d 1230 (1987).

NATURE OF CASE: Appeal from grant of injunction preventing interference with use of easement.

FACT SUMMARY: Granite Properties Limited Partnerhsip (P) argued that it had acquired, by implied reservation, easements over two driveways providing access to its properties when it sold an adjoining parcel of land to Manns (D).

🏛 RULE OF LAW
If a previous use is continuous and apparent, the degree of necessity required to create an implied easement is reduced.

FACTS: Granite Properties Limited Partnership (Granite) (P) held three contiguous parcels in common ownership from 1963 to 1982, when it sold the middle parcel to Manns (D). About five times a week, trucks servicing a shopping center located on Granite's (P) easternmost parcel used a driveway located partially on Manns's (D) property. Another driveway, also located on Manns's (D) property, serviced an apartment building on Granite's (P) property to the west. Manns (D) saw the driveways, which had been used by Granite (P) since the 1960s, before he bought the middle parcel. After his purchase, finding no recorded easements following a title search, Manns (D) notified Granite (P) to discontinue its use of the driveways. Granite (P) subsequently brought an action to enjoin Manns (D) from interfering with Granite's (P) use and enjoyment of the two driveways. The trial court denied injunctive relief as to the shopping center driveway, but found an implied easement for Granite (P) as to the apartment complex driveway. The appellate court found acquired easements for both driveways. Manns (D) appealed.

ISSUE: If a previous use is continuous and apparent, is the degree of necessity required to create an implied easement reduced?

HOLDING AND DECISION: (Ryan, J.) Yes. If a previous use is continuous and apparent, the degree of necessity required to create an implied easement is reduced. An easement implied from a prior existing use arises when an owner of two or more adjoining parcels sells part of the property without mentioning any incidental benefit one parcel may convey on another. This benefit must be obvious, continuous, and permanent, and the claimed easement must be necessary to the enjoyment of the parcel retained by the grantor. Proof of the prior use is evidence that the parties probably intended an easement. In this case, any alternatives to the two driveways would be expensive and impractical. Given the strong evidence of Granite's (P) prior use of the driveways and Manns's (D) knowledge thereof, the evidence was sufficient to fulfill the elastic necessity requirement. Affirmed.

▶ ANALYSIS

There is one other type of implied easement—the easement by necessity. The easement by necessity usually arises when an owner of land conveys to another an inner portion that is entirely surrounded by lands owned either by the grantor or the grantor plus strangers. Unless a contrary intent is manifested, the grantee is found to have a right-of-way across the retained land of the grantor for ingress and egress to the land-locked parcel.

Quicknotes

EASEMENT The right to utilize a portion of another's real property for a specific use.

IMPLIED EASEMENT An easement that is not expressly stated in a deed, but which is inferred upon conveyance, that a portion of one parcel had been used to benefit the other parcel and that upon sale the buyer of the benefited parcel could reasonably expect such benefits to continue.

Finn v. Williams

Landlocked landowner (P) v. Surrounding landowner (D)

Ill. Sup. Ct., 33 N.E.2d 226 (1941).

NATURE OF CASE: Appeal from judgment establishing an easement by necessity.

FACT SUMMARY: Finn's (P) land was entirely landlocked after its purchase from Williams (D).

🏛 RULE OF LAW
An easement by necessity is created when an owner conveys a portion of his land that has no outlet except over the retained land of the grantor or over the land of strangers.

FACTS: Charles Williams owned 140 acres of land. In 1895, he conveyed 40 acres of his holdings to Bacon, and in 1937, Finn (P) acquired title to those 40 acres. Zelphia Williams (D) inherited the remaining 100 acres from Charles, who was her husband. The 40 acres acquired by Finn (P) were entirely landlocked, but for many years access was gained over private roads of strangers and a road over the Williams land. In 1939, Williams (D) refused Finn (P) any further access over her land. By that time all of the other private roads leading out had been closed. Finn (P) was unable to take his stock and produce to market and had to walk to the highway on a footpath carrying what produce he could.

ISSUE: Is an easement by necessity created when an owner conveys a portion of his land that has no outlet except over the retained land of the grantor or over the land of strangers?

HOLDING AND DECISION: (Wilson, J.) Yes. An easement by necessity is created when an owner conveys a portion of his land that has no outlet except over the retained land of the grantor or over the land of strangers. If at one time there had been unity of title, the easement by necessity will pass with each transfer as appurtenant to the dominant estate and may be exercised at any time by the holder. It makes no difference that the easement was not used earlier. The easement came into existence when the unity of title was split. Where an owner of land conveys a parcel that has no outlet except over the remaining lands of the grantor or over the land of strangers, a right of way by necessity exists over the remaining lands of the grantor. When permission to go over the land of strangers is denied, the subsequent grantees of the dominant estate may avail themselves of the dominant easement implied in the deed severing the dominant and servient estates. Affirmed.

▶ ANALYSIS

A landlocked parcel of land was about the only situation that the common-law courts would recognize as creating an easement by necessity. This was the strict necessity view of such easements. In recent years, some American courts have refused to create an easement by necessity even for landlocked parcels. Their reasoning was that to do so would be to sanction a form of private eminent domain. Since only a governmental unit holds the power of eminent domain, it was the obligation of the landlocked owner to prevail upon the appropriate governmental unit to condemn a right of way and build a public road.

■—■

Quicknotes

APPURTENANT A burden attached to real property that either benefits or burdens the owner's right to utilize that property.

EASEMENT BY NECESSITY An easement that arises by operation of law without which the owner of the benefited property is deprived of the use and enjoyment of his property.

■—■

Neponsit Property Owners' Association, Inc. v. Emigrant Industrial Savings Bank

Covenantor's assignees (P) v. Subsequent purchaser (D)

N.Y. Ct. App., 15 N.E.2d 793 (1938).

NATURE OF CASE: Action to foreclose a lien upon land.

FACT SUMMARY: Neponsit Property Owners (P) claim Emigrant Bank's (D) deed to certain property conveyed such property subject to a covenant contained in the original deed that provided for the payment by all subsequent purchasers of an annual improvements charge.

🏛 RULE OF LAW
A covenant in deed subjecting land to an annual charge for improvements to the surrounding residential tract is enforceable by the property owners' association against subsequent purchasers if: (1) grantor and grantee so intended; (2) it appears that the covenant is one touching or concerning the land; and (3) privity of estate is shown between the party claiming benefit of the covenant and the party under the burden of such covenant.

FACTS: Neponsit Property Owners' (P) assignor, Neponsit Realty Company, conveyed the land now owned by Emigrant Bank (D) to R. Deyer and wife by deed. That original deed contained a covenant providing: (1) that the conveyed land should be subject to an annual charge for improvements upon the entire residential tract then being developed; (2) that such charge should be a lien; (3) such charge should be payable by all subsequent purchasers to the company or its assigns, including a property owners' association which might thereafter be organized; and (4) such covenant runs with the land. Neponsit Property Owners (P) brought action based upon the above covenant to foreclose a lien upon the land that Emigrant Bank (D) now owns, having purchased it at a judicial sale. Emigrant Bank (D) appealed from an order denying their motion for judgment on the pleadings.

ISSUE: Does a covenant in the original deed subjecting land to an annual charge for improvements run with the land and create a lien that is enforceable against subsequent owners by Neponsit Property Owners (P)?

HOLDING AND DECISION: (Lehman, J.) Yes. A covenant will run with the land and will be enforceable against a subsequent purchaser if: (1) the grantor and grantee intend that the covenant run with the land; (2) the covenant touches or concerns the land with which it runs; (3) there is privity of estate between the party claiming benefit of the covenant and the party who rests under the burden of the covenant. In the instant case, the grantor and grantee manifested their intent that the covenant

run with the land by so stating in the original deed. The covenant touches or concerns the land in substance if not in form, i.e., the covenant alters the legal rights of ownership of the land, by providing that the burden of paying the cost of maintaining public improvements is inseparably attached to the land that enjoys the benefits of such improvements. The concept of privity of estate between parties usually requires that the party claiming benefit from the enforcement of a covenant own the property that benefits from such enforcement. Although Neponsit Property Owners (P), the corporation, does not own the property that would benefit from enforcement, the corporation is acting as the agent of property owners and should therefore be considered in privity in substance if not in form. Since the covenant complies with the legal requirements for one that runs with the land and is enforceable against subsequent purchasers, the order that denied Emigrant Bank's (D) motion for judgment on the pleadings is affirmed.

▶ ANALYSIS

It has been suggested that the technical requirements that determine the enforceability of covenants as to future parties, e.g., *Neponsit*, might well be abandoned and that the intention of the covenanting parties be the sole criterion. This suggestion is supported by the following developments: (1) the benefit of a contract may now be assigned, or even created, initially for the benefit of a third person; (2) recording systems, though imperfect, afford much protection to the purchaser of land against outstanding burdens of which he may be unaware. It should be noted, however, that the unrestricted enforcement of covenants may seriously impair the usefulness of land. A student reading this case should keep in mind that *Neponsit* is not concerned with the enforcement of covenants between original covenanting parties. That question of enforceability is left to the contracts course.

Quicknotes

COVENANT A written promise to do, or to refrain from doing, a particular activity.

FORECLOSURE An action to recover the amount due on a mortgage of real property where the owner has failed to pay their debt, terminating the owner's interest in the property which must then be sold to satisfy the debt.

Continued on next page.

JUDICIAL SALE   A sale of property by a sheriff pursuant to a judgment.

LIEN   A claim against the property of another in order to secure the payment of a debt.

PRIVITY OF ESTATE   Common or successive relation to the same right in property.

"RUN WITH THE LAND"   Covenants that are binding on successor in interest to the property to which they are attached.

Evans v. Pollock

Landowner (P) v. Developer (D)

Tex. Sup. Ct., 796 S.W.2d 465 (1990).

NATURE OF CASE: Appeal from defense verdict in declaratory, equitable, and injunctive relief.

FACT SUMMARY: Evans (P) sought to enjoin the commercial use of unrestricted lots within a restricted subdivision under the implied reciprocal negative easement doctrine.

RULE OF LAW
A general plan of subdivision restriction need not apply to all tracts in a subdivision for the doctrine of implied reciprocal negative easements to apply.

FACTS: Evans's (P) predecessors bought the subdivision in question, platted it, and then further subdivided the plats. The majority of the plats contained a restriction against commercial use and limited construction to single family homes. Many of these lots were sold. Pollock (D) sought to buy some of the unrestricted lots for use as a marina, a private club, and condominiums. Evans (P) sought to enjoin the sale of the land without imposition of the restrictions. He also sought a declaration that the restrictive covenants on his property were implied on the other properties by reciprocity. The trial court found that restrictions were intended to apply to all lots in the subdivision. The court of appeals reversed. Evans (P) appealed.

ISSUE: Must a general plan of subdivision restriction apply to all tracts in a subdivision for the doctrine of reciprocal negative easement to apply?

HOLDING AND DECISION: (Ray, J.) No. A general plan of subdivision restriction need not apply to all tracts in a subdivision for a general plan of subdivision restriction to apply. Evans (P) is asking that we imply a reciprocal negative easement on the land Pollock (D) seeks to buy. A court may imply such an easement on a showing that the subdivider had a general development scheme for the subdivision. Here, the restricted lots are all similarly situated. They need not encompass the whole subdivision, so long as the restrictions apply to well-defined lots. Since that is the case here, reciprocal negative easements may be implied. Reversed and remanded.

▌ ANALYSIS

Note that the doctrine of implied reciprocal negative servitudes binds the buyers even though the grantor omits to include the mutual restrictions in subsequent deeds. The state of California, for one, has refused to recognize the doctrine on the grounds that it fails to protect buyer expectations, fosters uncertainty, and circumvents the orderly development of subdivisions. Instead, state law requires that only restrictive covenants must be in writing or on the deed in order to be enforceable.

■≡■

Quicknotes

NEGATIVE EASEMENT Refers to the duty to refrain from conducting a specific lawful activity on the servient estate because it interferes with the use of the dominant estate.

RESTRICTIVE COVENANT A promise contained in a deed to limit the uses to which the property will be made.

■≡■

Appel v. Presley Cos.

Homeowner (P) v. Developer (D)

N.M. Sup. Ct., 806 P.2d 1054 (1991).

NATURE OF CASE: Appeal from suit for permanent injunction.

FACT SUMMARY: The Appels (P) sought a permanent injunction to prevent Presley (D) from building four townhouses on a tract in their subdivision.

🏛 RULE OF LAW
Provisions allowing amendment of subdivision restrictions are subject to a requirement of reasonableness.

FACTS: The Appels (P) owned a home in a subdivision owned by Presley (D). Presley (D) proposed to replat the property in order to build townhouses on the subdivision, which consisted of single-family dwellings. The Appels (P) brought suit to enjoin such replatting and building claiming breach of restrictive covenants, negligent and fraudulent misrepresentation, and unfair trade practices, as well as seeking an injunction of development on the property. Judgment was entered for Presley (D) and the Appels (P) appealed.

ISSUE: Are provisions allowing amendment of subdivision restrictions subject to a requirement of reasonableness?

HOLDING AND DECISION: (Franchini, J.) Yes. Provisions allowing amendment of subdivision restrictions are subject to a requirement of reasonableness. A court of equity will not enforce restrictions if the circumstances render them inequitable. The determination of whether the restrictions were reasonable or destroyed the value of the property is a factual matter, and thus summary judgment must be reversed and the cause is remanded.

▶ ANALYSIS

Note that there is an inherent inconsistency in the establishment of restrictive covenants upon which purchasers may rely, and the reservation of the right to change such restrictions. Thus such amendments may be upheld, so long as the developer exercises them reasonably.

━━━

Quicknotes

EQUITABLE Just; fair.

PERMANENT INJUNCTION A remedy imposed by the court ordering a party to cease the conduct of a specific activity until the final disposition of the cause of action.

RESTRICTIVE COVENANT A promise contained in a deed to limit the uses to which the property will be made.

SUBDIVISION PLOT A parcel of land that is divided into portions to be resold or developed.

SUMMARY JUDGMENT Judgment rendered by a court in response to a motion by one of the parties, claiming that the lack of a question of material fact in respect to an issue warrants disposition of the issue without consideration by the jury.

━━━

Davidson Brothers, Inc. v. D. Katz & Sons, Inc.

Seller (P) v. Buyer (D)

N.J. Super. Ct. App. Div. 643 A.2d 642 (1994), *on remand from* N.J. Sup. Ct., 579 A.2d 288 (1990).

NATURE OF CASE: Appeal from decision rendering a restrictive covenant unenforceable.

FACT SUMMARY: The trial court, applying a reasonableness test, determined that a covenant prohibiting the use as a supermarket of property in downtown New Brunswick was unenforceable.

RULE OF LAW
No covenant can be sustained if it is inconsistent with the public interest or detrimental to the public good.

FACTS: Davidson Brothers, Inc. (Davidson) (P), a supermarket operator in N.J., opened a store on George Street in downtown New Brunswick. The store was later closed because it had opened another location two miles away. Davidson sold the George Street location to D. Katz & Sons, Inc. (Katz) (D), a rug merchant. The deed contained a covenant prohibiting its use as a supermarket. The city acquired the property from Katz (D) and attempted to procure another supermarket. The Housing Authority leased the store to C-Town for $1 per year on the condition they make certain improvements. Davidson (P) brought suit to enforce the covenant. The trial court, applying a reasonableness test promulgated by the New Jersey Supreme Court, determined that a covenant prohibiting the use as a supermarket of property in downtown New Brunswick was unenforceable. Davidson (P) appealed.

ISSUE: Can a covenant be sustained if it is inconsistent with the public interest or detrimental to the public good?

HOLDING AND DECISION: (D'Annunzio, J.) No. No covenant can be sustained if it is inconsistent with the public interest or detrimental to the public good. New Jersey courts have refused to enforce covenants that violate public policy. The rehabilitation of inner cities is a public policy of the state often expressed in relevant legislation. The covenant was so contrary to public policy that it should not be recognized as a valid, enforceable obligation. Affirmed.

ANALYSIS

The closing of the George Street location created an extreme hardship on the residents of downtown New Brunswick. Experts and testimony were introduced to show that many persons had no access to motor vehicles and that lack of markets in downtown areas make food more expensive for inner city residents.

Quicknotes

COVENANT A written promise to do, or to refrain from doing, a particular activity.

DEED A signed writing transferring title to real property from one person to another.

Nahrstedt v. Lakeside Village Condominium Association, Inc.

Cat lover (P) v. Homeowners association (D)

Cal. Sup. Ct., 878 P.2d 1275 (1994).

NATURE OF CASE: Suit challenging the validity of a provision in a common interest development's covenants, conditions and restrictions that prohibited the keeping of pets in the development.

FACT SUMMARY: A resident of a common interest development in California kept three cats in her condominium in violation of the development's governing covenants, conditions and restrictions. The homeowners association therefore assessed continuing penalties against her for the violations.

> ### 🏛 RULE OF LAW
> A recorded use restriction imposed by a common interest development in California must be enforced uniformly against all residents of the development unless the restriction is unreasonable.

FACTS: Nahrstedt (P) owned and lived in a condominium in Lakeside Village, a 530-unit common interest development in Los Angeles County overseen by the Lakeside Village Condominium Association (the homeowners association) (D). Nahrstedt's (P) ownership of her condominium gave her membership in the homeowners association (D). One of the homeowners association's (D) duties was to enforce Lakeside Village's governing, duly recorded covenants, conditions and restrictions (CC&Rs). One clause of the CC&Rs provided that "[n]o animals (which shall include dogs and cats) . . . shall be kept in any unit." Nahrstedt (P), who alleged that she did not know of the pet restriction when she bought her condominium, lived in her unit with her three cats, but she did not let her cats have free run of Lakeside Village's common areas. When the homeowners association (D) learned that Nahrstedt (P) was keeping the cats in her home, it started assessing monthly fines against her for violating the CC&Rs. Nahrstedt (P) sued the homeowners association (D), asking the trial court to invalidate the assessments already imposed against her, to enjoin the homeowners association (D) from making such assessments against her in the future, and to declare the pet restriction in the CC&Rs "unreasonable" as applied to situations involving non-disturbing, essentially entirely in-home pet ownership like hers. The homeowners association (D) filed a demurrer to Nahrstedt's (P) complaint [i.e., the homeowners association (D) moved to dismiss her complaint for failing to state a claim upon which relief could be granted]. The trial court agreed with the homeowners association (D) and dismissed Nahrstedt's (P) complaint. On Nahrstedt's (P) appeal, the intermediate appellate court reversed the trial court's judgment, agreeing with Nahrstedt (P) that the

reasonableness of a recorded use restriction in a common interest development must be determined on a case-by-case basis. The homeowners association (D) petitioned the California Supreme Court for further review.

ISSUE: Must a recorded use restriction imposed by a common interest development in California be enforced uniformly against all residents of the development unless the restriction is unreasonable?

HOLDING AND DECISION: (Kennard, J.) Yes. A recorded use restriction imposed by a common interest development in California must be enforced uniformly against all residents of the development unless the restriction is unreasonable. Homeowners in a common interest development sacrifice certain freedoms in exchange for, among other things, their ability to enforce restrictive covenants against other homeowners in the development. These restrictions are enforceable, though, only if they qualify as equitable servitudes or as covenants running with the land. In Section 1354(a) of the California Civil Code, California's legislature has established the test for determining whether a common interest development's use restrictions are enforceable: under Section 1354(a), a recorded declaration's use restrictions are "enforceable . . . unless unreasonable." Some states have reached similar conclusions through the courts. For example, in *Hidden Harbour Estates v. Basso*, 393 So. 2d 637 (Fla. Ct. App. 1981), a Florida appellate court held that a recorded declaration's stated use restrictions are entitled to a heavy presumption of validity, so much so that even somewhat unreasonable restrictions should nevertheless be enforced. The *Hidden Harbour Estates* court concluded further that arbitrary restrictions or those that violate public policy or a fundamental constitutional right should not be enforced. In a case involving a pet restriction, *Noble v. Murphy*, 612 N.E.2d 266 (Mass. App. Ct. 1993), the court agreed with the *Hidden Harbour Estates* rationale that otherwise-valid use restrictions should be enforced unless they violate constitutional rights or public policy. This court concludes, then, that recorded restrictive covenants should not be enforced when they violate public policy, as in *Shelley v. Kramer*, 334 U.S. 1 (1948) (racial restriction), or when they are arbitrary and bear no rational relation to a purpose involving the land. In such cases, the harm resulting from enforcement of arbitrary use restrictions or restrictions that violate fundamental public policy always outweighs any benefit that such restrictions might confer. Such principles also inform Section 1354(a) of the California Civil Code, which this court interprets as requiring enforcement of use

Continued on next page.

restrictions unless they are arbitrary, violate public policy, or impose burdens outweighing any benefit. This presumption of validity for recorded restrictive covenants means that homeowners associations can enforce their covenants without fear of instigating litigation. The presumption also relieves the judicial system from making case-by-case determinations of whether covenants are reasonable as applied to a particular homeowner. The presumption thus in turn means that homeowners in common interest developments will have the assurance that their covenants will be enforced uniformly and predictably. In this particular case, the appellate court failed to apply the pertinent rules governing equitable servitudes and erroneously relied on two opinions, *Portola Hills Community Assn. v. James*, 5 Cal. Rptr. 2d 580 (Cal. Ct. App. 1993), and *Bernardo Villas Management Corp. v. Black*, 235 Cal. Rptr. 509 (Cal. Ct. App. 1987), both of which are hereby disapproved because those courts did not use appropriately deferential review of the covenants at issue in those cases. Whether a use restriction is reasonable or unreasonable must be determined by referring to the entire common interest development, not by referring to the particular facts of a specific complaining homeowner. More specifically, the court holds that the Lakeside Village pet restriction is not arbitrary because it rationally promotes the other owners' legitimate concerns about health, sanitation, and noise; Nahrstedt (P) has failed to allege that the restriction's burden is so disproportionate to the legitimate benefits that the pet restriction is unreasonable. Moreover, no fundamental public policy requires that pets be kept in a condominium development, and no constitutional provision or California statute grants the right to keep pets in such a situation, either. Reversed and remanded.

DISSENT: (Arabian, J.) The majority's reasoning has technical merit, but the application of that analysis to these facts reveals a narrow understanding of the relationship between the law and the human spirit. The pet restriction at issue here violates Section 1354(a). It is arbitrary and unreasonable, within the meaning of Section 1354(a), because it imposes an undue burden on owners who keep their pets within their units and do not permit their pets to disturb the use of other homeowners' properties. The restriction's burden on such homeowners outweighs those homeowners' quality of life in the common interest development, and indeed the restriction only worsens the breakdown of our social fabric. All that the majority has done today is to accept, uncritically, the homeowners association's (D) assurances that uniform enforcement will promote all owners' "health and happiness." The first question in an appropriately probing inquiry should be to recognize that the burden on the particular use at issue here goes well beyond the impersonal and mundane issues normally covered by restrictive covenants. The majority instead asks only whether the use restriction at issue was stated in the original recorded declaration. If it was, it now shall be presumed valid unless it violates public policy.

Such a standard means that almost all recorded use restrictions are valid, a status that only the commandments issued by Moses have enjoyed before today. Further, the proscribed activity here, pet ownership that is wholly confined to one's own home, deprives homeowners of the American dream, a notion that has always included the ownership and full enjoyment of one's home. Courts should rule with more humanity and strive to create harmony, not division, within the populace.

▶ ANALYSIS

Despite the emotionalism of Justice Arabian's dissent, and despite the intermediate appellate court's contrary ruling (relying on two now-invalidated opinions), today this case seems relatively easy for all the reasons cited by the majority. Public policy argues heavily against Nahrstedt's (P) position because that position would create great instability within homeowners associations, and because the burden of deciding enforceability of use restrictions on a case-by-case basis would substantially increase the caseloads of a judicial system that is already over-burdened. Under the rationale of *Nahrstedt* and cases like it, homeowners now can know that, when they sign a development's recorded covenants and use restrictions, those covenants and restrictions will almost certainly be enforced.

Quicknotes

CC&Rs Covenants, conditions, and restrictions that residents of a condominium development agree to abide by when they take ownership of a unit in that development.

DECLARATORY RELIEF A judgment of the court establishing the rights of the parties.

O'Buck v. Cottonwood Village Condominium Association, Inc.

Condominium owners (P) v. Homeowners' association (D)

Alaska Sup. Ct., 750 P.2d 813 (1988).

NATURE OF CASE: Appeal concerning action seeking damages and an injunction against adoption of condominium rules.

FACT SUMMARY: The Cottonwood Village Association (D) found that roof leakage was caused in part by badly mounted television antennae and foot traffic on the roof related to the antennae and adopted a rule prohibiting the mounting of television antennae anywhere on the building. Consequently, the O'Bucks (P) lost reception in three of their four televisions.

🏛 RULE OF LAW
Condominium declarations and bylaws granting a board the authority to enact rules banning television antennae will withstand judicial scrutiny if they are deemed reasonable.

FACTS: The Board of Directors (the Board) of the Cottonwood Village Association (the Association) (D) found that roof leakage was caused in part by badly mounted T.V. antennae and foot traffic on the roof related to the antennae and adopted a rule prohibiting the mounting of television antennae anywhere on the building. The purpose of this rule was to protect the roof and to enhance the marketability of the condominium units. The Board (D) also decided to make a cable system available as an alternative to antennae. Without the antennae, the O'Bucks (P) lost reception in three of their four televisions. It would cost $10 per month per set to hook up to the newly offered cable. The O'Bucks (P) filed a complaint against the Association (D) seeking damages and an injunction against enforcement of the rule. The lower court decided in favor of the Association (D) and the O'Buck's (P) appealed.

ISSUE: Will condominium declarations and bylaws granting a board the authority to enact rules banning television antennae withstand judicial scrutiny if they are deemed reasonable?

HOLDING AND DECISION: (Rabinowitz, C.J.) Yes. Condominium declarations and bylaws granting a board the authority to enact rules banning television antennae will withstand judicial scrutiny if they are deemed reasonable. In evaluating the reasonableness of a condominium association rule, it is necessary to balance the importance of the rule's objective against the importance of the interest infringed upon. In a case where a rule seriously curtails an important civil liberty, the court will look with suspicion on the rule and require a compelling justification. However, the antennae ban in the instant case curtails no significant interests. The only loss suffered is that the O'Bucks (P) and the other owners must now pay a small fee to receive television. Affirmed.

▶ ANALYSIS

The absence of any provision explicitly authorizing a board to ban or prohibit certain uses or activities is not fatal to the board's right to do so. In *Beachwood Villas Condominium v. Poor*, 448 So. 2d 1143 (Fla. Dist. Ct. App. 1984), the court held that "it would be impossible to list all restrictive uses in a declaration of condominium." As mentioned above, determinations in these situations are based on a reasonableness standard where the competing interests are balanced and analyzed.

Quicknotes

INJUNCTION A remedy imposed by the court ordering a party to cease the conduct of a specific activity.

Neuman v. Grandview at Emerald Hills, Inc.

Condominium unit owners (P) v. Condominium association (D)

Fla. Dist. Ct. App., 861 So. 2d 494 (2003).

NATURE OF CASE: Appeal from denial of a request for injunctive and declaratory relief.

FACT SUMMARY: Neuman (P), along with other condominium unit members, sought declaratory and injunctive relief to prevent enforcement of an amendment to the condominium rules prohibiting religious services and activities in the common elements of the condominium.

🏛 RULE OF LAW
A categorical prohibition of all religious services in a common area to a condominium does not unreasonably restrict any unit owner's right to peaceably assemble.

FACTS: In 1982, the condominium association for Grandview at Emerald Hills, Inc. (Grandview) (D) enacted a rule allowing its common auditorium to be used for meetings including social gatherings and religious groups providing that at least 80% of those in attendance were condominium residents. In 2001, after the auditorium had become reserved every Saturday morning for religious services, other unit owners complained to the Board of Directors that such meetings should be restricted. A meeting was held and 70% of the owners voted to prohibit religious activities of any kind from being held in the common areas of the condominium. The purpose of the new rule was to prevent conflicts between competing religious groups. Neuman (P) brought suit against Grandview (D) alleging the rule violated his constitutional rights and § 718.123 of the Florida State Statutes. The court granted a temporary injunction prohibiting enforcement of the rule because of its ban on "any kind" of religious activity. Subsequently, Grandview (D) amended the rule to prohibit the holding of religious services in their auditorium. Neuman (P) then moved for a permanent injunction arguing that religious services fell under the constitutional protection of the right to peaceably assemble. The permanent injunction was denied and this appeal resulted.

ISSUE: Does a categorical prohibition of all religious services in a common area to a condominium unreasonably restrict any unit owner's right to peaceably assemble?

HOLDING AND DECISION: (Warner, J.) No. A categorical prohibition of all religious services in a common area to a condominium does not unreasonably restrict any unit owner's right to peaceably assemble. Grandview's (D) action as a condominium association does not constitute state action, and, consequently, does not implicate the constitutional rights of freedom of speech and religion.

Section 718.123 of the Florida Statutes applies a reasonableness test for any restrictions imposed by a condominium association in relation to its common elements, and because Grandview (D) has articulated a reasonable reason for the restriction, i.e., serious conflict between religious groups competing for use of the common areas, it does not violate the statute. The right to peaceably assemble has traditionally been interpreted to apply only to the rights of citizens to meet and discuss public or governmental affairs. Even if the court were to assume, *arguendo*, that religious activities fell under this umbrella, the rule at hand does not restrict the right to assemble, but rather only prohibits one type of assembly. The rule would have to ban all forms of assembly to violate Florida law. Prohibiting types of activities that may have a particularly divisive effect on the condominium community is a reasonable restriction. The judgment of the trial court is affirmed.

▶ ANALYSIS

The court recognizes the uniqueness of the condominium community, a creature of statute, when balancing the importance of the condominium's rules against any infringement upon the rights of the owner-members. The test is that of reasonableness, not a higher test that would apply to state actors where the constitution would be implicated. Unit owners in condominiums contractually bind themselves to follow the rules of the condominium's declaration. Condominium owners are put on notice of the condominium rules and the requirements to amend those rules prior to the purchase of any given unit. An individual always has the option not to buy into any condominium community, and once purchasing a unit, the owners always have the option to sell and move if they are unable to tolerate the rules adopted by the majority of the owner-members. It is also doubtful that a successful argument could be raised that the rule in this instance constitutes a restraint on alienation.

Quicknotes

CONDOMINIUM RESTRICTIONS Commonly known as CRRs, rules and regulations promulgated by the condominium association to govern the use of the property that comprises the condominium dwellings.

PEACEFUL ASSEMBLY Right of people to meet and gather for any purpose, usually connected with government, including policies and ideas.

Shelley v. Kraemer

Property owners (D) v. Neighbors (P)

334 U.S. 1 (1948).

NATURE OF CASE: On writ of certiorari in action to enjoin a sale of property.

FACT SUMMARY: The Kraemers (P) sought to oust the Shelleys (D), a black family, from their recently purchased property on the grounds that it was subject to a racially restrictive covenant.

🏛 RULE OF LAW
The Equal Protection Clause of the Fourteenth Amendment prohibits judicial enforcement by state courts of restrictive covenants based on race or color.

FACTS: In 1945, the Shelleys (D), a black family, purchased property that, unknown to them, was subject to a racially restrictive covenant signed in 1911 for a 50-year period by the majority of property owners on the block. The Kraemers (P), also owners of property subject to the covenant, sued in the state court to restrain the Shelleys (D) from taking possession and to revest the title in others. The state court denied relief on the grounds that the covenant had never been finalized. However, the Missouri Supreme Court reversed. The U.S. Supreme Court granted the Shelleys (D) certiorari. They argued that the Equal Protection Clause of the Fourteenth Amendment prevented the judicial enforcement by state courts of racially restrictive covenants.

ISSUE: Does the Equal Protection Clause of the Fourteenth Amendment prohibit judicial enforcement by state courts of racially restrictive covenants?

HOLDING AND DECISION: (Vinson, C.J.) Yes. The Equal Protection Clause of the Fourteenth Amendment prohibits judicial enforcement by state courts of racially restrictive covenants. Equality in the enjoyment of property rights was clearly among the civil rights intended to be protected from discriminatory state action by the framers of the Fourteenth Amendment. And although past cases have struck down such discrimination when enacted by state legislatures or city councils, it may not be said that such discrimination, as in the instant case, may escape on the grounds that it was only an agreement between private individuals. Indeed, were it no more than that, no violation would exist. However, in this case state action is clearly present by reason of the active intervention of the state court to enforce the covenant. As early as 1880, in *Ex parte Virginia*, 100 U.S 339, 347, this Court found state action in violation of the Fourteenth Amendment when a state judge restricted jury service to whites. Nor is the amendment ineffective simply because this action was taken according to the state's common law policy. We hold that in granting judicial enforcement of these restrictive covenants, the state has denied the Shelleys (D) equal protection of the laws. Reversed.

▶ ANALYSIS

In the 1961 case of *Burton v. Wilmington Parking Authority*, 365 U.S 715, a state agency had built and owned a parking garage, and rented space in the garage to a private restaurant. The Supreme Court held that the restaurant's exclusion of blacks from service amounted to state action under the Fourteenth Amendment. The test announced was that of significant state involvement in private discrimination.

Quicknotes

EQUAL PROTECTION A constitutional guarantee that no person shall be denied the same protection of the laws enjoyed by other persons in life circumstances.

RESTRICTIVE COVENANT A promise contained in a deed to limit the uses to which the property will be made.

STATE ACTION Actions brought pursuant to the Fourteenth Amendment claiming that the government violated the plaintiff's civil rights.

Northwest Real Estate Co. v. Serio

Property seller (D) v. Buyer (P)

Md. Ct. App. 144 A. 245 (1929).

NATURE OF CASE: Action for specific performance to compel the sale of real property.

FACT SUMMARY: Northwest Real Estate (D) prevented the sale of property to the Serios (P) based on a covenant restricting the alienation of the property.

🏛 RULE OF LAW
Covenants restraining a grantee's ability to sell property are inconsistent with a grant of fee simple and are thus invalid.

FACTS: Northwest Real Estate (Northwest) (D) included a covenant in a deed preventing its grantees from selling a property before a certain date without its consent. The grantees attempted to sell the property to the Serios (P) before the required date, and Northwest (D) refused to consent. The Serios (P) sued Northwest (D) for specific performance of the contract for sale.

ISSUE: Are covenants restraining a grantee's ability to sell property inconsistent with a grant of fee simple and thus invalid?

HOLDING AND DECISION: (Urner, J.) Yes. Covenants restraining a grantee's ability to sell property are inconsistent with a grant of fee simple and thus invalid. Freedom to alienate is essential to a grant of title in fee simple. The restriction imposed on the deed by Northwest (D) was designed to temporarily deprive the grantees of the unrestrained power of alienation and was clearly repugnant to the fee simple title conveyed by the grants.

DISSENT: (Bond, C.J.) The court's holding would hinder a developer's plan to create a city as a single large enterprise and thus is contrary to public policy.

▶ ANALYSIS

The purpose of the covenant in question was to develop a high-class neighborhood. By retaining the right to approve of sales, developers can attempt to keep out undesirables.

■=■

Quicknotes

FEE SIMPLE An estate in land characterized by ownership of the entire property for an unlimited duration and by absolute power over distribution.

RESTRAINT AGAINST ALIENATION A provision restricting the transferee's ability to convey interests in the conveyed property.

■=■

Woodside Village Condominium Association, Inc. v. Jahren

Condominium association (P) v. Condominium member (D)

Fla. Sup. Ct., 806 So. 2d 452 (2002).

NATURE OF CASE: Appeal from an injunction barring enforcement of condominium leasing restrictions.

FACT SUMMARY: Woodside Village Condominium Association, Inc. (P) brought an action against a condominium member, Jahren (D), seeking enforcement of condominium leasing restrictions.

RULE OF LAW
Restrictions passed by a condominium association will be presumed valid unless shown to be arbitrary, against public policy, or in violation of a fundamental constitutional right.

FACTS: In 1997, members of Woodside Village Condominium Association, Inc. (Woodside) (P) amended their Declaration of Condominium to prohibit owners from leasing their units during their first twelve months of ownership. Lease terms were also restricted to no more than nine months in any twelve-month period and no more than three units owned by any member could be leased at any one time. These restrictions were adopted by a two-thirds vote of the members in order to address concerns that non-owner occupied condos were negatively impacting the quality of life at Woodside (P). Jahren (D) failed to comply and Woodside (P) sought an injunction to enforce the restrictions. Jahren (D) counterclaimed for injunctive and declaratory relief asserting the lease restrictions were unreasonable, arbitrary and capricious, and that they served no reasonable purpose. The district court enjoined the enforcement of the restrictions, and the Second District Court of Appeals affirmed. This appeal followed.

ISSUE: Will restrictions passed by a condominium association be presumed valid unless shown to be arbitrary, against public policy, or in violation of a fundamental constitutional right?

HOLDING AND DECISION: (Anstead, J.) Yes. Restrictions passed by a condominium association will be presumed valid unless shown to be arbitrary, against public policy, or in violation of a fundamental constitutional right. Condominiums and their forms of ownership are strictly created by statute. A condominium is created by recording a declaration governing the relationships among the unit owners and the condominium association. Courts have recognized the unique living arrangement in condominiums and their corresponding greater degree of restriction upon individual owners. Florida Stat., § 718.110 provides broad authority for amending a declaration of condominium. Restrictions to the amendment process

only pertain to the size of each unit and the creation of timeshares, which require a unanimous vote by all of the owners. Jahren (D) was on notice of the unique form of ownership when he acquired his purchase. The Declaration of Condominium states that his units are subject to any lease restrictions and that each owner shall comply with the Declaration. The Declaration was amended appropriately by a two-thirds vote and the lease restrictions are not of the category that would require a unanimous vote. The restrictions are not arbitrary, are not against public policy, and do not violate any fundamental constitutional right. The injunction issued by the Second District Court of Appeals is quashed.

CONCURRENCE: (Quince, J.) The legislature should consider placing restrictions on the authority of condominium associations to alter the rights of the existing condominium owners. At the time of purchase, Jahren (D) was not subject to the new lease restrictions. One of the owners enjoyed unrestricted leasing rights for eighteen years before the Declaration was amended. The district court correctly observed that the amendments deprived the owners of a valuable right that existed at the time of purchase. Some type of "escape provision" should exist for owners whose substantial property rights are altered after the purchase of their units.

ANALYSIS

As a general rule, the courts will show deference to condominium restrictions duly adopted by their members unless they reach the threshold of being a restraint on alienation. Retroactive application of such restrictions has also been universally accepted, with the exception of North Dakota. The Restatement (Third) requires unanimous approval for any amendment to a condominium declaration that would restrict use or occupancy or deprive any owner of a significant property right; however, this rule is subject to being disclaimable if so provided in the declaration.

━━━

Quicknotes

CONDOMINIUM Separate ownership of individual units in a multiple-unit building. Most often located in urban or retirement community areas.

CONDOMINIUM ASSOCIATION Structured association of condominium owners with rules and bylaws that govern the common areas.

Continued on next page.

CONDOMINIUM RESTRICTIONS Commonly known as CRRs, rules and regulations promulgated by the condominium association to govern the use of the property that comprises the condominium dwellings.

LEASE An agreement or contract that creates a relationship between a landlord and tenant (real property) or lessor and lessee (real or personal property).

El Di, Inc. v. Town of Bethany Beach

Restaurant operator (D) v. City (P)

Del. Sup. Ct., 477 A.2d 1066 (1984).

NATURE OF CASE: Appeal of injunction en-forcing a restrictive covenant.

FACT SUMMARY: Bethany Beach (P) sought to enforce a restrictive covenant prohibiting the sale of alcoholic beverages, even though the nature of the neighborhood had changed greatly since the creation of the covenant.

🏛 RULE OF LAW

A restrictive covenant will not be enforced where a fundamental change in the nature of the neighborhood has made the purpose sought by the covenant unattainable.

FACTS: The Town of Bethany Beach (P) was originally established by a church and was intended to be a quiet, residential community. The property originally forming the town had a restrictive covenant placed on it preventing commercial use and the sale of alcoholic beverages. Over the years, the community grew. The covenant against non-residential use was ignored; in fact, the original center of town was zoned for commercial use. In 1981, El Di, Inc. (D), operator of a restaurant, applied for and received a license to sell alcohol, which it began to do. Bethany Beach (P) obtained an injunction enforcing the restrictive cove-nant. El Di (D) appealed.

ISSUE: Will a restrictive covenant be enforced where a fundamental change in the nature of the neighborhood has made the purpose sought by the covenant unattainable?

HOLDING AND DECISION: (Herrmann, C.J.) No. A restrictive covenant will not be enforced where a fundamental change in the nature of the neighborhood has made the purpose sought by the covenant unattainable. Courts will not enforce a restrictive covenant to no purpose. Here, the purpose of the covenant was to ensure that Bethany Beach (P) remained a quiet, residential community. This has not occurred, however. Rather, commercial development has occurred, and the town is now a seaside resort. Therefore, the community is no longer that envisioned by its founders, and the covenant has outlived its purpose. Reversed.

DISSENT: (Christie, J.) Despite its growth, Bethany Beach (P) still remains a quiet family-oriented community, justifying the continued enforcement of the restrictions. The tolerance of public consumption of alcohol does not negate the prohibition on its sale.

▶ ANALYSIS

"Changed conditions" is conceptually distinct from "aban-donment," another rationale for extinguishment of a servitude. The former refers to changes in the community outside the restricted land. Abandonment occurs when the use of the dominant tenement is altered so as to make enforcement of the covenant unreasonable.

■==■

Quicknotes

PERMANENT INJUNCTION A remedy imposed by the court ordering a party to cease the conduct of a specific activi-ty until the final disposition of the cause of action.

RESTRICTIVE COVENANT A promise contained in a deed to limit the uses to which the property will be made.

■==■

Blakeley v. Gorin

Property owner (P) v. Adjacent apartment owner (D)

Mass. Sup. Jud. Ct., 313 N.E.2d 903 (1974).

NATURE OF CASE: Appeal from action to remove building restrictions.

FACT SUMMARY: Blakeley (P) wanted to build a hotel to be connected by a passageway over an alley with an existing structure owned by him.

🏛 RULE OF LAW
Building restrictions will not be specifically enforced, even when they convey an actual and substantial benefit to the person seeking enforcement, if they impede reasonable use of the land for its most suitable purposes.

FACTS: Massachusetts placed certain restrictions on land sold to private parties. Blakeley (P) owned property subject to these restrictions. One parcel had a hotel built on it. Behind the property, separated by an alley, Blakeley (P) owned a vacant lot. Blakeley (P) wanted to build an addition to the hotel on this lot and to connect the two buildings by a walkway over the alley. Gorin (D), who owned an eight-story apartment building adjacent to the vacant lot, objected to the building of the walkway, alleging that it would infringe on light and air rights. Gorin (D) also alleged that the new construction would violate the no mercantile restriction and the 16-foot distance requirement between abutting buildings contained in the original deeds issued by Massachusetts. The court found that the restrictions were no longer valid and should not be enforced since they would unreasonably impede the most reasonable use of the property. The court found authority for its position under a state law that allowed the court to deny specific enforcement of outdated restrictions or that money damages could, where appropriate be awarded in lieu of enforcement. Gorin (D) appealed, alleging that the statute allowed for a taking of property rights without compensation, and he had been denied damages for loss of air and light rights.

ISSUE: Will building restrictions be specifically enforced when they convey an actual and substantial benefit to the person seeking enforcement if they impede reasonable use of the land for its most suitable purposes?

HOLDING AND DECISION: (Hennessey, J.) No. Building restrictions will not be specifically enforced, even when they convey an actual and substantial benefit to the person seeking enforcement, if they impede reasonable use of the land for its most suitable purposes. The legislature may provide that outdated or unnecessary building restrictions may be denied specific enforcement by the court. If the person asserting that the restriction should be enforced can establish damages, a money award in lieu of enforcement may be allowed. Any mercantile businesses established in the new structure are merely subsidiary to the primary business of operating the hotel. They will have no effect on the property owner. The passageway between the buildings does constitute an infringement on Gorin's (D) property rights, but it is not so substantial as to require enforcement of the restriction. Rather than deprive Blakeley (P) of the best and most reasonable use of his property, money damages are sufficient to compensate him. Private building restrictions are not the equivalent of constitutionally protected rights. Reasonable government regulation and control are permissible if it serves a valid public purpose. The valid public purpose served by the new hotel is the beneficial effect on the city's tax base. Reversed and remanded for a determination of damages to be awarded.

DISSENT: (Quirico, J.) The statute allowing nonenforcement of private restrictions is unconstitutional as applied herein. It allows private parties to deprive others of valuable property rights for a very large number of reasons.

▶ ANALYSIS

Normally, if any of the following conditions exist, building restrictions/covenants may be avoided (depending on the jurisdiction): (1) change in the neighborhood's character rendering the restriction unfair/unnecessary, (2) conduct of the party imposing the condition constituting waiver, (3) the party claiming enforcement owns no land in the parcel subdivision and the restrictions are not required to achieve a common plan, and/or (4) the restriction serves no public/private interest and would inhibit growth of the neighborhood and/or best use of the land.

■═■

Quicknotes

INFRINGEMENT Conduct in violation of a statute or contract that interferes with another's rights pursuant to law.

RESTRICTIVE COVENANT A promise contained in a deed to limit the uses to which the property will be made.

■═■

Concurrent, Family, and Entity Property

Quick Reference Rules of Law

Olivas v. Olivas

Husband (D) v. Wife (P)

N.M. Ct. App., 780 P.2d 640 (1989).

NATURE OF CASE: Appeal of the property division in a divorce action.

FACT SUMMARY: Because of a lengthy delay between the Olivases' divorce decree and the property division, Mr. Olivas (D) waited several years before seeking rent from Mrs. Olivas (P), who had remained in their home.

🏛 RULE OF LAW
When a spouse departs a residence held as community property due to marital friction, a constructive ouster is effected.

FACTS: Caroline (P) and Sam Olivas (D) were divorced by a partial decree entered December 18, 1984, but the district court did not enter its final order dividing property until August 31, 1987. The district court found that Sam Olivas (D) chose to move out of the family home and live in a separate home with another woman. The district court failed to find that he had been constructively ousted from the family home. Sam Olivas (D) requested findings and conclusions that the constructive ouster by Caroline (P) entitled him to half of the reasonable rental value of the home from the time of the initial separation.

ISSUE: When a spouse departs a residence held as community property due to marital friction, is a constructive ouster effected?

HOLDING AND DECISION: (Hartz, J.) Yes. When a spouse departs a residence held as community property due to marital friction, a constructive ouster is effected. The husband and wife held the family home as community property during their marriage. After the dissolution of their marriage, they held it as tenants in common until the property was finally judicially divided. There was a three-year gap between the time when the dissolution was made final and when the marital property was divided. During this time the husband had vacated the premises. While an ouster of a cotenant normally suggests an affirmative physical act, a constructive ouster can occur when the emotions of a divorce make it impossible for the former spouses to continue to share the marital residence. Under these circumstances, the remaining spouse is obligated to pay rent to the constructively oustered, cotenant spouse who can no longer be expected to benefit from the his share of the marital home. The husband bears the burden of proving his claim that he was oustered. Under the facts of this case, the evidence revealed that the husband left the marital home prior to its final disposition to be with his new girlfriend, not because of the hostility that had developed between the spouses. As such, he failed to meet his burden of proving a constructive ouster. He was not "pushed out, he was pulled." The district court's ruling must be sustained. Affirmed.

▶ ANALYSIS

Common law precedents support the proposition that the remaining spouse should pay rent to the cotenant when both cannot be expected to live together on the property. For example, when it is impractical for all cotenants to occupy the premises jointly, it is unnecessary that those claiming rent from the cotenant in possession first demand the right to move in and occupy the premises.

■■■

Quicknotes

COMMUNITY PROPERTY In community property jurisdictions, the term refers to all money or property acquired during the term of the marriage in which each spouse has an undivided one-half interest.

CONSTRUCTIVE OUSTER The unlawful dispossession of a party lawfully entitled to possession of real property.

OUSTER The unlawful dispossession of a party lawfully entitled to possession of real property.

■■■

Carr v. Deking

Property owner (P) v. Lessee (D)

Wash. Ct. App., 765 P.2d 40 (1988).

NATURE OF CASE: Appeal from decision declaring that a valid lease existed between one cotenant and a third party.

FACT SUMMARY: George Carr, owner of a parcel of land with his son, Joel Carr (P), as tenants in common, executed a written lease agreement with Deking (D) without Joel's (P) authorization.

🏛 RULE OF LAW
A cotenant may lawfully lease his own interest in the common property to another without the consent of the other tenant and without his joining in the lease.

FACTS: George Carr and his son, Joel Carr (P), owned a parcel of land as tenants in common. From 1974 to 1986 they leased the land to Deking (D) pursuant to a year-to-year oral agreement, receiving one-third of the annual crop as rent. In 1986, Joel Carr (P) informed Deking (D) he wanted cash rent in place of crop rent. Shortly thereafter, George Carr (P) executed a written lease agreement with Deking (D) without his son's authorization. Joel Carr (P) commenced this action to declare that no valid lease existed and that Deking (D) had no right to farm the land.

ISSUE: May a cotenant lawfully lease his own interest in the common property to another without the consent of the other tenant and without his joining in the lease?

HOLDING AND DECISION: (Green, J.) Yes. A cotenant may lawfully lease his own interest in the common property to another without the consent of the other tenant and without his joining in the lease. It is established law that each tenant in common of real property may use, benefit from, and possess the entire property subject only to the equal rights of the other cotenant. While a cotenant may lawfully lease his interest to another without the consent of the other cotenant, the nonjoining cotenant is not bound by the lease to the third person. The lessee, in effect, "steps into the shoes" of the leasing cotenant and becomes a tenant in common for the duration of the lease. A cotenant that does not join in the lease may not demand exclusive possession against the lessee, but may only demand to be let into the co-possession. Under these circumstances, the lease with Deking (D) is valid, and Carr (P) is not entitled to eject him. The proper remedy for Carr (P) to seek if he does not wish to let Deking (D) into the co-possession is that of physical partition. Until the land is partitioned, Deking (D) is entitled to farm the land pursuant to the terms of the lease. The trial court's judgment denying the eviction is affirmed. On remand, the trial court must determine Carr's (P) intentions as to whether he wants to accept the new lease with Deking (D) or if Carr (P), as a cotenant, desires a return to the terms of his prior oral lease with Deking (D).

▶ ANALYSIS

It is well settled that each tenant in common of real property may use, benefit, and possess the entire property subject only to the equal rights of cotenants. Thus, a cotenant may lawfully lease his own interest in the common property to another without the consent of the other tenant and without his joining in the lease.

Quicknotes

EJECTMENT An action to oust someone in possession of real property unlawfully and to restore possession to the party lawfully entitled to it.

PARTITION The division of property held by co-owners, granting each sole ownership of his or her share.

TENANCY IN COMMON An interest in property held by two or more people, each with equal right to its use and possession. Interests may be partitioned, sold, conveyed, or devised.

Tenhet v. Boswell

Property owner (P) v. Lessee (D)

Cal. Sup. Ct., 554 P.2d 330 (1976).

NATURE OF CASE: Joint tenant's action to have a lease declared invalid.

FACT SUMMARY: Johnson, a joint tenant with Tenhet (P), leased his interest in the joint tenancy property to Boswell (D) for a term of years and died during that term.

🏛 RULE OF LAW
(1) A lease entered into by a joint tenant does not sever the joint tenancy.
(2) A lease entered into by a joint tenant expires upon the death of that tenant.

FACTS: Johnson and Tenhet (P) owned a parcel of property as joint tenants. Without Tenhet's (P) knowledge or consent, Johnson leased the property to Boswell (D) for a period of ten years. Johnson died three months after execution of the lease, and Tenhet (P) sought to establish her sole right to possession of the property as the surviving joint tenant. After an unsuccessful demand upon Johnson (D) to vacate the premises, Tenhet (P) brought an action to have the lease declared invalid.

ISSUE:
(1) Does a lease entered into by a joint tenant sever the joint tenancy?
(2) Does a lease entered into by a joint tenant expire upon the death of that tenant?

HOLDING AND DECISION: (Mosk, J.)
(1) No. A lease entered into by a joint tenant does not sever the joint tenancy. A joint interest is one owned by two or more individuals in equal shares. Four unities are required to create a joint tenancy: unity of interest, unity of time, unity of title, and unity of possession. There is but one estate, which is taken jointly, and destruction of one of the unities destroys the joint tenancy. A joint tenancy carries with it the right of survivorship that is an expectancy that is not irrevocably fixed, but rather depends on survival without a prior breach of any of the unities. A partial alienation of one of the joint tenants interests, i.e., the lease, does not breach any of the four unities because it only conveys, at most, a life estate *pur autre vie*. Thus, it is only valid during that joint tenant's lifetime.
(2) Yes. A lease entered into by a joint tenant expires upon the death of that tenant. A joint tenancy must be expressly declared by a written instrument or a tenancy in common results. Likewise, severing a joint tenancy requires a demonstration of a clear and unambiguous intent to terminate the estate. This would have required

written conversion into a tenancy in common, or a conveyance of the property to a third person and a splitting of the proceeds. A joint tenancy can also be severed by the actions of one of the joint tenants by conveying his entire interest in the property to another, or by bringing an action to partition the property. In this instance, nothing was done to sever the joint tenancy. Because the joint tenants did nothing to sever their joint tenancy, the most Johnson could have conveyed in the lease was a life estate *pur autre vie*. This interest in the property, however, dies with the joint tenant and any encumbrances placed on the property by this tenant are unenforceable as to the other.

▶ *ANALYSIS*

California Civil Code § 683 provides in part, "A joint interest is one owned by two or more persons in equal shares, by a title created by a single will or transfer, when expressly declared in the will or transfer to be a joint tenancy." This statute, requiring an express declaration for the creation of joint interests, does not abrogate the common law rule that four unities are essential to an estate in joint tenancy: unity of interest, unity of time, unity of title, and unity of possession.

Quicknotes

FEE SIMPLE An estate in land characterized by ownership of the entire property for an unlimited duration and by absolute power over distribution.

JOINT TENANCY An interest in property whereby a single interest is owned by two or more persons and created by a single instrument; joint tenants possess equal interests in the use of the entire property and the last survivor is entitled to absolute ownership.

RIGHT OF SURVIVORSHIP Between two or more persons, such as in a joint tenancy relationship, the right to the property of a deceased passes to the survivor.

Sawada v. Endo

Injured car accident victims (P) v. Driver of car (D)

Haw. Sup. Ct., 561 P.2d 1291 (1977).

NATURE OF CASE: Appeal from refusal to set aside a conveyance of land.

FACT SUMMARY: The Sawadas (P), who were injured when struck by a car driven by Endo (D) and unable to obtain satisfaction of their judgments from Endo's (D) personal property, sought to set aside a conveyance by Endo (D) and his wife of some land that had been held by them as tenants by the entirety.

🏛 RULE OF LAW
The interest of one spouse in real property, held in tenancy by the entirety, is not subject to levy and execution by his or her individual creditors absent consent of both spouses.

FACTS: In 1968, Endo (D) struck Masako and Helen Sawada (P) while driving his car. After Helen Sawada (P) filed suit, Endo (D) and his wife conveyed to their sons some real property that they held as tenants by the entirety. Masako Sawada (P) filed suit, and both she and Helen Sawada (P) obtained judgments against Endo (D). Unable to satisfy the judgments from Endo's (D) personal property, the Sawadas (P) sought to set aside the conveyance of land. The court refused to do so, and the Sawadas (P) appealed.

ISSUE: Is the interest of one spouse in real property, held in tenancy by the entirety, subject to levy and execution by his or her individual creditors absent consent of both spouses?

HOLDING AND DECISION: (Menor, J.) No. The interest of one spouse in real property, held in tenancy by the entirety, is not subject to levy and execution by his or her individual creditors absent consent of both spouses. The tenancy by the entirety is an estate held by a husband and wife in single ownership; both and each hold the whole estate. At common law this unity was unequal and the husband maintained exclusive control and dominion of the possession and profits of the estate. The husband had the right to convey the estate in its entirety subject only to the possibility that the wife may become entitled to it upon surviving him, and the estate in its entirety was also subject to levy by the husband's individual creditors. Following the passage of the Married Women's Property Acts, this estate became indivisible except by joint action of the spouses. These Acts did not abrogate this type of estate, but rather placed the wife on an equal level with the husband with regard to ownership of the entire estate. Now, neither the husband nor wife has a separate divisible interest in the property that can be conveyed or reached by execution. A joint tenancy may be severed by voluntary alienation, partition, or by levy and execution. A tenancy by the entireties may not. The spouses can jointly convey the property free of any judgment liens against the husband or wife as individuals. This is in accord with the purpose of the estate; to protect a spouse from the other spouse's improvident debts. The tenancy of the entirety carries an indestructible right of survivorship, an inability for one spouse to alienate his interest in the estate, and broad immunity from the claims of separate creditors. Since the land in question was held by Endo (D) and his wife in tenancy by the entirety, it was immune from claims by Endo's (D) separate creditors, the Sawadas (P). Affirmed.

DISSENT: (Kidwell, J.) The effect of the Married Women's Act, if properly interpreted, was not to take from the husband his common law right to transfer his interest but to give the wife the same right to alienate her interest in the estate. Thus, judgment creditors of either spouse should be able to levy and execute on the separate interests, at least to the extent of the husband's or wife's right of survivorship.

▶ ANALYSIS

About half the states continue to recognize tenancy by the entirety as a valid institution. The majority of these states are aligned with *Sawada v. Endo* on the interpretation of the Married Women's Act: one spouse alone cannot assign his or her interest in a tenancy by the entirety. This is of great significance for general creditors, as they can only reach property that the debtors can voluntarily assign. This consequence of tenancy by the entirety is one of its primary attractions.

━■━

Quicknotes

FEE SIMPLE An estate in land characterized by ownership of the entire property for an unlimited duration and by absolute power over distribution.

HOMESTEAD A dwelling house and its surrounding property.

JOINT TENANCY An interest in property whereby a single interest is owned by two or more persons and created by a single instrument; joint tenants possess equal interests in the use of the entire property and the last survivor is entitled to absolute ownership.

TENANCY BY THE ENTIRETY The ownership of property by a husband and wife whereby they hold undivided interests in the property with right of survivorship.

━■━

Ark Land Company v. Harper

Coal mining company (P) v. Property heirs (D)

W. Va. Sup. Ct. App., 599 S.E.2d 754 (2004).

NATURE OF CASE: Appeal of order directing the partition and sale of property.

FACT SUMMARY: A company tried to acquire land owned by a family and the company in order to mine it for coal, and when they refused, sought to have the land partitioned.

RULE OF LAW
In a partition proceeding in which a party opposes the sale of property, the economic value of the property is not the exclusive test for deciding whether to partition in kind or by sale.

FACTS: The Caudill family (D) owned 75 acres of West Virginia land for nearly 100 years. The property consists of a farmhouse, several small barns, and a garden. In 2001, Ark Land Company (P) bought a 67.5% undivided interest in the land by purchasing property interests of several Caudill family members (D). When the remaining heirs refused to sell their interests, Ark Land (P) filed a complaint to have the land partitioned and sold. The court found that the property could not be partitioned in kind and ordered the partition and sale of the property.

ISSUE: In a partition proceeding in which a party opposes the sale of property, is the economic value of the property the exclusive test for deciding whether to partition in kind or by sale?

HOLDING AND DECISION: (Davis, J.) No. In a partition proceeding in which a party opposes the sale of property, the economic value of the property is not the exclusive test for deciding whether to partition in kind or by sale. In this case, the Caudill heirs (D) were not concerned with money, but with their emotional desire to keep their ancestral family home within the family. Economic and sentimental attachment must be considered in actions to partition. In addition, an expert testified that the house could be partitioned from the property so as to not deprive Ark Land (P) of any coal, and the circuit court erroneously dismissed this uncontradicted fact because of the increased costs that Ark Land (P) would incur as a result of partition in kind. Its economic burden is not determinative, however, because such a rule would allow commercial entities to always evict pre-existing co-owners since a commercial entity will always be able to show that its interest will always increase the property's value. Reversed and remanded.

CONCURRENCE: (Maynard, J.) Evidence of long-standing ownership along with emotional attachment to property are factors that should be considered and, in some cases, control the decision of whether to partition in kind or sale, but in this case, the evidence does not support the application of those factors. None of the Caudill family members (D) lived in the property for years, except for weekend retreats, and only a minority of the family has refused to sell its interest. Also, the majority may not have ruled the way it did if the company were pursuing some other use than coal mining, which it views as not important, economically.

ANALYSIS

Most jurisdictions will order partition in kind where possible because of the devastating effect partition by sale can have on property owners, particularly in cases such as this one, where a family home is at stake. That said, a critical economic requirement that might benefit many people could support a court's decision to order a partition by sale.

Quicknotes

PARTITION IN KIND A separation of undivided interests in land so that the parties may possess their interests separately.

PARTITION SALE A court-ordered sale of property held in joint tenancy, as a co-tenant or in tenancy by the entirety, if the property is incapable of being divided; the income is distributed in proportion to the parties' interests in the sold property.

O'Brien v. O'Brien

Husband (P) v. Wife (D)

N.Y. Ct. App., 489 N.E.2d 712 (1985).

NATURE OF CASE: Review of property division ordered pursuant to marital dissolution.

FACT SUMMARY: The divorcing wife (D) of Dr. O'Brien (P) claimed a marital property interest in his medical license.

🏛 RULE OF LAW
A professional license may constitute marital property.

FACTS: While the O'Briens were married, the husband (P) attended medical school full-time. Ms. O'Brien (D) worked and contributed most of the funds to maintain the household and the husband's (P) studies. Not long after Dr. O'Brien (P) obtained his license to practice, he filed for divorce. The trial court held Dr. O'Brien's (P) license to be marital property and awarded Ms. O'Brien (D) 40% of the present value of Dr. O'Brien's (P) expected lifetime earnings. The appellate division reversed, holding that a professional license was not marital property. Ms. O'Brien (D) appealed.

ISSUE: May a professional license constitute marital property?

HOLDING AND DECISION: (Simons, J.) Yes. A professional license may constitute marital property. New York's Equitable Distribution Law is not bound by traditional concepts of property. It provides that spouses have an equitable claim to things of value arising out of the marital relationship, whether or not such things of value fit into the common law notion of property. In fact, one of the reasons for the adoption of the law was the realization that application of traditional property concepts had led to inequities upon dissolution of a marriage. Here, Dr. O'Brien's (P) professional license constitutes the most valuable marital asset, and an equitable division of its value was proper. Reversed.

CONCURRENCE: (Meyer, J.) A court needs to be able to retain jurisdiction to modify an award of this nature in the event that circumstances force the licensed former spouse into a less remunerative situation than originally anticipated.

▶ ANALYSIS

Whether a professional license is "property" has been a hotly debated topic during the 1980s. This is because it has some attributes of traditional property but not all. Like property, it has value that can be measured. Unlike prop-erty, it cannot be alienated and becomes nonexistent upon the licensee's death or loss of license.

Quicknotes

EQUITABLE DISTRIBUTION The means by which a court distributes all assets acquired during a marriage by the spouses equitably upon dissolution.

MARITAL PROPERTY Property accumulated by a married couple during the term of their marriage.

SEPARATE PROPERTY Property that is owned by one spouse prior to the marriage, or any income derived therefrom, and any property that is received by one spouse pursuant to a gift, devise, bequest, or descent.

Watts v. Watts

Parent (P) v. Parent (D)

Wis. Sup. Ct., 405 N.W.2d 303 (1987).

NATURE OF CASE: Appeal in a breach of contract action by an unmarried cohabitant to obtain an equal share in the wealth accumulated during the relationship.

FACT SUMMARY: When the nonmarital cohabitation of Sue Ann Evans Watts (P) and James Watts (D) ended after a 12-year relationship that produced two children, Sue Ann (P) brought suit to share equally in the wealth accumulated during the relationship through the joint efforts of both parties.

🏛 RULE OF LAW
An unmarried cohabitant may assert a contract claim against the other cohabitant so long as the claim is independent of the sexual relationship and is supported by separate consideration.

FACTS: Sue Ann Evans (P) and James Watts (D) lived together for 12 years, holding themselves out to the public as husband and wife. During that time, Sue Ann (P) assumed James's (D) surname and gave birth to two children, who also assumed James's (D) surname. Sue Ann (P) contributed childcare and homemaking services and also assisted James (D) in his business, later starting a business of her own. After 12 years, Sue Ann (P) moved from their home. Subsequently, James (D) barred Sue Ann (P) from returning to her business. Sue Ann (P) filed suit, alleging that she and James (D) had a contract to share equally in the wealth accumulated through their joint efforts and that James (D) would be unjustly enriched if he were allowed to retain the benefit of services Sue Ann (P) provided during the relationship.

ISSUE: May an unmarried cohabitant assert a contract claim against the other cohabitant so long as the claim is independent of the sexual relationship and is supported by separate consideration?

HOLDING AND DECISION: (Abrahamson, J.) Yes. An unmarried cohabitant may assert a contract claim against the other cohabitant so long as the claim is independent of the sexual relationship and is supported by separate consideration. Sue Ann (P) has pleaded the facts necessary to state a claim for damages resulting from James's (D) breach of an express or an implied-in-fact contract to share the property accumulated through the efforts of both parties during their relationship. Moreover, if Sue Ann (P) can prove the elements of unjust enrichment to the satisfaction of the circuit court, she will be entitled to demonstrate that a constructive trust should be imposed as a remedy. Finally, Sue Ann (P) has alleged sufficient facts to state a claim for partition of all property accumulated during the relationship.

▶ ANALYSIS

State courts have taken three different approaches to the problem illustrated in this case. First, in *Hewitt v. Hewitt*, 394 N.E.2d 1204 (Ill. 1979), the Illinois Supreme Court denied any remedy to unmarried cohabitants. Second, in *Marvin v. Marvin*, 557 P.2d 106 (Cal. 1976), the California Supreme Court allowed for enforcement of a written or oral agreement between the parties. Finally, *Pickens v. Pickens*, 490 So. 2d 872 (Miss. 1986), provided for property distribution between unmarried cohabitants due to the creation of a relationship akin to a partnership.

Quicknotes

CONSTRUCTIVE TRUST A trust that arises by operation of law whereby the court imposes a trust upon property lawfully held by one party for the benefit of another, as a result of some wrongdoing by the party in possession so as to avoid unjust enrichment.

PARTITION The division of property held by co-owners, granting each sole ownership of his or her share.

UNJUST ENRICHMENT The unlawful acquisition of money or property of another for which both law and equity require restitution to be made.

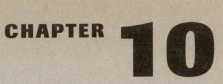
Present Estates and Future Interests

Quick Reference Rules of Law

Wood v. Board of County Commissioners of Fremont County

Land grantor (P) v. Grantee (D)

Wyo. Sup. Ct., 759 P.2d 1250 (1988).

NATURE OF CASE: Appeal from summary judgment for defense in action for reversion.

FACT SUMMARY: Wood (P) claimed that a grant of land to the Board of Commissioners of Fremont County (D) was subject to a condition subsequent that the land be used as a hospital.

 RULE OF LAW
A grant of fee simple determinable must clearly state that the estate will terminate if not used in accordance with the grant.

FACTS: Wood (P) gave a parcel of land to the Board of Commissioners of Fremont County (County) (D). The transfer stated that the purpose of the grant was that it be used for a hospital, but it did not express what would happen to the estate if it were not so used. The County (D) operated a hospital on the land for nearly 40 years before putting it up for sale. Wood (P) then brought suit, claiming a right to a reversion in the grant, which became effective when the land ceased to be used for the intended purpose. The trial court granted summary judgment to the County (D). Wood (P) appealed.

ISSUE: Must a grant of fee simple determinable clearly state that the estate will terminate if not used in accordance with the grant?

HOLDING AND DECISION: (Brown, C.J.) Yes. A grant of fee simple determinable must clearly state that the estate will terminate if not used in accordance with the grant. A fee simple determinable is characterized by its expiration upon the happening of an uncertain event. However, the grant must clearly state that the estate will expire automatically upon the happening of the uncertain event. The grant from Wood clearly stated the condition but failed to state that the grant would not continue to be valid if the condition were not met. Nor did Wood (P) grant a fee simple subject to a condition subsequent, because the grant made no clear provision for termination. Wood (P) retained no interest in the property. The trial court is affirmed.

▶ *ANALYSIS*

There is a presumption against forfeiture in the law. Thus any grant purporting to cause such a forfeiture will be strictly construed against the grantor absent clear intent otherwise. Although the grantor's intent, if realizable, typically prevails, ambiguous grants give rise to public policy considerations—in the above case, the free alienability of property.

■■■

Quicknotes

FEE SIMPLE DETERMINABLE A fee simple interest in property that may last forever or until the happening of a specified event.

REVERSION An interest retained by a grantor of property in the land transferred, which is created when the owner conveys less of an interest than he or she owns and which returns to the grantor upon the termination of the conveyed estate.

■■■

Edwards v. Bradley

Mother (D) v. Daughter (P)

Va. Sup. Ct., 315 S.E.2d 196 (1984).

NATURE OF CASE: Appeal from suit for injunction on the sale of property.

FACT SUMMARY: Bradley (P) brought suit against her mother's estate seeking to enjoin the sale of certain property devised by her grandmother.

RULE OF LAW
A conditional limitation imposed on a life estate is valid.

FACTS: Lilliston died testate leaving her farms to her daughter, Edwards (D), on the basis that she not sell the property. In such case her interest would be forfeited. Edwards (D) sought to have her children and their spouses sign an agreement to consent to her selling the farm. Bradley (P) declined and Edwards (D) died leaving her $1. Bradley (P) filed a complaint against the executors and her siblings seeking to enjoin the sale of the farm. The trial court ruled that Edwards (D) owned a life estate. Edwards (D) appealed, claiming a fee simple interest.

ISSUE: Is a conditional limitation imposed on a life estate valid?

HOLDING AND DECISION: (Cochran, J.) Yes. A conditional limitation imposed on a life estate is valid. The draftsman clearly did not use the words "fee simple"; however, such words are not necessary in order to create a fee simple estate where real estate is devised without words of limitation unless a contrary intent appears in the will. This is the case here. The testatrix clearly intended to create a life estate in Edwards (D) with a fee simple remainder in her children. Affirmed.

ANALYSIS

Note that the court recognized the testatrix created a spendthrift trust in other portions of her will, and could have chosen that vehicle here if she intended to. The court will uphold the apparent intent of the testatrix if possible where it does not otherwise violate another rule of law.

Quicknotes

DEVISE The conferring of a gift of real or personal property by means of a testamentary instrument.

FEE SIMPLE An estate in land characterized by ownership of the entire property for an unlimited duration and by absolute power over distribution.

LIFE ESTATE An interest in land measured by the life of the tenant or a third party.

REMAINDER An interest in land that remains after the termination of the immediately preceding estate.

McIntyre v. Scarbrough

Life tenant (D) v. Property owners (P)

Ga. Sup. Ct., 471 S.E.2d 199 (1996).

NATURE OF CASE: Petition to establish title and terminate a life estate.

FACT SUMMARY: The Scarbroughs (P) brought a petition to establish title and to terminate Ms. McIntyre's (D) interest in a portion of the land they purchased from her.

 RULE OF LAW
A life tenant is entitled to the full use and enjoyment of the property if in such use he or she exercises the ordinary care of a prudent person for its preservation and protection and commits no acts that would permanently injure the remainder interest.

FACTS: The Scarbroughs (P) purchased a tract of land from McIntyre (D) by warranty deed, with the reservation of a life estate for McIntyre (D) of 1.2 acres of the land for her natural life. She (D) was also to be responsible for the maintenance and upkeep of the property, all improvements thereon, and the payment of ad valorem taxes. The Scarbroughs (P) brought a petition to establish title and terminate the life estate and moved for summary judgment, claiming waste and violation of the warranty deed. The trial court first denied summary judgment, then reversed on the basis that McIntyre (D) failed to exercise ordinary care for the preservation of the property and thereby forfeited her interest to the remaindermen, who are entitled to immediate possession.

ISSUE: Is a life tenant entitled to the full use and enjoyment of the property if in such use he or she exercises the ordinary care of a prudent person for its preservation and protection and commits no acts that would permanently injure the remainder interest?

HOLDING AND DECISION: (Thompson, J.) Yes. A life tenant is entitled to the full use and enjoyment of the property if in such use he or she exercises the ordinary care of a prudent person for its preservation and protection and commits no acts that would permanently injure the remainder interest. This court has held that failure to pay burdens imposed by law on the property during the term constitutes such lack of ordinary care as a prudent person should exercise for its protection and preservation and would tend to divest the fee interest by subjecting it to sale. Here McIntyre (D) failed to pay the ad valorem property taxes on the tract for the years 1991–93 or the improvements for the years 1992–94, which was also a requirement of the warranty deed. Such failure results in forfeiture of the life estate as a matter of law. Affirmed.

DISSENT: (Benham, C.J.) The issue of waste is ordinarily one for the jury to decide. The question of whether McIntyre's (D) conduct with regard to the life estate was so egregiously wasteful as to warrant forfeiture of her interest in the property was inappropriate for summary judgment and should have been submitted to the jury.

▶ *ANALYSIS*

The court here concluded that while the trial court too narrowly construed the definition of occupancy, it correctly determined that the life estate was terminated under the doctrine of waste. The trial court defined occupancy as "dwelling" in the subject premises. This court recognized that the term "occupy" is more expansive and encompasses those situations in which a person holds possession of property for use.

■▬■

Quicknotes

LIFE ESTATE An interest in land measured by the life of the tenant or a third party.

LIFE TENANT An individual whose estate in real property is measured either by his own life or by that of another.

REMAINDER INTEREST An interest in land that remains after the termination of the immediately preceding estate.

■▬■

Evans v. Abney

State, municipality, and residents (D) v. Board managers of local park (P)

396 U.S. 435 (1970).

NATURE OF CASE: Appeal from state supreme court decision finding that because a trust settlor's intention of creating a whites-only public park could no longer be carried out lawfully, the park should close and the trust property should revert to the heirs of the trust settlor.

FACT SUMMARY: In 1911, Senator A. O. Bacon of Georgia conveyed property in trust to Macon, Georgia, to be used as a public park for whites only. In a prior decision, the United States Supreme Court ruled the park's white-only designation was discriminatory. The Georgia Supreme Court then ruled that because Bacon's intentions could no longer be carried out lawfully, the park should close and the trust property should revert to the heirs of the trust settlor.

🏛 RULE OF LAW
When a valid charitable bequest may no longer be carried out in the same manner as provided by the testator or donor, a court sitting in equity may revise the bequest in such a manner that it adheres as closely as possible to the testator or donor's intention.

FACTS: In 1911, Senator A. O. Bacon of Georgia conveyed property in trust to Macon, Georgia, to be used as a public park for whites only. Just six years prior, the Georgia legislature modified a statute to allow for the dedication of land for use by one race only. Macon (D) initially operated the park for whites only. However, it then opened the park to all residents. In response, several of the Board of Managers of the park brought this suit to remove the city as trustee and to appoint new trustees, who presumably would run the park again as whites-only. The case eventually reached the United States Supreme Court after African American residents intervened to keep the park open. In the prior decision, *Evans v. Newton*, 382 U.S. 296 (1966), the Court ruled the park's whites only designation was discriminatory. On remand, the African American residents and the Georgia Attorney General's office argued that the state court should apply the doctrine of cy pres and modify the trust to allow all residents to use the park. The Georgia Supreme Court ruled, however, that because Bacon's intentions could no longer be carried out lawfully, the park should close and the trust property should revert to Bacon's heirs, 224 Ga. 826, 165 S.E.2d 160 (1968). The United States Supreme Court granted the state Attorney General's petition for further review.

ISSUE: When a valid charitable bequest may no longer be carried out in the same manner as provided by the testator or donor, may a court sitting in equity revise the bequest in such a manner that it adheres as closely as possible to the testator or donor's intention?

HOLDING AND DECISION: (Black, J.) Yes. When a valid charitable bequest may no longer be carried out in the same manner as provided by the testator or donor, a court sitting in equity may revise the bequest in such a manner that it adheres as closely as possible to the testator or donor's intention. Most states follow this doctrine, known as cy pres. When the testator's fundamental purpose is thwarted or no longer possible and trust funds or property remain, courts are free to modify the trust document for the public's benefit. However, the doctrine of cy pres is not applicable in all cases. Where the evidence is clear via the trust document that the settlor of the trust only desires a certain outcome, the trust may cease and trust property may revert to the heirs of the trust when that outcome becomes impossible. Here, Senator Brown was clear that he had limitations for the public park. He specifically stated that the park should not be used for anything other than a whites-only public park. His trust stated that he did not believe that whites and African Americans could coexist. The Georgia trial courts and Georgia Supreme Court concluded that Bacon's limitation on use of the park was quite clear and that no modification was allowed. Trusts and wills are matters of state law. These state court decisions respecting a particular trust present no violation of any constitutionally protected rights. Separately, this case is distinguishable from a case where a city closes a public park. In that case, there is state action that could lead to a colorable constitutional claim, such as an equal protection violation. Here, the state courts are interpreting a private trust and no state action is present. Affirmed.

DISSENT: (Brennan, J.) State action is present in this case via a number of avenues. First, the city accepted title to the park and operated it for fifty years as a desegregated public park. Second, a state court decision to prevent willing parties to associate with one another is itself a form of state action. Third, the Georgia legislature itself enabled Bacon to create this whites-only park when it modified state statutes to allow the practice. This is also a form of state action. Accordingly, the petitioners have stated a colorable claim for an equal protection violation. A city should not be able to close a public park when forced to desegregate it.

▌ *ANALYSIS*

Whenever the United States Supreme Court grants certiorari to parties appealing a state court decision, the case

Continued on next page.

must include a significant federal issue. Here, the presence of a possible equal protection violation was likely enough for the court to grant the petition for review. However, the crux of this case, an interpretation of trust law, is essentially a state law matter.

■■■

Quicknotes

CERTIORARI A discretionary writ issued by a superior court to an inferior court in order to review the lower court's decisions; the United States Supreme Court's writ ordering such review.

COLORABLE CLAIM A claim sufficient to withstand a motion to dismiss; a claim valid on its face without the resolution of factual disputes.

CY PRES DOCTRINE Equitable doctrine applied in order to give effect to an instrument as close to the drafter's intent as possible without violating the law, which effect would be unlawful if strictly enforced.

■■■

Johnson v. Whiton

Purchaser (D) v. Seller (P)

Mass. Sup. Jud. Ct., 34 N.E. 542 (1893).

NATURE OF CASE: Action for recovery of deposit for defective title.

FACT SUMMARY: Johnson (P) claimed a deed to him was invalid because Whiton (D), having received only a qualified fee from her grandfather's will, could not convey a fee simple absolute.

🏛 RULE OF LAW
Grantors may not create new types of inheritance, and any attempt to do so will result in the full fee being conveyed.

FACTS: Royal Whiton executed a will bequeathing one-third of his property to Sarah Whiton (D) "and her heirs on her father's side," remainder over to his four other grandchildren. All five grandchildren contracted to sell the land to Johnson (P), who then refused to accept the deed, claiming that Sarah Whiton (D) could not convey a fee simple absolute. Johnson (P) sued to recover his deposit.

ISSUE: May grantors create new types of inheritance?

HOLDING AND DECISION: (Holmes, Jr., J.) No. Grantors may not create new types of inheritance, and any attempt to do so will result in the full fee being conveyed. Under old English law, to take land by descent a person had to be "of the blood of the first purchaser," that is, the closest relative on the father's side, if the father was the grantor. Therefore, it was permissible to restrict inheritance to particular lineal decedents using words of limitation such as those contained in Royal Whiton's will. However, under modern Massachusetts law, inherited property may pass from one line to the other. Therefore, Royal Whiton's attempt to create an estate descending only to heirs on the father's side was a new kind of inheritance. As such, it must be rejected, leaving the estate a fee simple. Furthermore, the policy against restraints on alienation militates against depriving Sarah Whiton (D) of her ability to convey an unqualified fee. Judgment for defendant.

▶ ANALYSIS

An estate in fee tail, which operates to keep land in the grantee's family until the line of heirs becomes extinct, is considered inconsistent with the values of a democratic society. As such, it has been prohibited, either statutorily or constitutionally, in 33 states. Depending on the state, a fee tail is automatically converted into a fee simple estate either absolute or with limitations.

Quicknotes

FEE SIMPLE ABSOLUTE An estate in land characterized by ownership of the entire property for an unlimited duration and by absolute power over distribution.

FEE TAIL A limitation in either a deed or will limiting succession of property to a grantee and the heirs of his body.

Symphony Space, Inc. v. Pergola Properties, Inc.

Buyer (P) v. Seller (D)

N.Y. Ct. App., 669 N.E.2d 799 (1996).

NATURE OF CASE: Suit for declaratory judgment.

FACT SUMMARY: Symphony Space, Inc. (P) sought a declaratory judgment that an option clause in its agreement to purchase property from Broadwest Realty Corp. was unenforceable in violation of the Rule Against Perpetuities.

🏛 RULE OF LAW
Commercial option agreements are not exempted from the Rule Against Perpetuities.

FACTS: Symphony Space, Inc. (Symphony) (P), a non-profit organization dedicated to the arts, leased a theatre from Broadwest Realty Corp (Broadwest). Broadwest sold the building to Symphony (P) and leased back the income producing property, minus the theatre, for one year. The purpose of the agreement was to provide Symphony (P) with a tax exemption. The agreement also contained an option clause allowing Broadwest to purchase the property during specified periods. Pergola Properties, Inc. (Pergola) (D), a nominee of Broadwest, notified Symphony (P) of its intent to exercise the option, and Symphony (P) brought suit seeking a declaratory judgment that the option violated New York's Rule Against Perpetuities. The Appellate Division held the clause unenforceable.

ISSUE: Are commercial option agreements exempted from the Rule Against Perpetuities?

HOLDING AND DECISION: (Kaye, C.J.) No. Commercial option agreements are not exempted from the Rule Against Perpetuities. Options to purchase are to be treated differently than preemptive rights, which impede transferability only minimally in contrast to purchase options, which vest substantial control over the alienability of the property upon the option holder. Only where the preemptive right arises in a governmental or commercial agreement is the minor restraint offset by the holder's incentive to improve the property. The option agreement here creates the type of control over the transferability over property that the rule against remote vesting has sought to prevent. An option "appurtenant" to purchase land that originates in a lease provision that is not exercisable after the expiration of the lease, and is incapable of separation from the lease agreement, is still generally valid even though the holder's interest may vest beyond the perpetuities period. Here the option does not qualify as an option appurtenant, since it significantly deters the development of the property. Affirmed.

▶ ANALYSIS

The exception to the Rule Against Perpetuities for preemptive rights was developed in order to provide an incentive for the development of property. At common law, options to purchase land were subject to the rule, since they worked as a disincentive to such development. Although such options are typically found in commercial contracts, they are still subject to the rule against remote vesting.

Quicknotes

FREE ALIENABILITY Unrestricted transferability.

OPTION A contract pursuant to which a seller agrees that property will be available for the buyer to purchase at a specified price and within a certain time period.

RULE AGAINST PERPETUITIES The doctrine that a future interest that is incapable of vesting within twenty-one years of lives in being at the time it is created is immediately void.

VESTING The attaining of the right to pension or other employer-contribution benefits when the employee satisfies the minimum requirements necessary in order to be entitled to the receipt of such benefits in the future.

Estate of Guidotti

Wife (P) v. Trustee (D)

Cal. Ct. App., 109 Cal. Rptr. 2d 674 (2001).

NATURE OF CASE: Appeal from lower court decision finding that testator could permissibly terminate income support to his wife in the event she remarried after his death.

FACT SUMMARY: Earl Guidotti's will created a testamentary trust for the benefit of his wife, Darlene Guidotti (P). The trust document stated she would receive the net income from the trust for life unless and until she remarried.

RULE OF LAW
Conditions in testamentary instruments that impose restraints on marriage are typically void as against public policy, unless the intent of the provision was not to forbid marriage but only to provide support until the surviving spouse remarries.

FACTS: Earl Guidotti's will created a testamentary trust for the benefit of his wife, Darlene Guidotti (P). The trust document stated she would receive the net income from the trust for life unless and until she remarried or cohabited with another man as though they were man and wife. Earl passed away in 1999. In 2000, Darlene (P) petitioned the court to reform the will. Darlene (P) did so because the provision terminating her income interest upon her remarriage precluded her from obtaining the federal estate tax marital deduction. At the lower court, Darlene (P) produced evidence from the attorney who drafted Earl's will. The attorney declared that Earl was very jealous of Darlene (P) and desired that she not remarry. The attorney included the income termination provision in the will even though he thought it might be void as against public policy. The lower court found that the provision was not a restraint on marriage. Rather that court found the intent of the provision was only to provide for Darlene (P) until she did remarry. Darlene (P) appealed to an intermediate appellate court.

ISSUE: Are conditions in testamentary instruments that impose restraints on marriage typically void as against public policy, unless the intent of the provision was not to forbid marriage but only to provide support until the surviving spouse remarries?

HOLDING AND DECISION: (Gilbert, J.) Yes. Conditions in testamentary instruments that impose restraints on marriage are typically void as against public policy, unless the intent of the provision was not to forbid marriage but only to provide support until the surviving spouse remarries. The interpretation of written instruments, from contracts to wills, is typically a question of law. A reviewing court may construe testamentary instruments provided that any extrinsic evidence is not conflicting with the documents. The intention of the testator is paramount and courts will strive to construe testamentary instruments in a manner consistent with that intent. California, as well as most states, invalidate provisions in wills that impose a restraint on marriage of a surviving spouse or heir. In this case, the evidence from Earl's attorney is dispositive that Earl's provision barring Darlene (P) from remarriage is an improper restraint on marriage. The attorney declared that Earl was jealous of Darlene (P). It is clear Earl did not simply wish to provide for Darlene (P) until the time she remarried. Rather, he sought, impermissibly, to bar her from marriage entirely. The case is remanded to the trial court with the order that the will should be reformed consistent with this opinion. Reversed.

ANALYSIS

There is a fine distinction between impermissible provisions restraining marriage and permissible provisions that seek to provide support until a surviving spouse remarries. The determining factor is the intent of the testator. Typically, extrinsic evidence will be required to determine that intent. Often the best evidence will come from the attorney who drafted the testamentary instrument.

Quicknotes

EXTRINSIC EVIDENCE Evidence that is not contained within the text of a document or contract, but which is derived from the parties' statements or the circumstances under which the agreement was made.

TESTAMENTARY INSTRUMENT An instrument that takes effect upon the death of the maker.

Quick Reference Rules of Law

Vásquez v. Glassboro Service Association, Inc.

Farmworker (P) v. Employer (D)

N.J. Sup. Ct., 415 A.2d 1156 (1980).

NATURE OF CASE: Appeal from a judgment in an action seeking to enjoin farm owners from depriving farmworkers of the use of their quarters except through judicial process.

FACT SUMMARY: After Vásquez's (P) employment as a migrant farmworker was terminated, he was not allowed to remain overnight in the employer-provided barracks until he could find alternative housing.

RULE OF LAW
When a migrant farmworker's employment is terminated, he may be removed from employer-provided housing only through a judicial proceeding.

FACTS: Glassboro Service Association, Inc. (Glassboro) (D) contracted to bring migrant farmworkers to New Jersey from Puerto Rico, supplying living quarters for those workers at its labor camp. No extra charge was imposed for such housing. Vásquez (P), who was recruited in Puerto Rico, worked for Glassboro (D). Later, Glassboro's (D) foreman told Vásquez (P) that his work was unsatisfactory and that he was to be discharged. After a hearing and discharge, Vásquez (P) was not allowed to remain in the camp overnight. Unable to speak English and without funds to return to Puerto Rico, Vásquez (P) sought the assistance of the Farmworkers Corporation. He also consulted with the Farmworkers Rights Project, which filed a complaint, seeking an order permitting Vásquez (P) to reenter his living quarters and enjoining Glassboro (D) from depriving him of the use of the quarters except through judicial process.

ISSUE: When a migrant farmworker's employment is terminated, may he be removed from employer-provided housing without a judicial proceeding?

HOLDING AND DECISION: (Pollock, J.) No. When a migrant farmworker's employment is terminated, he may not be removed from employer-provided housing without a judicial proceeding. The contract under which Vásquez (P) was brought from Puerto Rico is a contract of adhesion. The unconscionability of the contract inheres not only in its failure to provide a worker with a reasonable opportunity to find alternative housing, but in its disregard for his welfare after termination of his employment. In the absence of any concern demonstrated for the worker in the contract, public policy requires the implication of a provision for a reasonable time to find alternative housing. By abolishing self-help in such situations, the court provides a forum for an equitable resolution of a controversy between a farm labor service and a migrant farmworker on termination of employment.

ANALYSIS

A migrant farmworker has even less bargaining power than a residential tenant. Although Vásquez (P) had found housing at the time of this court decision, other workers had been evicted, some at odd hours of the night. The lack of alternative housing emphasized the inequality between Glassboro (D) and the migrant farmworkers. Once his employment ended, a farmworker lost not only his job but his shelter. Moreover, a migrant farmworker is not a tenant under the applicable New Jersey statute.

Quicknotes

COVENANT OF HABITABILITY A warranty implied by a landlord that the premises are suitable, and will remain suitable, for habitation.

EJECTMENT An action to oust someone in possession of real property unlawfully and to restore possession to the party lawfully entitled to it.

"EJUSDEM GENERIS" Belonging to the same class or type; rule of construction applied when general words follow a specified class of persons or items, then the words are not to be applied in their broad meaning but are to apply only to those persons or items listed.

RESTRICTIVE COVENANT A promise contained in a deed to limit the uses to which the property will be made.

TENANT An individual who enjoys the use and occupation of the property of another for a specified period.

Kendall v. Ernest Pestana, Inc.

Prospective buyer (P) v. Leaseholder (D)

Cal. Sup. Ct., 709 P.2d 837 (1985).

NATURE OF CASE: Appeal from judgment in an action for declaratory and injunctive relief for a landlord's refusal to consent to a lease assignment.

FACT SUMMARY: When Ernest Pestana, Inc. (Pestana) (D) refused to allow Bixler to assign his interest in a commercial leasehold to Kendall (P) and two others, they filed suit, seeking a declaration that Pestana's (D) refusal was unreasonable.

> ## 🏛 RULE OF LAW
> Where a lease provides for assignment only with the prior consent of the lessor, such consent may be withheld only where the lessor has a commercially reasonable objection to the assignment.

FACTS: Ernest Pestana, Inc. (Pestana) (D) held an assigned lease interest in hangar space at the San Jose Municipal Airport. The original holders of the lease had also entered into a 25-year sublease with Bixler, who was to use the premises for an airplane maintenance business. Bixler later decided to sell the business to Kendall (P) and two others. The proposed sale included the existing lease. Kendall (P) had a stronger financial statement and greater net worth than Bixler and was willing to be bound by the terms of the lease. However, Pestana (D) refused to consent to the assignment, maintaining that it had an absolute right arbitrarily to refuse any such request. Kendall (P) and the others brought suit, seeking a declaration that Pestana's (D) refusal was unreasonable and an unlawful restraint on the freedom of alienation. This appeal followed the lower court's decision.

ISSUE: Where a lease provides for assignment only with the prior consent of the lessor, may such consent be withheld only where the lessor has a commercially reasonable objection to the assignment?

HOLDING AND DECISION: (Broussard, J.) Yes. Where a lease provides for assignment only with the prior consent of the lessor, such consent may be withheld only where the lessor has a commercially reasonable objection to the assignment. Some of the factors that the trier of fact may properly consider in applying the standards of good faith and commercial reasonableness are (1) financial responsibility of the proposed assignee, (2) suitability of the use for the particular property, (3) legality of the proposed use, (4) need for alteration of the premises, and (5) the nature of the occupancy. Pestana (D) is trying to get more than it bargained for in the lease. A lessor is free to build periodic rent increases into a lease, as was done here. Any increased value of the property beyond this belongs to the lessor only in the sense that the lessor's reversionary estate will benefit from it upon the expiration of the lease. The minority rule applied here is the preferable one.

DISSENT: (Lucas, J.) The weight of authority should be followed, which allows the commercial lessor to withhold his consent to an assignment or sublease arbitrarily or without reasonable cause.

▌ANALYSIS

The impetus for change in the majority rule has come from two directions, reflecting the dual nature of a lease as a conveyance of a leasehold interest and a contract. The Restatement (Second) of Property adopts the minority rule on the validity of approval clauses in leases, requiring that withholding of consent be reasonable. In addition, where a contract confers on one party a discretionary power affecting the rights of the other, a duty is imposed to exercise that discretion in good faith and in accordance with fair dealing.

Quicknotes

LEASEHOLD INTEREST The interest of a landlord or tenant pursuant to a lease agreement.

RESTRAINT AGAINST ALIENATION A provision restricting the transferee's ability to convey interests in the conveyed property.

Slavin v. Rent Control Board of Brookline

Landlord (P) v. Rent control board (D)

Mass. Sup. Jud. Ct., 548 N.E.2d 1226 (1990).

NATURE OF CASE: Appeal from a ruling refusing to issue an eviction certificate requested by a landlord.

FACT SUMMARY: When Slavin (P) sought a certificate of eviction in an attempt to evict a tenant for violation of a lease provision requiring the landlord's consent for another person to occupy the premises, the Rent Control Board of Brookline (D) refused to issue the certificate on the ground that Slavin (P) had acted unreasonably.

RULE OF LAW
A lease provision requiring the landlord's consent to an assignment or sublease permits the landlord to refuse arbitrarily or unreasonably.

FACTS: Slavin (P) applied to the Rent Control Board of Brookline (the Board) (D) for a certificate of eviction, seeking to evict a tenant, Myers (D), on the ground that Myers (D) violated an obligation of his tenancy by allowing an unauthorized person to occupy his apartment without first obtaining Slavin's (P) written consent as stipulated in the lease. The Board (D) refused to issue the certificate on the ground that Slavin (P) had acted unreasonably because she had categorically refused to allow Myers (D) to bring in someone new after the original cotenant had moved out. Thus, Myers (D) could not be said to have violated the lease. Slavin (P) appealed.

ISSUE: Does a lease provision requiring the landlord's consent to an assignment or sublease permit the landlord to refuse arbitrarily or unreasonably?

HOLDING AND DECISION: (O'Connor, J.) Yes. A lease provision requiring the landlord's consent to an assignment or sublease permits the landlord to refuse arbitrarily or unreasonably. All but two of the cases cited by the Board (D) involved a commercial, not a residential lease. In several of the cases, the court specifically states that its holding is limited to the commercial lease context. In *68 Beacon St., Inc. v. Sohier*, 194 N.E. 303 (Mass. 1935), this court ruled that a commercial lease provision requiring a landlord's consent prior to an assignment, with no limitation on the landlord's ability to refuse, is not an unreasonable restraint on alienation. In light of that decision and in the absence of a demonstrable trend involving residential leases in other jurisdictions, there appears no need to impose on residential landlords a reasonableness requirement. The question is one of public policy, which the legislature is free to address. Reversed.

▶ ANALYSIS

The court noted that in *Kruger v. Page Management Co.*, 432 N.Y.S.2d 295 (Sup. Ct. 1980)—the only purely residential lease case cited by the Board (D)—the reasonableness requirement in New York has been statutorily imposed. Valid arguments can be made in support of a reasonableness rule in the residential context. But there are also valid counter-arguments, not the least of which is that such a rule would be likely to engender a plethora of litigation about whether the landlord's withholding of consent was reasonable.

━■━

Quicknotes

RENT CONTROL A municipal ordinance limiting the maximum rent that may be lawfully charged for rental property.

RESTRAINT AGAINST ALIENATION A provision restricting the transferee's ability to convey interests in the conveyed property.

━■━

Sommer v. Kridel

Apartment owner (P) v. Lessee (D)

N.J. Sup. Ct., 378 A.2d 767 (1977).

NATURE OF CASE: Appeal from intermediate appellate court's decision in favor of defendant.

FACT SUMMARY: Sommer (P) did not attempt to relet the premises he had leased to Kridel (D), even though the opportunity to do so existed and Kridel (D) had specifically informed Sommer (P) that he was unable to go through with the leasing for personal reasons and asked for acceptance of his surrender.

🏛 RULE OF LAW
A landlord has an obligation to make a reasonable effort to mitigate damages when a lessee "surrenders," meaning that the landlord must make a reasonable effort to relet the premises.

FACTS: Sommer (P) and Riverview Realty Co. (Riverview) (P) were both landlords who leased to tenants, Kridel (D) and Perosio (D), respectively, who were forced by personal circumstances to attempt "surrenders." Sommer (P) received a letter explaining the situations and stating Kridel's (D) desire to surrender. Neither landlord made an attempt to relet their vacated units, even though a party expressed interest in renting the unit from Sommer (P). Instead, both landlords brought suits to recover damages from their respective "defaulting" tenants. Noting that Sommer (P) never responded to Kridel's (D) written offer of surrender and finding that such was tantamount to an acceptance of that offer, the court found that Kridel's (D) tenancy had been terminated along with his obligation to pay rent. From an appellate reversal of the judgment dismissing Sommer's (P) complaint and the counterclaim for return of the security deposit, Sommer (P) appealed. His appeal was consolidated with that of Perosio (D), there having been an appellate affirmance of the trial court decision granting Riverview (P) summary judgment.

ISSUE: Must a landlord make a reasonable effort to mitigate damages by attempting to relet the premises when a lessee "surrenders" same?

HOLDING AND DECISION: (Pashman, J.) Yes. If a lessee has effected a "surrender" of the leased premises, the landlord is under an obligation to make a reasonable effort to mitigate damages by attempting to relet the premises. Such mitigation of damages is his duty when he seeks to recover rents due from a defaulting tenant. While the historical rule, and that still followed in a majority of states, is that no such duty exists, the modern trend is in favor of finding such a duty. This trend is based on the recognition that a lease is no longer simply a conveyance giving the tenant control over an estate and making his abandonment of as little concern to the landlord as would be the tenant's abandonment of property he owned outright and not simply for a term. Leases now also are of contractual nature; the changes in society have created diverse problems that have come to be dealt with by utilizing specific clauses in residential leases to fit each particular set of circumstances. Thus, a contractual ingredient has been reintroduced into the law of estates for years. Contractual obligations bespeak a duty to mitigate damages, and in the case of a residential lease, this is accomplished, upon "surrender" by the lessee, by an attempt to relet the premises. As the landlord is in a better position to prove that he has used reasonable diligence in attempting to relet the premises, the burden of proof on that issue lies with him. The facts show that Sommer (P) was not diligent in that regard; thus, that judgment must be reversed. As to Riverview (P), the lack of a factual determination as to any attempt to relet requires that the case be remanded for a determination of whether a reasonable attempt to mitigate damages was made.

▶ ANALYSIS

Some courts have found that such mitigation is not required when a landlord simply sues to recover unpaid rent. For example, in *Winshall v. Ampco Auto Parks, Inc.*, 417 F. Supp. 334 (E.D. Mich. 1976), the court specifically held that mitigation was a concept applicable only to suits for damages and then went on to state that an action to recover unpaid rent was not a suit for damages.

Quicknotes

IMPLIED WARRANTY OF HABITABILITY A warranty implied by a landlord that the premises are suitable, and will remain suitable, for habitation.

MITIGATION OF DAMAGES A plaintiff's implied obligation to reduce the damages incurred by taking reasonable steps to prevent additional injury.

Minjak Co. v. Randolph

Landlord (P) v. Tenant (D)

N.Y. App. Div., 528 N.Y.S.2d 554 (1988).

NATURE OF CASE: Appeal from reversal of an award in tenant's favor of rent abatement and punitive damages in a landlord's action for nonpayment of rent.

FACT SUMMARY: After Randolph (D) and Kikuchi (D) withheld their rent due to the condition of the loft space they were leasing, Minjak Co. (P), the landlord, brought this action for nonpayment, and Randolph (D) and Kikuchi (D) counterclaimed for breach of warranty of habitability.

🏛 RULE OF LAW
A tenant may assert the defense of constructive eviction for the nonpayment of rent, even if he or she has abandoned only a portion of the demised premises due to the landlord's acts.

FACTS: Randolph (D) and Kikuchi (D) leased a loft in a building owned by Minjak Co. (P). Two-thirds of the loft space was used as a music studio by Kikuchi (D), and the remainder of the space was used as their residence. At one point, water poured into the bedroom and closets from the tenant's loft above them. After Minjak (P) started construction on the building, huge clouds of dust came pouring into the loft, settling everywhere. Kikuchi's (D) musical equipment had to be covered at all times to protect it from the dust. When Randolph (D) and Kikuchi (D) withheld their rent payments, Minjak (P) commenced a summary nonpayment proceeding against them. Randolph (D) and Kikuchi (D) counterclaimed for breach of warranty of habitability. After trial, the jury awarded Randolph (D) and Kikuchi (D) a rent abatement as compensatory damages on the theory of constructive eviction, along with punitive damages. The appellate term reversed. This appeal followed.

ISSUE: May a tenant assert the defense of constructive eviction for the nonpayment of rent, even if he or she has abandoned only a portion of the demised premises due to the landlord's acts?

HOLDING AND DECISION: (Memorandum Decision) Yes. A tenant may assert the defense of constructive eviction for the nonpayment of rent, even if he or she has abandoned only a portion of the demised premises due to the landlord's acts. The evidence fully supported a finding that Randolph (D) and Kikuchi (D) had to abandon the music studio portion of the loft due to the Minjak's (P) wrongful acts. Moreover, the record supports the jury's finding of morally culpable conduct allowing punitive damages in light of the dangerous and offensive manner in which the landlord permitted the construction work to be performed. Accordingly, the award of punitive damages is sustained.

▶ ANALYSIS

The appellate term held that the doctrine of constructive eviction could not provide a defense to the nonpayment proceeding because Randolph (D) and Kikuchi (D) had not abandoned possession of the demised premises. However, the appellate division found that compelling considerations of social policy and fairness dictated the rule it applied here. Punitive damages may be awarded in breach of warranty of habitability cases where the landlord's actions were intentional and malicious.

Quicknotes

ABATEMENT A decrease or lessening of something; in equity, a suspension or dismissal of a cause of action.

CONSTRUCTIVE EVICTION An action whereby the landlord renders the property unsuitable for occupancy, either in whole or in part, so that the tenant is forced to leave the premises.

PUNITIVE DAMAGES Damages exceeding the actual injury suffered for the purposes of punishment, deterrence and comfort to plaintiff.

WARRANTY OF HABITABILITY An implied warranty owed by a landlord to a tenant to provide leased premises is properly maintained in a habitable condition prior to leasing the premises and during the duration of the lease.

3000 B.C. v. Bowman Properties Ltd.

Tenant (P) v. Landlord (D)

No. 1968, 2008 WL 5544414 (Pa. Com. Pl. 2008).

NATURE OF CASE: Trial court's consideration of tenant's claim that landlord breached the implied covenant of quiet enjoyment.

FACT SUMMARY: 3000 B.C. (P), a professional spa, brought suit against Bowman Properties, Ltd. (Bowman) (D) for breach of the covenant of quiet enjoyment after Bowman (D) entered into a lease with a children's hair salon in the apartment above. The noise from the children allegedly disrupted 3000 B.C.'s (P) business.

🏛 RULE OF LAW

All residential leases include an implied covenant of quiet enjoyment and any act of the landlord that interferes with the tenant's possession of the premises, in whole or in part, may constitute an eviction for which the landlord may be liable in damages to the tenant.

FACTS: 3000 B.C. (P), a professional spa, brought suit against Bowman Properties, Ltd. (Bowman) (D) for breach of the covenant of quiet enjoyment after Bowman (D) entered into a lease with a hair salon for children in the apartment above. 3000 B.C.'s (P) business required a serene, quiet, and tranquil setting. The business had operated successfully for 12 years until the children's hair salon moved in. The noise from the children allegedly disrupted 3000 B.C.'s (P) business. In this action, the court conducted a nonjury trial to determine if Bowman (D) breached the covenant of quiet enjoyment and, if so, the appropriate damages to be awarded to 3000 B.C. (P).

ISSUE: Do all residential leases include an implied covenant of quiet enjoyment and does any act of the landlord that interferes with the tenant's possession of the premises, in whole or in part, constitute an eviction for which the landlord may be liable in damages to the tenant?

HOLDING AND DECISION: (Bernstein, J.) Yes. All residential leases include an implied covenant of quiet enjoyment and any act of the landlord that interferes with the tenant's possession of the premises, in whole or in part, may constitute an eviction for which the landlord may be liable in damages to the tenant. The breach of the covenant can be shown through a constructive eviction. A court may find a constructive eviction if the tenant can prove that use of the premises has been substantially impaired or disrupted. A tenant may recover for losses that he has actually sustained, including lost profits. The purpose of damages is to return the tenant to the same financial position as if the constructive eviction had not occurred.

The court finds that Bowman's (D) lease to the children's hair salon breached 3000 B.C's (P) covenant of quiet enjoyment. The lease to the hair salon began in February of 2005 and 3000 B.C. (D) left the premises in December of 2005. 3000 B.C. (P) may recover for lost profits during that timeframe, including attorneys' fees, reasonable moving expenses, and any additional rent it needed to pay. 3000 B.C. (P) should be reimbursed for loss of the value of the business, which it had been providing customers with successful treatments for over 12 years at the location. Totaling these damages, 3000 B.C. (P) is awarded $236,233.45 in damages.

▶ ANALYSIS

The implied covenant of quiet enjoyment exists in all jurisdictions, either by operation of law or via state statute. A typical residential or commercial lease will include a specific provision regarding the covenant. Often, those provisions will include specific remedies for the tenant in the case of a breach. There may also be notice obligations on the part of the tenant, which, if not followed, may limit the tenant's right to damages.

Quicknotes

CONSTRUCTIVE EVICTION An action whereby the landlord renders the property unsuitable for occupancy, either in whole or in part, so that the tenant is forced to leave the premises.

COVENANT OF QUIET ENJOYMENT A promise contained in a lease or a deed that the tenant or grantee will enjoy unimpaired use of the property.

Javins v. First National Realty Corp.

Tenant (D) v. Landlord (P)

428 F.2d 1071 (D.C. Cir. 1970).

NATURE OF CASE: Appeal from actions to recover past-due rents.

FACT SUMMARY: Javins (D) refused to pay rent due to numerous housing code violations.

> 🏛 **RULE OF LAW**
> Leases of urban dwelling units contain an implied warranty of habitability, and breach of this warranty gives rise to the usual remedies for breach of contract.

FACTS: Javins (D) and other tenants refused to pay rent due to approximately 1,500 housing code violations in the building. The landlord, First National Realty (First National) (P), brought suit to recover possession and past-due rent. The trial court refused Javins's (D) offer of proof as to the violations, finding that their presence was not a defense. Judgment was rendered for First National (P).

ISSUE: Do leases of urban dwelling units contain an implied warranty of habitability, the breach of which gives rise to the usual remedies for breach of contract?

HOLDING AND DECISION: (Wright, J.) Yes. Leases of urban dwelling units contain an implied warranty of habitability, and breach of this warranty gives rise to the usual remedies for breach of contract. The old common law rule that the lessor is not obligated to effectuate repairs unless he covenants to do so in the lease is outdated and must be rejected. The value of the lease to a tenant is that it gives him a place to live; a home suitable for occupation. Because a lease contract specifies a time period during which the tenant has a right to use the apartment for shelter, there is a legitimate expectancy that the apartment be fit for habitation during the term of the contract. The common law must recognize the landlord's obligation to keep the premises in a habitable condition. Beyond the common law, the District's housing code also requires an implied warranty of habitability. The code establishes the standards for such housing and delineates the penalties for violations. The code specifically provides that every premises be maintained and kept in a state of repair to provide decent living conditions for the occupants. In the instant case, the landlord sued for possession for nonpayment of rent. However, the tenant's obligation to pay is dependent on the landlord's performance of his obligations, including maintaining the premises in a habitable condition. The case is remanded to determine what violations in the code existed during the time when the tenants withheld rent. The trial court must also determine if the tenant's obligation to pay rent was suspended, in full or in part, by the landlord's breach of the implied warranty. Should it be determined that any rental obligation exists, no judgment for possession shall be entered unless the tenant refuses to pay such obligation.

▶ ANALYSIS

The implied warranty of habitability is found to be coextensive with the requirements of the housing code in some jurisdictions. In others it is mere evidence of breach of warranty. The breach of one covenant by the landlord excuses the tenant's counterperformance (breaches of mutually dependent covenants). The lease is treated as a contract rather than as a conveyance of real property under these theories. Some states require that the rent withheld be placed in an escrow account pending repairs.

■═■

Quicknotes

WARRANTY OF HABITABILITY An implied warranty owed by a landlord to a tenant to provide leased premises is properly maintained in a habitable condition prior to leasing the premises and during the duration of the lease.

■═■

Hillview Associates v. Bloomquist

Landlord (P) v. Tenant (D)

Iowa Sup. Ct., 440 N.W.2d 867 (1989).

NATURE OF CASE: Summary action for eviction and detainer where the tenants raised the defenses of retaliatory eviction and waiver.

FACT SUMMARY: Following a physical altercation between a tenant and a manager at a tenant's meeting, a number of tenants (D) received eviction notices from Hillview Associates (P).

🏛 RULE OF LAW
Tenants may organize and join a tenant's association and may participate in activities designed to legitimately coerce a landlord into taking action to improve living conditions without fear of retaliation, but engaging in physical threats or violence is not a legitimate method of coercion.

FACTS: Tenants at Gracious Estates formed a tenant's association and contacted the Iowa Attorney General's office and their state representative regarding concerns over the physical condition of their trailer park and recent rent increases. At an April 15, 1987, meeting, a heated argument between tenants and management escalated into a physical altercation between tenant Davenport (D) and a manager. Hillview Associates (P) attempted to evict some of the tenants who attended the meeting in question, including Davenport (D). The tenants raised the defenses of retaliatory eviction and waiver.

ISSUE: May tenants organize and join a tenant's association and participate in activities designed to legitimately coerce a landlord into taking action to improve living conditions without fear of retaliation?

HOLDING AND DECISION: (Andreasen, J.) Yes. Tenants may organize and join a tenant's association and may participate in activities designed to legitimately coerce a landlord into taking action to improve living conditions without fear of retaliation. However, engaging in physical threats or violence is not a legitimate method of coercion, and termination due to this sort of activity will not be deemed retaliatory. The resolution of landlord-tenant grievances will normally involve some conflicts and friction between the parties. Arguments—even heated ones with raised voices—cannot fairly be described as being in violation of proper conduct. There is, however, a limit to the type of conduct that will be tolerated. Davenport (D) crossed this line, and his lease was appropriately terminated. Bloomquist (D) and the other tenants have established their affirmative defense of retaliatory eviction.

▶ ANALYSIS

In 1968, the United States Court of Appeals for the District of Columbia held that a landlord was not free to evict a tenant in retaliation for the tenant's report of housing code violations. As a matter of statutory construction and for reasons of public policy, such an eviction would not be permitted. See *Edwards v. Habib*, 397 F.2d 687 (D.C. Cir. 1968).

Quicknotes

DETAINER The unlawful withholding of real or personal property from an individual who is lawfully entitled to it.

FORCIBLE ENTRY The entry onto real property of another through the use of violence in order to oust that person from possession.

RETALIATORY EVICTION The removal of a tenant from possession of property due to the tenant's complaints or other conduct to which the landlord is opposed.

Imperial Colliery Co. v. Fout

Landlord (P) v. Tenant (D)

W. Va. Sup. Ct. App., 373 S.E.2d 489 (1988).

NATURE OF CASE: Appeal of a summary judgment dismissing claim of retaliatory eviction based on provisions of state summary eviction statute.

FACT SUMMARY: Imperial Colliery Co. (P) instituted an eviction proceeding against Fout (D), who claimed the eviction was in retaliation for his participation in a labor strike.

🏛 RULE OF LAW
(1) A residential tenant who is sued for possession may assert retaliatory eviction as a defense.
(2) A retaliatory eviction defense must relate to the tenant's exercise of rights incidental to the tenancy.

FACTS: Fout (D) worked for Milburn Colliery Company as a coal miner. For six years, Fout (D) had a month-to-month lease on a dwelling owned by Imperial Colliery Co. (P), an interrelated company. After several extensions, Imperial Colliery Co. (P) instituted an eviction proceeding that Fout (D) claimed was in retaliation for his participation in a labor strike and a violation of his First Amendment rights of speech and assembly. Fout (D) also counterclaimed, seeking an injunction against Imperial Colliery Co. (P) and damages for annoyance and inconvenience.

ISSUE:
(1) May a residential tenant who is sued for possession assert retaliatory eviction as a defense?
(2) Must a retaliatory eviction defense relate to the tenant's exercise of rights incidental to the tenancy?

HOLDING AND DECISION: (Miller, J.)
(1) Yes. A residential tenant who is sued for possession may assert retaliatory eviction as a defense. Retaliatory evictions by landlords can seriously jeopardize the effectiveness of local sanitation and safety codes. They can also render implied warranties of habitability meaningless. A tenant should not be punished for claiming benefits afforded by health and safety statutes or for requiring a landlord to fulfill his duties to perform maintenance and repair necessary to make a dwelling habitable. The court, therefore, holds that a defense of retaliatory eviction may be asserted as a defense against a summary eviction proceeding.
(2) Yes. A retaliatory eviction defense must relate to the tenant's exercise of rights incidental to the tenancy. Fout (D) raised his retaliatory eviction defense in the context of his union activities and a labor strike. He

claims that Imperial Colliery's (P) motive for the eviction proceeding are in violation of his rights to free speech and association. These fundamental rights, however, do not arise from the tenancy relationship, which is instead based in contract law. Any alleged violation of those rights may be addressed in an independent action, but they cannot provide the basis for a retaliatory eviction defense.

▶ ANALYSIS

A few courts recognize that even where a tenant's activity is only indirectly related to the tenancy relationship, it may be protected against retaliatory conduct if such conduct would undermine the tenancy relationship. Typical of these cases is *Windward Partners v. Delos Santos*, 577 P.2d 326 (Haw. 1978). In that case, a group of month-to-month tenants gave testimony before a state land use commission in opposition to a proposal to redesignate their farm property from "agricultural" to "urban" uses. The court determined that the legislative policy encouraging such input would be jeopardized if landlords were permitted to retaliate against tenants for opposing land use changes in a public form.

◼◼

Quicknotes

RETALIATORY EVICTION The removal of a tenant from possession of property due to the tenant's complaints or other conduct to which the landlord is opposed.

◼◼

CHAPTER 12

Real Estate Transactions

Quick Reference Rules of Law

Burns v. McCormick

Caretakers (P) v. Heir contesting promise (D)

N.Y. Ct. App., 135 N.E. 273 (1922).

NATURE OF CASE: Appeal from decision denying specific performance.

FACT SUMMARY: The Burnses (P) agreed to take care of Halsey (now deceased) for life in exchange for Halsey's house and furnishings after his death.

🏛 RULE OF LAW
Acts of part performance are not solely and unequivocally referable to a contract for the sale of land.

FACTS: Halsey told the Burnses (P) that if they would board and care for him during his life, he would give them his house and furniture at his death. Halsey died without will, deed, or memorandum of the alleged transfer. The Burnses (P) sued for specific performance of the oral contract, and other parties in interest raised the Statute of Frauds. McCormick (D) was successful and the trial court denied specific performance. The Burnses (P) appealed.

ISSUE: Are acts of part performance solely and unequivocally referable to a contract for the sale of land?

HOLDING AND DECISION: (Cardozo, J.) No. Acts of part performance are not solely and unequivocally referable to a contract for the sale of land. In general, the Statute of Frauds requires a written contract for the conveyance of real property. In order for performance alone to satisfy the Statute of Frauds, the performance must be unequivocally referable to the agreement. Not every act of part performance will move a court in equity to grant specific performance, even though legal remedies are deemed to be inadequate. The board and care of Halsey by the Burnses (P) could have been in exchange for rent or explained in any number of different ways. The performance in this case is not unequivocally referable to an agreement to convey the property and without more the Statue of Frauds cannot be satisfied. The trial court decision is affirmed.

▎ANALYSIS

Hardship, estoppel, and numerous casual remarks by a decedent may be recognized in various jurisdictions as proving the existence of the alleged oral contract to pass property after death. Some jurisdictions, notably California, have held that hardship alone may remove an oral contract from the statute through estoppel. However, a majority of courts still strictly construe the Statute of Frauds and the doctrine of part performance.

Quicknotes

SPECIFIC PERFORMANCE An equitable remedy whereby the court requires the parties to perform their obligations pursuant to a contract.

STATUTE OF FRAUDS A statute that requires specified types of contracts to be in writing in order to be binding.

■═■

Hickey v. Green

Buyer (P) v. Seller (D)

Mass. Ct. App., 442 N.E.2d 37 (1982).

NATURE OF CASE: Appeal from grant of specific performance of a real estate contract.

FACT SUMMARY: Green (D) contended that the real estate sales contract she orally entered into with Hickey (P) was unenforceable based on the Statute of Frauds.

🏛 RULE OF LAW
An oral contract for the transfer of interest in land may be specifically enforced despite the Statute of Frauds if the party seeking performance changed his position in reasonable reliance on the contract and injustice can be avoided only through specific performance.

FACTS: Green (D) orally agreed to sell a parcel to Hickey (P), and accepted a check as a deposit. In reliance on the contract Hickey (P) accepted a deposit on his home from a purchaser, intending to build a new home on the land he purchased from Green (D). Subsequently, Green (D), knowing Hickey (P) sold his house in reliance on the contract, refused to sell the land to Hickey (P). Hickey (P) sued for specific performance, and Green (D) defended, contending the contract was unenforceable under the Statute of Frauds. The trial court granted specific performance, and Green (D) appealed.

ISSUE: Can an oral contract for the sale of real estate be specifically enforced if the party seeking enforcement changed his position in reasonable reliance upon the contract?

HOLDING AND DECISION: (Cutter, J.) Yes. An oral contract for the transfer of an interest in land may be specifically enforced, despite the Statute of Frauds requirement of a writing, if the party seeking enforcement changed his position in reasonable reliance on the contract and injustice can be avoided only through specific performance. In this case, Hickey (P) clearly changed his position in reliance on the contract by selling his house in anticipation of occupying another on Green's (D) land. The reliance was reasonable, and Green (D) was fully aware of this change in position when she refused to honor the contract. As a result, it would be manifestly unjust to refuse specific performance in this case. Therefore, it must be ordered. Affirmed.

▶ ANALYSIS

This case could have been decided on different grounds. Some commentators, spurred by dicta in the opinion, contend that the check that Hickey (P) gave Green (D) as a deposit on the land constituted an adequate memorandum to satisfy the requirements of the Statute of Frauds.

Quicknotes

SPECIFIC PERFORMANCE An equitable remedy whereby the court requires the parties to perform their obligations pursuant to a contract.

STATUTE OF FRAUDS A statute that requires specified types of contracts to be in writing in order to be binding.

Johnson v. Davis

Seller (D) v. Purchaser (P)

Fla. Sup. Ct., 480 So. 2d 625 (1985).

NATURE OF CASE: Appeal from trial court decision finding fraudulent misrepresentation and granting respondents the return of their deposit.

FACT SUMMARY: The Davises (P) agreed to purchase the Johnsons' (D) home after the Johnsons (D) assured them that buckling around a family room window and stains on the ceiling resulted from a minor problem that had long since been fixed.

🏛 RULE OF LAW
Where the seller of a home knows of facts materially affecting the value of the property that are not readily observable and are not known to the buyer, the seller is under a duty to disclose them to the buyer.

FACTS: In May of 1982, the Davises (P) entered into a contract to buy the Johnsons' (D) home. The contract required a $5,000 deposit payment and an additional $26,000 deposit payment within five days. Before making the additional $26,000 payment, the Davises (P) noticed ceiling stains and buckling around a family room window. The Johnsons (D) assured them that these problems resulted from a minor problem that had long since been fixed. Several days later during a heavy rain, water came gushing into the house through various parts of the family room. Two roofers hired by the Johnsons (D) concluded that the problem could be solved for under $1,000. Three roofers hired by the Davises (P) determined that the roof was inherently defective and any repairs would be temporary because the roof was slipping. The Davises (P) filed a complaint alleging breach of contract, fraud, and misrepresentation and sought recession of the contract and return of their deposit. The trial court ruled for the Davises (P), and the Johnsons (D) appealed.

ISSUE: Where the seller of a home knows of facts materially affecting the value of the property that are not readily observable and are not known to the buyer, is he under a duty to disclose them to the buyer?

HOLDING AND DECISION: (Adkins, J.) Yes. Where the seller of a home knows of facts materially affecting the value of the property that are not readily observable and are not known to the buyer, he is under a duty to disclose them to the buyer. This duty is equally applicable to all forms of real property, new and used. In the case at bar, the evidence shows that the Johnsons (D) knew of and failed to disclose that there had been problems with the roof of the house. The Davises (P) detrimentally relied on this concealment. Affirmed.

DISSENT: (Boyd, Jr., C.J.) Homeowners who attempt to sell their houses are typically in no better position to measure the quality, value, or desirability of their houses than are the prospective purchasers with whom they come into contact. This ruling will give rise to a flood of litigation and will facilitate unjust outcomes in many cases.

▶ ANALYSIS

In the state of Florida, relief for a fraudulent misrepresentation may be granted only when the following elements are present: (1) a false statement concerning a material fact; (2) the representor's knowledge that the representation is false; (3) an intention that the representation induce another to act on it; and (4) consequent injury by the party acting in reliance on the representation. Those opposed to this sort of regulation argue that it is unnecessary since prudent purchasers inspect property, with expert advice if necessary, before they agree to buy, and prudent lenders require inspections before agreeing to provide purchase money.

■══■

Quicknotes

FRAUDULENT MISREPRESENTATION A statement or conduct by one party to another that constitutes a false representation of fact.

■══■

Commonwealth v. Fremont Investment & Loan

Massachusetts (P) v. Industrial Bank (D)

Mass. Sup. Jud. Ct., 897 N.E.2d 548 (2008).

NATURE OF CASE: Appeal from trial court's granting of preliminary injunction to state.

FACT SUMMARY: Fremont Investment & Loan (D) was selling subprime, adjustable rate mortgages to thousands of Massachusetts residents. Massachusetts' Attorney General's (P) office brought suit alleging the sale of such mortgages was a violation of the Massachusetts Consumer Protection Act.

🏛 RULE OF LAW
Mortgage loans with the following four characteristics would likely be "unfair" under Massachusetts' Consumer Protection Act: (1) the loans were adjustable with a preliminary rate for three years; (2) the initial rate was typically three points lower than the usual mortgage rate on 30-year loans; (3) the debt-to-income ratio would exceed 50% after the introductory period expired; and (4) the loan-to-value ratio was 100%.

FACTS: Fremont Investment & Loan (Fremont) (D) was selling loans to thousands of Massachusetts' residents. There is no dispute the loans in question all had the four characteristics as mentioned above. In March 2007, Fremont (D) entered into an agreement with the Federal Deposit Insurance Corporation (FDIC) to cease granting subprime loans to customers without considering whether the customer would be able to pay the monthly loan amounts after the rate increased. Subsequently, Massachusetts (P) entered into a similar agreement with Fremont (D). Accordingly, Fremont (D) had to give the Massachusetts Attorney General's (P) office 90 days notice before any foreclosures. If the Attorney General (P) objected, Fremont (D) would attempt to resolve the matter short of foreclosure. As it turned out, the Attorney General (P) objected to all foreclosure requests. It then filed this action to enjoin Fremont (D) from foreclosing on such loans because the loans were "unfair" under Chapter 93A of the Massachusetts Consumer Protection Statute. The judge granted the preliminary injunction. The court ordered Fremont (D) to give notice to the Attorney General (P) prior to foreclosures and ordered it to resolve any foreclosure issues with the Attorney General (P). If there was no resolution, Fremont (D) had to go to court for an order of foreclosure. Fremont (D) appealed on the grounds that its loans were customary in the industry and therefore were not unfair.

ISSUE: Are mortgage loans with the following four characteristics likely to be "unfair" under Massachusetts' Consumer Protection Act: (1) the loans were adjustable with a preliminary rate for three years; (2) the initial rate

was typically three points lower than the usual mortgage rate on 30-year loans; (3) the debt-to-income ratio would exceed 50% after the introductory period expired; and (4) the loan-to-value ratio was 100%?

HOLDING AND DECISION: (Botsford, J.) Yes. Mortgage loans with the following four characteristics would likely be "unfair" under Massachusetts' Consumer Protection Act: (1) the loans were adjustable with a preliminary rate for three years; (2) the initial rate was typically three points lower than the usual mortgage rate on 30-year loans; (3) the debt-to-income ratio would exceed 50% after the introductory period expired; and (4) the loan-to-value ratio was 100%. First, Fremont's (D) argument that the adjustable rate mortgage (ARM) loans were not unfair because it was standard practice in the industry is without merit. The record at the preliminary injunction stage revealed that Fremont (D) knew or should have known that loans that had the four characteristics stated above would most likely be difficult to repay. In addition, the record reveals that Fremont (D) did not attempt to determine if borrowers would be able to pay the monthly loan amounts after the rate increased. FDIC's actions in this matter underscore its belief that these loans constitute unsafe and unsound banking practices. Regarding the Massachusetts Predatory Home Loan Practices Act, Fremont (D) is correct that the statute technically does not apply because that statute only applies to high cost home mortgage loans. However, the judge used the statute for policy support to conclude that loans are unfair where the lender should know the borrower will be unable to repay the loan. Lastly, that the loans in question are technically allowed by state and federal regulations does not mean they are not unfair. It has long been held that a determination of whether conduct is permitted by statute is just one aspect of the fairness analysis. It is not dispositive. The preliminary injunction is affirmed.

▶ ANALYSIS

This case is an example of a successful government action against the subprime lenders in the wake of the mortgage crisis. However, surprisingly, other states have not followed Massachusetts' tactic of using a local consumer protection act. Rather, a handful of other states have brought actions against subprime lenders under the federal Securities Act of 1933.

▬▬■

Continued on next page.

Quicknotes

MORTGAGE An interest in land created by a written in-strument providing security for the payment of a debt or the performance of a duty.

PRELIMINARY INJUNCTION A judicial mandate issued to require or restrain a party from certain conduct; used to preserve a trial's subject matter or to prevent threatened injury.

U.S. Bank National Association v. Ibanez

Purported Mortgage Holder (P) v. Homeowner (D)

Mass. Sup. Jud. Ct., 941 N.E.2d 40 (2011).

NATURE OF CASE: Appeal from lower court decision finding that purported mortgage holders, attempting to foreclose on two properties, failed to demonstrate they actually held the mortgage on the properties at issue.

FACT SUMMARY: U.S. Bank National Association (P) and Wells Fargo (P) foreclosed on two properties. The mortgages on each of the properties had been sold and assigned multiple times during their existence. After the foreclosure process, U.S. Bank National Association (P) and Wells Fargo (P) brought actions in state court seeking a declaration that they were the owners in fee simple of the two properties.

⬛ RULE OF LAW
Any foreclosure proceeding initiated by a party that lacks the jurisdiction and authority to conduct the foreclosure shall be null and void.

FACTS: Antonio Ibanez (D) purchased a home in Springfield, Massachusetts, for $103,500 with a loan secured by a mortgage to the lender, Rose Mortgage, Inc. The mortgage was then assigned multiple times to different mortgage companies. In 2006, the latest holder of the mortgage pooled it with 1,200 other mortgages into a trust known as a mortgage-backed security. This process, known as a securitization, allowed these trusts to be bought and sold by investors. Eventually, U.S. Bank purchased a mortgage-backed security that allegedly included Ibanez's (D) mortgage. That transaction occurred via a private placement memorandum. That document states the trust would include all mortgages placed into it and those mortgages would be reflected on an attached schedule of mortgages. A similar scenario played out with a mortgage taken out by Mark and Tammy LaRace (D). It was also pooled into a mortgage-backed security and eventually purchased by Wells Fargo (P). U.S. Bank (P) and Wells Fargo (P) foreclosed on the two properties in 2007, a process that does not require judicial approval. The foreclosure process included the properties being placed up for sale and then purchased by U.S. Bank (P) and Wells Fargo (P), respectively. (There is no dispute both homeowners defaulted on their loans.) After the foreclosure process, U.S. Bank (P) and Wells Fargo (P) brought actions in state court seeking a declaration that they were the owners in fee simple of the two properties. At the trial court level, the judge found both plaintiffs failed to prove they had the authority to foreclose on the properties. Specifically, using U.S. Bank (P) as an example, that entity did not provide the court with a schedule or any documentation that the Ibanez (D) mortgage was

actually included in the mortgage-backed security that U.S. Bank (P) purchased in 2006. U.S. Bank (P) and Wells Fargo (P) appealed and the case was transferred to the Massachusetts Supreme Judicial Court.

ISSUE: Is any foreclosure proceeding initiated by a party that lacks the jurisdiction and authority to conduct the foreclosure null and void?

HOLDING AND DECISION: (Gants, J.) Yes. Any foreclosure proceeding initiated by a party that lacks the jurisdiction and authority to conduct the foreclosure shall be null and void. In these actions to quiet title to property, U.S. Bank (P) and Wells Fargo (P) have the burden of proving they were the fee simple owners of the properties. To do so, they (Ps) need to demonstrate that they properly adhered to the statutory foreclosure process in Massachusetts. Massachusetts, like many states, does not require judicial approval before an entity forecloses on a property. The mortgagor/homeowner may petition a court to enjoin the foreclosure if he or she desires. Any mortgage includes a power of sale. However, one who sells under a power of sale must strictly follow the terms. Powers of sale have restrictions on who can actually foreclose on the property. A power of sale can be exercised only by a mortgagee or its successors or assigns. U.S. Bank (P) claims that the private placement memorandum it received when it purchased the mortgage-backed security in 2006 made U.S. Bank (P) the holder of the Ibanez (D) mortgage. However, U.S. Bank (P) did not provide the lower court with a schedule or any documentation that the Ibanez (D) mortgage was actually included in the mortgage-backed security that U.S. Bank (P) purchased in 2006. Read closely, the private placement memorandum reveals an intent that certain mortgages would be included in the pool, but there simply was no evidence attached to that document stating which mortgages were included, if any. The last assignment on the record of Ibanez's (D) mortgage was to an entity called Option One. Accordingly, U.S. Bank (P) did not have the authority to foreclose on the mortgage. Wells Fargo (D) similarly could not demonstrate it actually held the mortgage on the LaRace (D) property. Affirmed.

CONCURRENCE: (Cordy, J.) Assignments of mortgages need not be recorded to be effective. However, the assignment or similar transaction must actually occur. In these complicated mortgage-backed security transactions, the onus is on the mortgage holders to demonstrate that the assignment has passed to them before a foreclosure can proceed.

Continued on next page.

▶ *ANALYSIS*

This litigation and others like it were spawned after the housing crisis began in 2008. With the rate of foreclosures skyrocketing around the country, courts began to examine more closely the complicated array of transactions that occur after a homeowner takes out a mortgage. This particular decision resulted in a large number of foreclosures being placed into legal limbo until the foreclosing parties could remedy the defects in the various transactions. Although assignment of a mortgage does not have to be recorded, it does have to actually occur via some written instrument, which neither bank in this case could prove was the case.

Quicknotes

FORECLOSURE An action to recover the amount due on a mortgage of real property where the owner has failed to meet the mortgage obligations, terminating the owner's interest in the property which must then be sold to satisfy the debt.

MORTGAGE An interest in land created by a written instrument providing security for the payment of a debt or the performance of a duty.

MORTGAGEE Party to whom an interest in property is given in order to secure a loan.

MORTGAGOR Party who grants an interest in property in order to secure a loan.

Baskurt v. Beal

Purchasers of real property (D) v. Foreclosed party (D)

Alaska Sup. Ct., 101 P.3d 1041 (2004).

NATURE OF CASE: Appeal from lower court decision finding that purchase and sale of foreclosed property should be voided.

FACT SUMMARY: After the foreclosure of Beal's (P) property, three individuals, including the holder of the promissory note that secured Beal's original loan, purchased Beal's (P) property for less than 15% of its market value.

🏛 RULE OF LAW
While inadequacy of price is typically not sufficient to set aside a foreclosure sale, a court may invalidate the sale if the sale price is so inadequate as to shock the conscience of the court or the inadequate sales price is coupled with other irregularities in the foreclosure sale process.

FACTS: The Marion and Mortimer Moore sold two pieces of property to Annette Beal (P) via a quitclaim deed. Beal (P) purchased Parcel A for $95,000 and secured it with a promissory note payable to Mortimer Moore. She purchased Parcel B for $135,000 and secured that parcel with a promissory note payable to Mortimer's former wife, Marion. The promissory notes were further secured by a deed of trust that covered both parcels of land. That document stated the Beal (P), the trustor, was aware that default on either of the two promissory notes would constitute default on the other note as well. The Trustee, Sarah Baskurt (D) (the Moores' daughter), would then be able to sell the property either in whole or in part at a public auction to the highest bidder. Beal (P) paid off the $95,000 amount to Mortimer Moore in 1994 with a lump sum payment. She then paid 80% of the $135,000 loan to Marion but began defaulting on the loan. The outstanding balance was $26,780.81. In the fall of 1999, Baskurt (D) commenced foreclosure proceedings on both Parcel A and Parcel B. A foreclosure sale took place on April 26, 2000. Baskurt (D) and two other partners were present and placed the only bid on the properties. Their successful bid amount was $26,781.81 for both properties, one dollar more than the amount Beal (P) owed on the loan. The sale amount was for approximately 15% of the properties' fair market value. Beal (P) then filed this action to set aside the foreclosure sale as void due to the inadequate sales price. A lower court agreed and voided the sale. Baskurt (P) and her partners appealed.

ISSUE: While inadequacy of price is typically not sufficient to set aside a foreclosure sale, may a court invalidate the sale if the sale price is so inadequate as to shock the conscience of the court or the inadequate sales price is coupled with other irregularities in the foreclosure sale process?

HOLDING AND DECISION: (Matthews, J.) Yes. While inadequacy of price is typically not sufficient to set aside a foreclosure sale, a court may invalidate the sale if the sale price is so inadequate as to shock the conscience of the court or the inadequate sales price is coupled with other irregularities in the foreclosure sale process. A trustee of a deed of trust securing real property may foreclose and sell the property. However, defects in the sale process may render the sale voidable. One potential defect is inadequacy of price. Gross inadequacy is measured by reference to the fair market value of the property. Jurisdictions vary on what percentage of fair market value would constitute a gross inadequacy. The Restatement uses a figure of 20%. In addition, a trustee of a deed of trust has a fiduciary responsibility to both the trustor of the property (Beal) and the beneficiary (Marion Moore). A trustee must take steps to avoid the sacrifice of the trustor's property unnecessarily. That did not occur in this case. First, the sales price for Parcel A and B was only 15% of the fair market value of roughly $225,000. The court below was correct that the sale price was grossly inadequate. Second, Baskurt (D) failed in her fiduciary duty to protect Beal's (P) interest in her property by foreclosing on both parcels, even though Beal (P) had paid off the $95,000 note relating to Parcel A. Baskurt (D) acted unreasonably by failing to sell only Parcel B. Accordingly, due to the inadequate sale price for the property and Baskurt's (D) failure to protect Beal's (P) interests in Parcel A, the lower court was correct to void the sale. Affirmed.

▶ ANALYSIS

Over the course of the past several years, many states have responded to the housing crisis in the United States by enacting new legislation to strengthen the rights of property owners faced with foreclosure. The legislative requirements vary from state to state, but most include requirements of public notice, providing the homeowner with the opportunity to obtain another lender and bid on the property, and preventing mortgagees from obtaining unjust enrichment resulting from a successful low bid on the property.

Quicknotes

FIDUCIARY DUTY A legal obligation to act for the benefit of another, including subordinating one's personal interests to that of the other person.

Continued on next page.

FORECLOSURE SALE Termination of an interest in property, usually initiated by a lienholder upon failure to tender mortgage payments, resulting in the sale of the property in order to satisfy the debt.

■=■

Sebastian v. Floyd

Buyer (D) v. Seller (P)

Ky. Sup. Ct., 585 S.W.2d 381 (1979).

NATURE OF CASE: Appeal from judgment enforcing a forfeiture.

FACT SUMMARY: Sebastian (D) sought to have an installment land contract treated as a mortgage after he defaulted.

> 🏛 **RULE OF LAW**
> The seller's interest in an installment land sale contract should be treated as a lien in order to protect the buyer from unfair forfeiture.

FACTS: Sebastian (D) contracted to buy real property from Floyd (P) for $3,800 down and the balance of $10,900 in monthly installments at 8% interest. The agreement contained a forfeiture clause providing that if Sebastian (D) defaulted on any payments, Floyd (P) could terminate the contract and retain all previous payments as liquidated damages. Sebastian (D) defaulted after paying out a total of $5,480 ($4,300 of principal). Floyd (P) sued to enforce the forfeiture. The trial court ruled for Floyd (P), and Sebastian (D) appealed.

ISSUE: Should the seller's interest in an installment land sale contract be treated as a lien in order to protect the buyer from unfair forfeiture?

HOLDING AND DECISION: (Aker, J.) Yes. The seller's interest in an installment land sale contract should be treated as a lien in order to protect the buyer from unfair forfeiture. In a typical installment land contract, legal title to the property remains with the seller until the buyer has paid the entire contract price, but equitable title is transferred at the outset of the agreement. There is no practical difference between this type of contract and a purchase money mortgage in which the buyer gets legal title immediately and the seller holds a lien on the property as security. However, under a mortgage, the buyer's interest in the property is not forfeited at default. Instead, the buyer is entitled to any remaining equity in the property after the seller has been paid the contract amount and any expenses. Since this arrangement protects both the buyer and seller, an installment land contract should be treated as giving the seller a lien on the property. Therefore, in the present case, the forfeiture clause may not be enforced by Floyd (P), and Sebastian (D) is entitled to any equity interest in the property that remains after Floyd (P) exercises his lien. Reversed.

▶ **ANALYSIS**

Other states treat only some installment land contracts as mortgages based on a range of factors, including the buyer's equity in the property and the length of the default period. See *Grombone v. Krekel*, 754 P.2d 777 (Colo. Ct. App. 1988). In that case, the court of appeals held the decision to be within the lower court's discretion pending an analysis of those factors.

━━■

Quicknotes

FORFEITURE The loss of a right or interest as a penalty for failing to fulfill an obligation.

INSTALLMENT CONTRACT A contract pursuant to which the parties are to render performance or payment in periodic intervals.

LIQUIDATED DAMAGES An amount of money specified in a contract representing the damages owed in the event of breach.

PURCHASE MONEY MORTGAGE A mortgage or other security in property taken in order to ensure the performance of a duty undertaken pursuant to the purchase of such property.

━━■

Koenig v. Van Reken

Seller (P) v. Buyer (D)

Mich. Ct. App., 279 N.W.2d 590 (1979).

NATURE OF CASE: Appeal from a dismissal of complaint.

FACT SUMMARY: Koenig (P) claimed an equitable mortgage should be imposed because she did not intend to grant an absolute deed to Van Reken (D).

🏛 RULE OF LAW
A conveyance of property by deed may be treated as a mortgage if it appears that the parties did not intend to make an absolute transfer.

FACTS: Koenig (P) owned a home with a market value of $60,000. There were three mortgages on the property totaling $26,000. Koenig (P) was unable to pay the property taxes and the mortgage payments. Van Reken (D) then approached Koenig (P) and proposed a complex arrangement whereby Van Reken (D) would purchase the property, redeem it from tax sale and foreclosure, and give Koenig (P) a lease with an option to repurchase the property. The lease agreement provided that Koenig (P) would pay $300 per month for three years, after which she could repurchase the premises for $32,000. Van Reken (D) prepared all of the contracts and deeds and Koenig (P) was unrepresented by counsel. After almost two years under the agreement, Koenig (P) defaulted and was evicted. Koenig (P) brought suit to impose an equitable mortgage based on the agreement with Van Reken (D). [The lower court dismissed Koenig's (P) complaint. Koenig (P) appealed that decision.]

ISSUE: May conveyances of property by deed be treated as mortgages if it appears that the parties did not intend to make an absolute transfer?

HOLDING AND DECISION: (Brennan, J.) Yes. Conveyances of property by deed may be treated as mortgages if it appears that the parties did not intend to make an absolute transfer. The intention of the parties determines whether an absolute deed should be construed as a mortgage. This intention may be determined by looking at the circumstances of the transaction and the relative positions of the parties. If the adverse financial position of the seller is combined with an inadequate purchase price, a deed should be considered a mortgage. In the present case, Koenig (P) was in financial distress and entered into an agreement whereby her $30,000 in equity was conveyed for less than $4,000. This indicates that the conveyance was not meant to be absolute and that an equitable mortgage should be imposed. The granting of the motion to dismiss was improper. Reversed.

▶ ANALYSIS

Equitable mortgages are not affected by the Statute of Frauds. Other courts have identified other factors that should be considered when imposing an equitable mortgage, such as the relationship of the parties, the sophistication of the parties, and who retained possession.

Quicknotes

EQUITABLE MORTGAGE A lien upon real property, enforceable in equity but not at law, in order to ensure that a specific sum of money is paid or a particular performance is rendered.

QUITCLAIM DEED A deed whereby the grantor conveys whatever interest he or she may have in the property without any warranties or covenants as to title.

WARRANTY DEED A deed that guarantees that the conveyor possesses the title that he purports to convey.

Sabo v. Horvath

Purchaser who recorded deed (D) v. Purchaser who did not record (P)

Alaska Sup. Ct., 559 P.2d 1038 (1976).

NATURE OF CASE: Action to determine title to real property.

FACT SUMMARY: Horvath (P) recorded his deed prior to a patent being granted the seller so that the recorded deed was outside the chain of title.

🏛 RULE OF LAW
A deed outside the chain of title is not constructive notice and a subsequently recorded deed will take priority.

FACTS: Lowery filed for a federal land patent on real property he was homesteading in Alaska. Prior to the issuance of the patent, Lowery conveyed his interest in the land to Horvath (P) by quitclaim deed. Horvath (P) recorded the deed, which was then outside the chain of record title since Lowery had not yet obtained patent title to the land. After patent title was obtained, Horvath (P) did not re-record the deed. Lowery subsequently "sold" the land a second time to Sabo (D) by quitclaim deed. Sabo (D) recorded his deed. Sabo (D) had no notice of the earlier conveyance. Horvath (P) brought a quiet title action. Sabo (D) alleged that a deed recorded out of chain of title was not constructive notice and that under the state's notice recording law he had no notice of the earlier sale and should be given preference.

ISSUE: Is a deed recorded outside the chain of title given preference to a subsequent bona fide purchaser without actual notice?

HOLDING AND DECISION: (Boochever, C.J.) No. A deed outside the chain of title is not constructive notice and a subsequently recorded deed will take priority. The purpose of our recording statute is to protect innocent purchasers without notice of an earlier unrecorded sale. Normally, a recordation gives the subsequent purchaser constructive notice of the earlier conveyance. However, we hold that a deed recorded outside the chain of title is not constructive notice to an innocent purchaser for value without actual notice. It is less burdensome for one recording outside the chain of title to re-record than to force purchasers to check all conveyances outside the chain of the title. Quitclaim deedholders are entitled to protection under the recording statutes (the majority rule). While Horvath (P) originally received Lowery's equitable interest in the land, his failure to re-record after the patent was granted requires us to find for Sabo (D). Reversed.

▶ ANALYSIS

Sabo would be useful only where the jurisdiction does not use a tract index system. Under a tract index system, every

document affecting land is recorded. Some jurisdictions hold that the grantee of a quitclaim deed is not a bona fide purchaser. In *Crossly v. Campion Mining Co.*, 1 Alaska 391 (1901), a quitclaim grantee with knowledge of a superior unrecorded claim was held not to be in good faith.

Quicknotes

ACTION TO QUIET TITLE Equitable action to resolve conflicting claims to an interest in real property.

BONA FIDE PURCHASER A party who purchases property in good faith and for valuable consideration without notice of a defect in title.

CONSTRUCTIVE NOTICE Knowledge of a fact that is imputed to an individual who was under a duty to inquire and who could have learned of the fact through the exercise of reasonable prudence.

QUITCLAIM DEED A deed whereby the grantor conveys whatever interest he or she may have in the property without any warranties or covenants as to title.

Brock v. Yale Mortgage Corporation

Husband (P) v. Former wife (D) and Mortgage lender (D)

Ga. Sup. Ct., 700 S.E.2d 583 (2010).

NATURE OF CASE: Appeal from lower court decision finding that husband ratified a forged quitclaim deed that his former wife drafted granting her full title to the property.

FACT SUMMARY: To avoid foreclosure, Brock's (P) wife, Joyce (D), forged a quitclaim deed that granted her full title to their home. Without Brock's (P) knowledge, she then took out a new mortgage with Yale Mortgage Company (Yale) (D). When Brock (P) and Joyce (D) divorced several years later, their settlement agreement acknowledged the existence of a liability on the home in the amount of the loan from Yale (D).

🏛 **RULE OF LAW**
One holding property with another as tenants in common cannot convey the other person's interests in the property without his or her consent.

FACTS: Brock (P) and his wife, Joyce (D), did not have a joint checking account. Each month he would give her money to make the monthly mortgage payments on their home. On several different occasions, Joyce (D) spent the money in other ways. Eventually, foreclosure proceedings were commenced against the property, all with Brock (P) having no knowledge of any of the proceedings. To avoid foreclosure, Joyce (D) forged a quitclaim deed that granted her full title to their home. Again without Brock's (P) knowledge, Joyce (D) then took out a new mortgage with Yale Mortgage Company (Yale) (D). The new mortgage was secured via a promissory note and another deed in favor of Yale (D). The parties divorced several years later after Brock (P) alleged that Joyce (D) removed $200,000 from his checking account. At some point, Brock (P) became aware of the forged deed and the Yale (D) mortgage. The parties' divorce settlement agreement acknowledged the existence of a liability on the home in the amount of the loan from Yale (D). Brock (P) commenced this action to void the forged deed and set aside the subsequent deed granted to Yale (D) as part of the new mortgage transaction. The lower court found that Brock (P) ratified the forged deed by virtue of the provision in the divorce settlement agreement acknowledging the existence of a liability in the property. Brock (P) appealed.

ISSUE: Can one holding property with another as tenants in common convey the other person's interests in the property without his or her consent?

HOLDING AND DECISION: (Hunstein, C.J.) No. One holding property with another as tenants in common cannot convey the other person's interests in the property without his or her consent. A deed may be voided if it is proven to be a forgery. While a tenant in common cannot encumber other tenants without their consent, one tenant may encumber his own interest in the property. If a tenant purports to convey the entire property, the forged deed will still affect his own interest but will not bind the others. Accordingly, the forged deed resulted in Yale (D) receiving only a one-half interest in the property. Yale (D) argues it is a bona fide purchaser. Typically, a bona fide purchaser is protected against any outstanding interests of which the purchaser is not aware. However, a bona fide purchaser cannot obtain title to property via a forged deed, which is a nullity. Accordingly, Yale (D) cannot obtain title over the entire property using that argument. Turning to the ratification issue, a forged signature may become binding if ratified by the person whose name was fraudulently signed. The lower court found that the settlement agreement was evidence of Brock's (P) acknowledgment and ratification of the quitclaim deed and the mortgage transaction to Yale (D). However, the provision only states that the parties acknowledge that "Joyce has incurred a $50,000 liability on the property." While the parties may have been contemplating the Yale (D) mortgage, there is no specific identifying information confirming that is the case. Accordingly, this factual dispute needs to be determined in light of any available extrinsic evidence. Affirmed in part, reversed in part, and remanded for further proceedings.

▶ **ANALYSIS**

A bona fide purchaser who receives a valid title to property will typically have greater rights to property over other claimants of which the purchaser was not aware. These situations arise where an heir or other claimant fails to record his or her interest properly in the local registry or there is some other defect in the title. However, as noted here, to gain status as a bona fide purchaser, the purchaser cannot have simply received a forged deed.

Quicknotes

BONA FIDE PURCHASER A party who purchases property in good faith and for valuable consideration without notice of a defect in title.

FORGERY The false preparation or modification of a written document with an intent to defraud another.

Continued on next page.

RATIFICATION Affirmation of a prior action taken by either the individual himself or by an agent on behalf of the principal, which is then treated as if it had been initially authorized by the principal.

■≡■

McCoy v. Love

[Parties not identified.]

Fla. Sup. Ct., 382 So. 2d 647 (1980).

NATURE OF CASE: Appeal from finding that a deed was voidable.

FACT SUMMARY: Russell drew up a fraudulent sales contract wherein Elliott (P) unknowingly conveyed all of her interest in mineral rights to Russell.

🏛 RULE OF LAW
Fraud in the inducement renders a legally effective deed merely voidable and not void.

FACTS: Elliott (P), who was unable to read or write, agreed to sell Russell a small portion of her mineral rights in a property. Russell drew up a sales contract wherein Elliott (P) unknowingly conveyed all of her interest to Russell. Russell notified Elliott (P) that a mistake had been made, but in the meantime sold part of Elliott's (P) mineral rights to other parties, including Love (D). Elliott (P) remained ignorant of these subsequent transactions until she wanted to sell more of her mineral rights and a title search revealed them. She sued for cancellation of the deed. The trial court concluded that the deed was void and granted summary judgment to Elliott (P). On appeal, the district court held the deed voidable rather than void. Elliott (P) appealed.

ISSUE: Does fraud in the inducement render a legally effective deed merely voidable and not void?

HOLDING AND DECISION: (Boyd, Jr., J.) Yes. Fraud in the inducement renders a legally effective deed merely voidable and not void. Where all essential legal requisites of a deed are present, it conveys legal title. In this case, Elliott (P) knew she was executing and delivering a deed of mineral rights. She was responsible for informing herself of its legal effect. The district court was correct in holding that the deed was merely voidable and that it conveyed a legal title to Russell. The case should be remanded for trial on the factual issue of whether Love (D) and the other buyers were bona fide purchasers.

▶ ANALYSIS

A deed is either void or voidable if obtained by forgery or fraud. The deed will be set aside at the previous owner's request if no further conveyances have occurred. Where the property has been conveyed to a bona fide purchaser (BFP), if the deed is void, no title is conveyed to the grantee; thus, the grantee cannot convey the title to another. If the deed is considered merely voidable by an owner who had a fraud perpetrated against him, a subsequent BFP will obtain good title.

Quicknotes

BONA FIDE PURCHASER A party who purchases property in good faith and for valuable consideration without notice of a defect in title.

FRAUD A false representation of facts with the intent that another will rely on the misrepresentation to his detriment.

INDUCEMENT Incentive or benefit motivating a party to enter into a contractual relationship.

Fair Housing Law

Quick Reference Rules of Law

Fair Housing Council of San Fernando Valley v. Roommate.com, LLC

Federal agency (P) v. Internet-based company (D)

666 F.3d 1216 (9th Cir. 2012).

NATURE OF CASE: Appeal from lower court decision finding that website's requirement that applicants disclose their sex, sexual orientation, and familial status while searching for roommates violated the Fair Housing Act.

FACT SUMMARY: The Fair Housing Council of San Fernando Valley (P) sued Roommate.com (D) in federal court alleging that the website's requirement that applicants disclose their sex, sexual orientation, and familial status and the website's subsequent use of that information to match roommates violated the Fair Housing Act.

RULE OF LAW

The Fair Housing Act, which prohibits discrimination on the basis of race, color, religion, sex, familial status and national origin in the sale or renting of a dwelling, does not apply to a tenant's choice of a roommate within the dwelling.

FACTS: Roommate.com (D) operates an internet-based business that helps people find roommates. Users of the website create a site profile indicating their sex, sexual orientation, and familial status. Users list their preferences for a roommate using the same criteria. Based upon the selected criteria, Roommate.com (D) then provides a list of potential roommate matches. The Fair Housing Council of San Fernando Valley (P) sued Roommate.com (D) in federal court. The suit alleged that the website's requirement that applicants disclose their sex, sexual orientation, and familial status and subsequent use of that information to match roommates violated the Fair Housing Act. The federal district court agreed and enjoined Roommate.com's (P) practice of using these characteristics to pair up roommates. Roommate.com (D) appealed to the United States Court of Appeals for the Ninth Circuit.

ISSUE: Does the Fair Housing Act, which prohibits discrimination on the basis of race, color, religion, sex, familial status and national origin in the sale or renting of a dwelling, apply to a tenant's choice of a roommate within the dwelling?

HOLDING AND DECISION: (Kozinski, J.) No. The Fair Housing Act (FHA), which prohibits discrimination on the basis of race, color, religion, sex, familial status and national origin in the sale or renting of a dwelling, does not apply to a tenant's choice of a roommate within the dwelling. The central issue in this case is the scope of the statutory phrase, "sale or rental of a dwelling." The FHA defines a dwelling as a single living unit such as a house or an apartment. It would be difficult to divide these single unit spaces into separate dwellings for the purposes of the statute. While the statute prohibits discrimination in the sale or renting of a living unit, it does not cover the choice of one's roommate inside that dwelling. Essentially, the coverage of the statute stops at the front door. A business transaction to buy or lease property is different from an arrangement by two people who wish to live together. In addition, constitutional concerns prohibit the statute from reaching one's choice of a roommate. The freedom to enter and carry on certain private or intimate relationships is a fundamental right protected by the Bill of Rights. To determine if a certain relationship is constitutionally protected, courts will examine the size, purpose, selectivity and whether others are excluded from the relationship. The roommate relationship qualified. People are selective about their roommates. Roommates share living spaces, bathrooms, and sometimes bedrooms. Because of a potential roommate's access to one's living space, the choice of a roommate implicates significant privacy and safety considerations. A government's ability to regulate and restrict a person's ability to choose a roommate thus improperly invades one's private home. The Constitution and Bill of Rights clearly protect a person from these unwarranted government intrusions into one's home. Restricting one's ability to choose a roommate based upon compatible lifestyles would be an invasion of privacy. For example, single women often seek other women for roommates out of security concerns. This type of private engagement should not be prohibited. Because the FHA does not apply to the sharing of individual dwelling units, Roommate.com's practice of pairing up roommates based on their sex, sexual orientation, and familial status is not prohibited. Reversed.

ANALYSIS

As further support, the decision also notes in dicta that, whenever possible, federal and state statutes will be interpreted to avoid any constitutional concerns. Courts will attempt to construe statutes to avoid these concerns unless the interpretation is clearly contrary to the statue. In this case, adopting the narrow interpretation that a dwelling is a single, indivisible unit allowed the court to avoid the constitutional issues such as invasion of privacy or interference with a protected intimate relationship.

Continued on next page.

Quicknotes

FAIR HOUSING ACT 42 U.S.C. § 3601 Prohibits housing discrimination on the basis of race, color, religion, sex, familial status or national origin.

FUNDAMENTAL RIGHT A liberty that is either expressly or impliedly provided for in the United States Constitution, the deprivation or burdening of which is subject to a heightened standard of review.

■=■

Asbury v. Brougham

Black renter (P) v. Housing complex (D)

866 F.2d 1276 (10th Cir. 1989).

NATURE OF CASE: Appeal from award of damages for illegal discrimination.

FACT SUMMARY: Asbury (P) claimed that she was denied an opportunity to rent a home at Brougham Estates (D) because she was black.

🏛 RULE OF LAW
The Fair Housing Act is violated where the plaintiff proves a prima facie case of intent to discriminate based on race and the defendant is unable to demonstrate legitimate nondiscriminatory reasons.

FACTS: Asbury (P), a black woman, went to Brougham Estates (Brougham) (D), a housing complex, looking to rent a home. Asbury (P) was told that there were no vacancies and was refused an application. The following day, a white woman inquired about the same housing and was told that there were immediate openings. Other evidence presented at trial also indicated that white persons were given different information than Asbury (P). Brougham Estates (D) responded that there was no appropriate housing available for Asbury (P) at the time she inquired. The jury awarded damages, including punitive damages, against Brougham (D) to Asbury (P), and Brougham (D) appealed.

ISSUE: Is the Fair Housing Act violated where the plaintiff proves a prima facie case of intent to discriminate based on race and the defendant is unable to demonstrate legitimate nondiscriminatory reasons?

HOLDING AND DECISION: (Parker, J.) Yes. The Fair Housing Act is violated where the plaintiff proves a prima facie case of intent to discriminate based on race and the defendant is unable to demonstrate legitimate nondiscriminatory reasons. Under the Fair Housing Act and § 1982, persons may not use race as a factor to discriminate against minority applicants for rental housing. The plaintiff has the burden of bringing proof of a prima facie case. Then the defendant has the burden of showing that the refusal to rent or provide information was motivated by legitimate nonracial reasons. Finally, the burden shifts back to the plaintiff to demonstrate that the reasons claimed by the defendant were not the true considerations. Asbury (P) made her prima facie case by proving that she was denied access to housing although it remained available to white applicants. Brougham Estates' (D) defense that Asbury (P) was not qualified for housing was rebutted by evidence that exceptions were often made for persons in her position and she was not even provided with the conditions for obtaining an exception. Thus, the jury had a valid basis for deciding that Brougham Estates' (D) reasons were not legitimate. Accordingly, the award of damages to Asbury (P) is affirmed.

▶ ANALYSIS

The award of punitive damages against Brougham (D), the owner of the complex, was upheld despite his assertion that he could not be held responsible for the actions of his employees. The court found that there was ample evidence that Brougham (D) had adopted the discriminatory policy and ratified the employees' actions.

Quicknotes

COMPENSATORY DAMAGES Measure of damages necessary to compensate victim for actual injuries suffered.

PRIMA FACIE CASE An action where the plaintiff introduces sufficient evidence to submit the issue to the judge or jury for determination.

PUNITIVE DAMAGES Damages exceeding the actual injury suffered for the purposes of punishment, deterrence, and comfort to plaintiff.

United States v. Starrett City Associates

Federal government (P) v. Public housing complex (D)

840 F.2d 1096 (2d Cir. 1988).

NATURE OF CASE: Appeal from grant of summary judgment and permanent injunction in housing discrimination case.

FACT SUMMARY: Starrett City Associates (Starrett) (D) appealed from a decision granting summary judgment and a permanent injunction in favor of the United States (P), preventing it from discriminating on the basis of race in the rental of apartments. Starrett (D) contended that its tenant selection procedures, designed to achieve racial integration, did not violate the Fair Housing Act.

🏛 RULE OF LAW
The Fair Housing Act may prevent the use of rigid racial quotas of indefinite duration to maintain a fixed level of integration in public housing when such practices restrict minority access to public housing.

FACTS: Starrett City Associates (Starrett) (D) owned and operated Starrett City, the largest public housing complex in the nation. To prevent "white flight" and to maintain a racial balance of 64% white, 22% black, and 8% Hispanic, Starrett (D) adopted a selection process whereby as vacancies arose, applicants of a similar race or national origin to those tenants departing were selected. It was undenied that this practice restricted minority access to the complex. The Government (P) brought suit against Starrett (D) alleging that the selection process discriminated on the basis of race, in violation of the Fair Housing Act. The parties made cross-motions for summary judgment. The Government's (P) motion was granted and the court permanently enjoined the selection process, which it determined had adversely impacted minority participation in the complex solely on the basis of race. From this decision, Starrett (D) appealed.

ISSUE: May the Fair Housing Act prevent the use of rigid racial quotas of indefinite duration to maintain a fixed level of integration in public housing when such practices restrict minority access to public housing?

HOLDING AND DECISION: (Miner, J.) Yes. The Fair Housing Act (FHA) may prevent the use of rigid racial quotas of indefinite duration to maintain a fixed level of integration in public housing when such practices restrict minority access to public housing. Housing practices violative of the FHA include not only those motivated by racially discriminatory purposes, but also those that disproportionately affect minorities. Quotas bring the dual goals of the FHA—antidiscrimination and integration—into conflict. A racial classification is presumptively discriminating, but a race-conscious affirmative action plan does not necessarily violate federal constitutional or statutory law. Such plans must be temporary in nature and must terminate when a defined goal is reached. Access quotas that increase or ensure minority participation are generally upheld, while integration maintenance plans that restrict minority participation are of doubtful validity. Finally, quotas, when used, address the history of racial discrimination or imbalance. In the present case, Starrett's (D) selection process has as its only goal integration maintenance. There is no adequate explanation as to why it was in force for over fifteen years. Furthermore, the selection process redresses no prior discrimination or racial imbalance. In fact, it acts as a ceiling on minority access to Starrett's (D) complex. Fear of "white flight" cannot justify the use of inflexible racial quotas in the present case. While race is not always an inappropriate factor, Starrett's (D) use of racial quotas in the present case is. Affirmed.

DISSENT: (Newman, J.) The FHA, which was promulgated to bar the perpetuation of segregation, was never designed or intended to apply to actions like Starrett's (D), which do not promote segregated housing, but rather maintain integrated housing.

▶ ANALYSIS

Housing practices need not be motivated by a racially discriminatory purpose to be violative of the FHA; they may also be violative if they disproportionately affect minorities. Race-based factors, which are not motivated by a racially discriminating purpose, may not be violative of the FHA, even if they adversely affect minorities. A justifiable rental increase may decrease minority participation in a complex, but the increase, if not racially motivated, may not run afoul of the FHA.

■=■

Quicknotes

AFFIRMATIVE ACTION A form of benign discrimination designed to remedy existing discrimination by favoring one group over another.

■=■

Quigley v. Winter

Tenant (P) v. Landlord (D)

598 F.3d 938 (8th Cir. 2010).

NATURE OF CASE: Appeal from jury verdict finding that, among other things, landlord's sexual harassment of plaintiff created a hostile housing environment, entitling the plaintiff to compensatory and punitive damages.

FACT SUMMARY: Quigley (P), a mother of four, rented an apartment from Winter (D) via a Section 8 housing voucher from the federal government. Quigley (P) alleged that Winter (D) sexually harassed her on many different occasions in and around her apartment, forcing Quigley (P) to terminate her lease and move out.

RULE OF LAW
A claim of a hostile housing environment created by sexual harassment may be demonstrated by evidence that a landlord or property owner subjected a tenant to unwelcome sexual harassment sufficiently severe so as to interfere with or deprive the tenant of his or her rights to use or enjoy the home.

FACTS: Quigley (P), a mother of four, rented an apartment from Winter (D) via a Section 8 housing voucher from the federal government. Quigley (P) alleged that Winter (D) sexually harassed her on many different occasions in and around her apartment. The harassment included two occasions of unwanted touching, various sexually suggestive comments, calls to Quigley's (P) home in the middle of the night, and repeated unannounced visits and unapproved entrances into Quigley's (P) apartment. Winter's (D) behavior eventually forced Quigley (P) to terminate her lease and move out. Quigley (P) filed a complaint in federal district court alleging sexual harassment, sex discrimination, and coercion and intimidation with her (P) rights in violation of the Fair Housing Act (FHA). Winter (D) filed a counterclaim alleging that Quigley (P) breached her lease when she vacated the apartment early. A jury found in favor of Quigley (P) on all counts and awarded her $13,685 in compensatory damages and $250,000 in punitive damages. The district court then lowered the punitive damage amount to $20,527.50. Both parties appealed to the United States Appeals Court for the Eighth Circuit.

ISSUE: May a claim of a hostile housing environment created by sexual harassment be demonstrated by evidence that a landlord or property owner subjected a tenant to unwelcome sexual harassment sufficiently severe so as to interfere with or deprive the tenant of his or her rights to use or enjoy the home?

HOLDING AND DECISION: (Riley, J.) Yes. A claim of a hostile housing environment created by sexual harassment may be demonstrated by evidence that a landlord or property owner subjected a tenant to unwelcome sexual harassment sufficiently severe so as to interfere with or deprive the tenant of his or her rights to use or enjoy the home. First, as a matter of law, a claim for hostile housing environment based on sexual harassment is allowed under the FHA and several other circuit courts have concluded the same. Winter (D) claims the evidence to establish the claim was insufficient at trial. Based upon the factual evidence presented at trial regarding the multiple instances of sexual harassment, the court concludes Quigley (P) presented sufficient evidence to support the claim. All of these instances occurred in and around Quigley's (P) own home, making the conduct even more egregious. The jury also found that Quigley (P) proved the separate legal claim of "quid pro quo" sexual harassment. For this claim, Quigley (P) must have shown that she was a member of a protected class, she was subjected to harassment based on sexual advances, and her submission to the advances was an implied condition of receiving some type of benefit. Here, Quigley (P) produced evidence that when she inquired with Winter (D) as to whether she would receive her security deposit back, Winter (D) put his hand on her stomach and said, "My eagle eyes have not seen everything yet." The jury could properly infer that Winter (D) was conditioning the return of the security deposit upon seeing more of Quigley's (P) body. This Court will not overturn that decision by the jury. Turning to Quigley's (P) third claim, 42 U.S.C. § 3617 prohibits use of coercion and intimidation to deny or limit benefits to a person in connection with the rental of a dwelling. Based upon the same evidence noted above supporting her hostile environment claim, Quigley (P) produced enough evidence to support her coercion claim. Lastly, the district court reduced the punitive damage award by too large of a degree. Punitive damages are appropriate in federal civil actions when the defendant's conduct included evil motive or intent or reckless indifference to federally protected rights. Here, Winter (D) admitted at trial he knew sexual harassment was unlawful. The only question on appeal is the reasonableness of the jury's damage award. To assess reasonableness, courts should consider: (1) the degree of reprehensibility of the defendant's conduct; (2) the ratio between compensatory damages and the punitive damages; and (3) any civil or criminal penalties that could be imposed for the conduct in question. There is no question Winter's (D) conduct was reprehensible. It occurred multiple times, in Quigley's (P) home and often in the presence of her children. Turning to

Continued on next page.

the ratio, the jury's $250,000 punitive damages award was 18 times the amount of compensatory damages. The court agrees with the trial court that this was excessive. The last factor is the amount of any civil or criminal penalties. A provision of the FHA states any person interfering with one's rights under the FHA may be subject to a penalty of $55,000 for first time offences. Accordingly, the court finds the compensatory damages should be multiplied by four. This will result in a punitive damages award of $54,750. Affirmed in part and reversed in part.

▶ ANALYSIS

The United States Supreme Court has recently issued several decisions that have limited the possibility of large punitive damage amounts in federal civil cases. The Court has said a four to one ratio of punitive damages to compensatory damages will normally suffice. The Court also stated that awards with a ratio higher than ten to one may be presumptively unconstitutional because they violate the Due Process Clauses of the Fifth and Fourteenth Amendment.

Quicknotes

PUNITIVE DAMAGES Damages exceeding the actual injury suffered for the purposes of punishment of the defendant, deterrence of the wrongful behavior or comfort to the plaintiff.

SEXUAL HARASSMENT The practice of subjecting persons to oppressive conduct on account of their gender.

Human Rights Commission v. LaBrie, Inc.

Mobile park homeowner (P) v. Mobile park owner (D)

Vt. Sup. Ct., 668 A.2d 659 (1995).

NATURE OF CASE: Appeal in a case alleging discrimination in housing.

FACT SUMMARY: The McCarthys (P) claimed the LaBries (D) unlawfully discriminated against them by prohibiting them to reside in their mobile home park with minor children.

RULE OF LAW
Privately imposed occupancy limits that limit or exclude persons with minor children are unreasonable and in violation of state and federal law.

FACTS: The LaBries (D) purchased a mobile home park. They changed the occupancy provisions of their leases to provide that no tenants be permitted to have children under the age of 18 reside in their mobile home. The McCarthys (P) purchased a home in the park; however, they were later forced to sell when Mrs. McCarthy learned she was pregnant. The McCarthys (P) brought suit against the LaBries (D), claiming violations of the Fair Housing and Public Accommodations Act by discriminating against persons intending to occupy a dwelling with one or more minor children. The court found in favor of plaintiffs and the LaBries (D) appealed.

ISSUE: Are privately imposed occupancy limits that limit or exclude persons with minor children unreasonable and in violation of state and federal law?

HOLDING AND DECISION: (Allen, C.J.) Yes. Privately imposed occupancy limits that limit or exclude persons with minor children are unreasonable and in violation of state and federal law. In addition, the LaBries' (D) argument that the occupancy limit is based on legitimate water and septic capacity considerations is without merit. The trial court properly rejected this argument on the grounds the LaBries (D) failed to present evidence that an increase in the number of occupants in the units would adversely affect their water and septic capacities. We agree with the trial court that this argument is merely a pretext to prohibit minors from the mobile home park. A privately enforced occupancy limit must at a minimum be reasonable. Defendants failed to make this showing. Affirmed.

▶ ANALYSIS

The defendants were guilty here of both disparate treatment and disparate impact discrimination. While such discrimination may be proven by extrinsic evidence, here there was direct evidence of the fact that no minor children had moved into the park. Moreover, the court held that the affirmative defense asserted by the LaBries (D) that an increase in occupancy would overburden their septic systems was unproven.

Quicknotes

AFFIRMATIVE DEFENSE A manner of defending oneself against a claim not by denying the truth of the charge but by the introduction of some evidence challenging the plaintiff's right to bring the claim.

DISPARATE TREATMENT Unequal treatment of employees or of applicants for employment without justification.

EXTRINSIC EVIDENCE Evidence that is not contained within the text of a document or contract but that is derived from the parties' statements or the circumstances under which the agreement was made.

State ex rel. Sprague v. City of Madison

Lessee (P) v. City (D)

Wis. Ct. App., 555 N.W.2d 409 (1996).

NATURE OF CASE: Appeal in a case alleging sexual discrimination in violation of municipal law.

FACT SUMMARY: Sprague (P) brought suit against Hacklander-Ready and Rowe for their retraction of an offer to rent her a room based on her sexual orientation.

> **RULE OF LAW**
> A statute is ambiguous if it may be construed in different ways by reasonably informed persons or if its literal meaning produces an absurd or unreasonable result.

FACTS: Hacklander-Ready leased a four-bedroom house. She had the owner's permission to lease rooms out to other persons to help her in paying the rent. She leased a room to Rowe, and they placed ads to find tenants to replace two women who were moving out. They agreed to rent a room to Sprague (P) and were aware of her sexual orientation. However, they retracted their offer on the basis that they were uncomfortable living with a person of her sexual orientation. Sprague (P) filed a complaint with the Madison Equal Opportunity Commission alleging discrimination on the basis of sexual orientation in violation of Madison General Ordinances. The trial court found Ready and Rowe in violation of the statute and they appealed.

ISSUE: Is a statute ambiguous if it may be construed in different ways by reasonably informed persons or if its literal meaning produces an absurd or unreasonable result?

HOLDING AND DECISION: (Sundby, J.) Yes. A statute is ambiguous if it may be construed in different ways by reasonably informed persons or if its literal meaning produces an absurd or unreasonable result. This is not the case here. The statute unambiguously prohibits any person having right of rental to refuse to rent to any person because of the person's sexual orientation. Hacklander-Ready has the right to rent the property to others and the sole reason she and Rowe withdrew their offer was due to Sprague's (P) sexual orientation. Affirmed.

▌ ANALYSIS

Note that all jurisdictions have ordinances that expressly prohibit discrimination in housing based on sexual orientation. Moreover, the definition of "family" for purposes of statutory construction may also differ from jurisdiction to jurisdiction. Some jurisdictions extend the definition to include a homosexual partner.

Quicknotes

AMBIGUOUS TERMS Contract terms that are capable of more than one interpretation.

SEXUAL HARASSMENT An employment practice subjecting persons to oppressive conduct on account of their gender.

DiLiddo v. Oxford Street Realty, Inc.

Tenant (P) v. Landlord (D)

Mass. Sup. Jud. Ct., 876 N.E.2d 421 (2007).

NATURE OF CASE: Appeal from granting of summary judgment in favor of defendant.

FACT SUMMARY: DiLiddo (P) sought to rent an apartment from Oxford Street Realty, Inc. (Oxford) (D) using a state assisted housing program, which required landlords to execute a form lease. Oxford (D) objected to the terms of the lease.

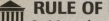 **RULE OF LAW**
In Massachusetts, a landlord may not refuse to rent an apartment to a participant in a state assisted housing program for temporary housing simply because the landlord considers certain terms of the program's standard lease form economically unfavorable.

FACTS: The Massachusetts Legislature created a program in 1995 whereby the state would subsidize temporary housing costs for qualified disabled persons of low income. The enabling statute created an alternate housing voucher program (AHVP) as well as a standard form lease for such short-term tenancies. The lease allowed tenants to provide one month's notice of termination if the tenant found more suitable, permanent housing. DiLiddo (P), disabled from an auto accident, sought to rent an apartment owned by Oxford Street Realty, Inc. (Oxford) (D). Oxford (D) objected on the grounds the one-month termination provision in favor of the tenant placed an unreasonable financial burden on the landlord. DiLiddo (P) brought suit, alleging that Oxford's (D) actions were discriminatory and in violation of state law that prohibited landlords from discriminating against tenants who receive public housing assistance or because of any requirement of the public assistance program. [The lower court granted Oxford (D) summary judgment and DiLiddo (P) appealed.]

ISSUE: In Massachusetts, may a landlord refuse to rent an apartment to a participant in a state assisted housing program for temporary housing simply because the landlord considers certain terms of the program's standard lease form economically unfavorable?

HOLDING AND DECISION: (Marshall, C.J.) No. In Massachusetts, a landlord may not refuse to rent an apartment to a participant in a state assisted housing program for temporary housing simply because the landlord considers certain terms of the program's standard lease form economically unfavorable. M.G.L. c. 151 Section 4(10) prohibits landlords from discriminating against tenants who receive public subsidies or because of any requirements of the subsidy program. The question here

is whether the AHVP's one-month notice of termination provision is a "requirement" of the AHVP program, therefore barring landlords from refusing to execute the lease. We hold the language of Chapter 151B is unambiguous. The landlord may not object to the lease's notice of termination provision because the provision constitutes a requirement of the subsidy program. In addition, the statute does not require the plaintiff to proffer evidence of a discriminatory animus. On this point, Chapter 151B does not require such a showing. Accordingly, Oxford's (D) objections to the lease run afoul of Chapter 151B. [The court reversed the summary judgment in favor of Oxford (D) and ordered judgment in favor of DiLiddo (P) as to liability.]

ANALYSIS

This case represented the first time the Massachusetts Supreme Judicial Court interpreted this particular statute in over twenty years. Essentially, the court held that landlords could no longer use economic reasons as grounds to reject tenants who receive public subsidies.

Quicknotes

SUMMARY JUDGMENT Judgment rendered by a court in response to a motion made by one of the parties, claiming that the lack of a question of material fact in respect to an issue warrants disposition of the issue without consideration by the jury.

Huntington Branch, NAACP v. Town of Huntington

National Association for the Advancement of Colored People (P) v. Town (D)

844 F.2d 926 (2d Cir.), *review declined in part and judgment aff'd sub nom.* Town of Huntington v. Huntington Branch, NAACP, 488 U.S. 15 (1988).

NATURE OF CASE: Appeal from judgment denying an injunction.

FACT SUMMARY: Huntington (D) zoning regulations did not allow housing projects in white neighborhoods.

RULE OF LAW
Town zoning regulations may not restrict multifamily housing projects to largely minority areas.

FACTS: Huntington (D), New York, was a town of 200,000 people in 1980. Ninety-five percent of the residents were white. The 3.35 percent of black residents were concentrated in two neighborhoods. Because there was a shortage of low-income housing in Huntington (D), Housing Help Inc. (HHI) (P) decided to sponsor an integrated housing project. HHI (P) determined that it could only foster integration by locating the project in a white neighborhood. HHI (P) purchased a parcel of land and obtained HUD approval for the project. However, Huntington (D) zoning regulations allowed this type of housing only in a single area already occupied by black residents. HHI (P) and the NAACP (P) brought suit against Huntington (D), claiming that it was violating the Fair Housing Act because its zoning regulations had a disparate impact on racial minorities. Specifically, 24 percent of blacks living in Huntington (D) required subsidized housing as opposed to only 7 percent of the white residents. The trial court ruled for Huntington (D), and the HHI (P) and the NAACP (P) appealed.

ISSUE: May town zoning regulations restrict multifamily housing projects to largely minority areas?

HOLDING AND DECISION: (Kaufman, J.) No. Town zoning regulations may not restrict multifamily housing projects to largely minority areas. Disparate impact analysis under the Fair Housing Act examines a facially neutral policy or practice that has a different impact on particular groups of people. Intent to discriminate is not necessary to prove illegal discrimination. The prima facie case is established by showing that the practice has a discriminatory effect. Then a court must weigh the adverse impact against legitimate government interests and any possible alternatives with less discriminatory effects. In the present case, Huntington (D) zoning regulations promote racial segregation in housing by refusing to permit projects in white neighborhoods. At trial, Huntington (D) presented no evidence as to why preventing projects in white neighborhoods would impair any legitimate interests.

Huntington's (D) objections to certain specific provisions of HHI's (P) plan could be resolved, and there was no support for evidence that the site chosen by HHI (P) was inappropriate for the housing project. Accordingly, the district court is ordered to direct judgment for HHI (P) and mandate that Huntington (D) re-zone the site to allow the project. Reversed.

ANALYSIS

The circuit courts are split on whether the Fair Housing Act requires discriminatory intent. Most agree with this case—that a plaintiff may make a prima facie case based on disparate impact only. But see *Metropolitan Housing Development Corp. v. Village of Arlington Heights*, 558 F.2d 1283 (7th Cir. 1977), for an opposing view.

Quicknotes

DISCRIMINATORY IMPACT The effect of an action that affects one group of persons more significantly than another; insufficient to prove discriminatory intent on its own.

PRIMA FACIE SHOWING An action in which the plaintiff introduces sufficient evidence to submit an issue to the judge or jury for determination.

ZONING ORDINANCE A statute that divides land into defined areas and that regulates the form and use of buildings and structures within those areas.

Janush v. Charities Housing Development Corp.

Tenant (P) v. Landlord (D)

169 F. Supp. 2d 1133 (N.D. Cal. 2000).

NATURE OF CASE: Federal district court's consideration of defendant's motion to dismiss plaintiff's claims of housing discrimination.

FACT SUMMARY: Janush (P) kept two birds and two cats in her apartment to help lessen the effects of her severe mental health disability. Her lease with Charities Housing Development Corp. (D) prohibited pets in the apartment.

RULE OF LAW
To establish a prima facie case of housing discrimination based upon a defendant/property owner's failure to provide a disabled person with a reasonable accommodation, the plaintiff must show: (1) the existence of a qualifying handicap; (2) the defendant/property owner was aware of the handicap; (3) the accommodation of the handicap may be necessary to afford the plaintiff the opportunity to use and enjoy the dwelling; and (4) the defendant/property owner refused to make the accommodation.

FACTS: Janush (P) kept two birds and two cats in her apartment to help lessen the effects of her severe mental health disability. Her lease with Charities Housing Development Corp. (D) (CHD) specifically prohibited pets in the apartment. In January of 2000, CHD (D) became aware of Janush's (P) pets and opened a dialogue with her as to whether she could keep the pets. Janush (P) alleges CHD (D) prohibited her from keeping the pets. CHD (D) alleges it offered Janush (P) the opportunity to keep the pets, but that Janush (P) failed to provide them with proof the animals had been vaccinated. CHD (D) eventually commenced the eviction process and Janush (P) moved out shortly thereafter. Janush (P) filed in federal court a housing discrimination claim based on CHD's (D) failure to provide her with a reasonable accommodation. CHD (D) moved to dismiss Janush's (P) claims on the ground that federal and state law only requires landlords to allow service dogs in apartments as reasonable accommodations. This decision is the federal district court's consideration of CHD's (D) motion to dismiss.

ISSUE: To establish a prima facie case of housing discrimination based upon a defendant/property owner's failure to provide a disabled person with a reasonable accommodation, must the plaintiff show: (1) the existence of a qualifying handicap; (2) the defendant/property owner was aware of the handicap; (3) the accommodation of the handicap may be necessary to afford the plaintiff the opportunity to use and enjoy the dwelling; and (4) the defendant/property owner refused to make the accommodation?

HOLDING AND DECISION: (Whyte, J.) Yes. To establish a prima facie case of housing discrimination based upon a defendant/property owner's failure to provide a disabled person with a reasonable accommodation, the plaintiff must show: (1) the existence of a qualifying handicap; (2) the defendant/property owner was aware of the handicap; (3) the accommodation of the handicap may be necessary to afford the plaintiff the opportunity to use and enjoy the dwelling; and (4) the defendant/property owner refused to make the accommodation. CHD (D) argues federal and state laws only require landlords to allow service dogs in apartments as reasonable accommodations. In addition, CHD (D) argues it will be inundated with similar requests if it must allow animals in apartments based upon vague allegations of reasonable accommodations. Although federal regulations do specifically cite seeing-eye dogs, there is nothing in the regulations or Fair Housing Act stating that accommodations for other animals are per se unreasonable. Under the regulations, "service animal" is given a broad definition. It includes dogs "or other animal" trained to perform tasks for the benefit of a disabled person. In addition, whether an accommodation is reasonable is typically a fact-intensive analysis. While a plaintiff's needs are considered, those needs must be balanced against the administrative and financial burdens placed upon the landlord to comply with the requested accommodations. At this stage of the litigation, CHD (D) has not produced any documents or evidence to support their claims of an unreasonable financial burden. This case requires additional discovery. Accordingly, Janush (P) has pled that she is handicapped and that CHD (D) was aware of the handicap. She has further alleged the accommodation may be necessary and that CHD (D) has refused. CHD's (D) motion to dismiss is denied.

ANALYSIS

When considering a motion to dismiss, a reviewing court takes the allegations in the plaintiff's complaint as true. It then reviews those allegations and makes a ruling of law whether the plaintiff has stated a prima facie legal claim that should proceed into the discovery phase of the litigation. A court only reviews the allegations in the complaint, does not consider any other outside evidence, and takes no notice of any factual disputes. If the plaintiff fails to state a claim, a court may dismiss the action.

Continued on next page.

Quicknotes

MOTION TO DISMISS   Motion to terminate an action based on the adequacy of the pleadings, improper service or venue, etc.

PRIMA FACIE CASE   An action where the plaintiff introduces sufficient evidence to submit the issue to the judge or jury for determination.

Familystyle of St. Paul, Inc. v. City of St. Paul

Group home operator (P) v. City (D)

923 F.2d 91 (8th Cir. 1991).

NATURE OF CASE: Appeal from validation of de-institutionalization ordinance.

FACT SUMMARY: When Familystyle of St. Paul, Inc. (P) was denied a permit to expand its capacity to house mentally ill persons by adding three homes to its existing campus, it challenged the City of St. Paul's (D) requirement that group homes be located at least a quarter mile apart.

🏛 RULE OF LAW
Legislation that requires dispersal of group homes is a legitimate means whereby a state may achieve its goal of deinstitutionalization of the mentally ill, and does not violate the Fair Housing Amendments Act of 1988.

FACTS: The State of Minnesota (D) required that all residential services for people with mental illness and retardation be licensed. In an attempt to deinstitutionalize the mentally ill and integrate them back into mainstream society, Minnesota (D) enacted a licensing regulation requiring new group homes to be spaced at least a quarter of a mile apart. The City of St. Paul's (D) zoning code contains the same dispersal requirement. Familystyle of St. Paul, Inc. (Familystyle) (P) operated group homes and provided rehabilitative services for mentally ill persons on its campus located in St. Paul. Familystyle (P) applied for a license to add three new homes to its campus, but the City of St. Paul (D) denied the application because it violated the dispersal requirement. Familystyle (P) filed suit alleging that Minnesota's (D) and the City of St. Paul's (D) dispersal requirements result in a disparate impact on and discriminatory treatment of the mentally ill, in violation of the Fair Housing Amendments Act of 1988. The district court found that the government's interest in deinstitutionalization sufficiently rebutted any discriminatory effect of the laws. Familystyle (P) appealed.

ISSUE: Is legislation that requires dispersal of group homes a legitimate means for a state to achieve its goal of deinstitutionalization of the mentally ill, and not a violation of the Fair Housing Amendments Act of 1988?

HOLDING AND DECISION: (Wollman, J.) Yes. Legislation that requires dispersal of group homes is a legitimate means whereby a state may achieve its goal of deinstitutionalization of the mentally ill and does not violate the Fair Housing Amendments Act of 1988. First of all, in a Title VIII case, the plaintiff has the initial burden of establishing the discriminatory effect of the challenged law. Once such an effect is shown to disparately impact a non-

suspect class like the mentally ill, the burden shifts to the government to demonstrate that its legislation was rationally related to a legitimate government purpose. In this case, although local and state dispersal requirements for group homes on their face limit housing choices for the mentally ill, the government's method of dispersing group homes was rationally related to its goal of integrating the mentally ill into the mainstream of society. Affirmed.

▶ ANALYSIS

The Fair Housing Act (FHA) prohibits discrimination on the basis of race, color, religion, sex, familial status, handicap, or national origin. Most FHA cases involve alleged discrimination on the basis of race, color, or national origin. Very few cases are brought under the FHA based on gender. However, in *Doe v. City of Butler*, 892 F.2d 315 (3d Cir. 1989), a zoning ordinance that limited group homes to six persons was challenged as gender discrimination when applied to a home for abused women. The court validated the ordinance, finding no intention to discriminate against women, since the provision applied equally to group homes for men. On the other hand, the court condemned as discriminatory a landlord's refusal to rent to a group of males because he believed that male tenants were dirtier than female tenants, in *Baumgardner v. HUD*, 960 F.2d 572 (6th Cir. 1992).

━■■

Quicknotes

DISCRIMINATORY IMPACT The effect of an action that affects one group of persons more significantly than another; insufficient to prove discriminatory intent on its own.

REBUT A defendant's refuting of evidence that raises a presumption as to his liability.

━■■

M & T Mortgage Corp. v. Foy

Mortgage company (P) v. Homeowner (D)

N.Y. Sup. Ct. 20 Misc. 3d 274 (2008).

NATURE OF CASE: Trial court's interim decision regarding applicable burden of proof in foreclosure proceeding.

FACT SUMMARY: M & T Mortgage Corp. (P) brought foreclosure proceedings against Major Jahn K. Foy (D). Foy (D), a reserve army officer on active duty, sought a hearing to reform the mortgage.

RULE OF LAW

A mortgage granted to a minority buyer with an interest rate that exceeds nine percent creates a rebuttable presumption of discriminatory practice.

FACTS: M & T Mortgage Corp. (M & T) (P) brought this foreclosure action against Major Jahn K. Foy (D), a reserve officer who has served several active duty tours in recent years. Foy (D), a minority living in a minority neighborhood of Brooklyn, sought to modify the terms of the mortgage. The mortgage had an interest rate of nine percent. The court granted a hearing on Foy's (D) motion and had previously ordered that Foy (D) prove that she was the victim of discriminatory lending. In this decision, the trial court now modifies that order.

ISSUE: Does a mortgage granted to a minority buyer with an interest rate that exceeds nine percent create a rebuttable presumption of discriminatory practice?

HOLDING AND DECISION: (Kramer, J.) Yes. A mortgage granted to a minority buyer with an interest rate that exceeds nine percent creates a rebuttable presumption of discriminatory practice. First, the court now modifies its previous order regarding burden of proof. It appears from the record that Foy (D) may have been a victim of "reverse redlining," the practice of extending unfair loans to minority communities. After researching the issue, the burden is now on M & T (P) to demonstrate that the loan is not a "higher priced loan" given as a result of discriminatory practices on the part of M & T (P). A higher priced loan has an interest rate that is three percentage points higher than the normal interest rate for 30-year loans. In 2005, the Federal Reserve published findings of interest rate data. From those findings, we learned that under-served minority groups were more likely than other populations to pay higher prices for mortgages. The mortgage in the instant case qualifies as a higher priced loan, due to its interest rate of nine percent. The court holds that loans exceeding nine percent create the rebuttable presumption of discrimination on the part of the lender. The burden is therefore placed on M & T (P) to produce evidence that the mortgage was granted for other, economic reasons.

▶ ANALYSIS

Many times the judiciary, rather than the executive branch of state government, will be the vehicle to protect underrepresented minority groups that are the victims of predatory lending. Here, the court, in an action brought by M & T (P), raised the issue of the high interest rate on its own. It then fashioned an equitable remedy to place the burden of proof on the foreclosing lender that the mortgage was not discriminatory.

Quicknotes

BURDEN OF PROOF The duty of a party to introduce evidence to support a fact that is in dispute in an action.

REBUTTABLE PRESUMPTION A rule of law, inferred from the existence of a particular set of facts, that is conclusive in the absence of contrary evidence.

CHAPTER 14

Equal Protection and Due Process

Quick Reference Rules of Law

Miller v. Schoene

[Parties not identified.]

276 U.S. 272 (1928).

NATURE OF CASE: Appeal from condemnation action.

FACT SUMMARY: Under the authority of a Virginia statute, a state official ordered the plaintiff in error to cut down certain infected cedar trees.

RULE OF LAW

The state does not exceed its constitutional powers by deciding upon the destruction of one class of property in order to save another that, in the judgment of the legislature, is of greater value to the public.

FACTS: A Virginia statute provided for the condemnation and destruction of cedar trees that were determined to be infected with cedar rust, a communicable plant disease, and that were located within a certain radius of an apple orchard. The statute allowed compensation of $100 to the owner of the trees to cover removal expense and permitted him to use the timber, but it provided no compensation for loss of the ornamental value of the trees or decrease in real estate value. The plaintiff in error was ordered to remove his cedars under the terms of the statute and appealed the order to the county circuit court. Evidence presented by Virginia showed that cedar rust was communicable between cedars and apple trees and that the commercial value of apple trees was far greater than that of cedars. [The Circuit Court, the Supreme Court of Appeals of Virginia, the state entomologist, and the plaintiff in error appealed to the United States Supreme Court.]

ISSUE: May a state constitutionally decide upon the destruction of one class of property in order to save another that, in the judgment of the legislature, is of greater value to the public?

HOLDING AND DECISION: (Stone, J.) Yes. The state does not exceed its constitutional powers by deciding upon the destruction of one class of property in order to save another that, in the judgment of the legislature, is of greater value to the public. One of the distinguishing features of the police power as it affects property is the preference of the public interest over the private property interests of the individual. Here, the state was forced to choose between preservation of the cedars and preservation of the nearby apple orchard. Since far greater public interest is attached to the preservation of the apple industry, the statute is constitutional.

ANALYSIS

Although "takings" of private property for public use require just compensation, regulation under the police power does not. A frequent issue arising under the Taking Clause is therefore whether the action in fact is a "taking" or is merely an exercise of the police powers. The Court adopted a common approach, balancing public need against private cost. In general, government actions that restrict the use of property that is harmful to others in some way are deemed to be regulatory and do not require compensation. But where the property is needed for some public purpose but is not harmful, there is a "taking" requiring compensation.

Quicknotes

POLICE POWERS The power of a state or local government to regulate private conduct for the health, safety, and welfare of the general public.

TAKING A governmental action that substantially deprives an owner of the use and enjoyment of his or her property, requiring compensation.

Village of Willowbrook v. Olech

Municipal government (D) v. Landowner (P)

528 U.S. 562 (2000).

NATURE OF CASE: Appeal from reversal of a dismissal in an equal protection claim.

FACT SUMMARY: Olech (P) brought suit against the Village of Willowbrook (D) alleging an equal protection violation in relation to an easement.

🏛 RULE OF LAW
An equal protection claim may be made by a "class of one" in instances where the plaintiff has been intentionally treated differently from similarly situated individuals and where there is no rational basis for the disparity in treatment.

FACTS: Olech (P) wanted to connect her property to the Village of Willowbrook's (the Village's) (P) water supply, but the Village (D) conditioned the connection on the grant of a 33-foot easement. Olech (P) objected because surrounding landowners were only subjected to a 15-foot easement. Olech (P) brought an action in the federal court alleging that the demand for the additional 18-feet of easement violated the Equal Protection Clause of the Fourteenth Amendment. Olech (P) claimed that the Village (D) was seeking revenge because Olech (P) had previously won a lawsuit against the Village (D). Olech (P) alleged that the Village (D) intentionally sought to deprive her of her rights. The district court dismissed pursuant to Rule 12(b)(6) for failure to state a claim, but the Seventh Circuit Court of Appeals reversed finding that Olech (P) sufficiently pled that the Village (D) was motivated solely by a spiteful effort to get even wholly unrelated to any legitimate state objective. The United States Supreme Court granted certiorari to determine if the Equal Protection Clause could give rise to a cause of action on behalf of a "class of one."

ISSUE: May an equal protection claim be made by a "class of one" in instances where the plaintiff has been intentionally treated differently from similarly situated individuals and where there is no rational basis for the disparity in treatment?

HOLDING AND DECISION: (Per curiam) Yes. An equal protection claim may be made by a "class of one" in instances where the plaintiff has been intentionally treated differently from similarly situated individuals and where there is no rational basis for the disparity in treatment. The purpose of the Equal Protection Clause is to secure every person within the state's jurisdiction against intentional and arbitrary discrimination. Olech's (P) complaint properly pled that the Village (D) intentionally demanded an easement far greater than that of similarly situated property owners and that the demanded was irra-

tional and wholly arbitrary. The decision of the Seventh Circuit Court of Appeals is affirmed.

CONCURRENCE: (Breyer, J.) Olech (P) alleged an extra factor, "ill will" or "illegitimate animus" that is sufficient to minimize any concern about transforming run-of-the-mill zoning cases into cases of a constitutional right.

▶ ANALYSIS

Different classifications of individuals receive different applications of the Equal Protection Clause. If the person alleging discrimination is a member of a "suspect class," such as race or religion, then the government action must survive a strict scrutiny analysis. Under those circumstances the government action or a statute must be narrowly tailored to promote a compelling governmental interest. If a person is a member of a "quasi-suspect class" such as gender, then intermediary review applies and the government action must bear a substantial relationship to an important government objective. If a person is not a member of either of these classes, then only rational basis review applies and the government action must only be rationally related to a legitimate governmental purpose. In this instance, the question was whether Olech (P) belonged to any type of class to have standing to bring an action pursuant to the Equal Protection Clause. The Court found that one person could be a representative class as long as similarly situated persons received different treatment and defined the appropriate standard of review as being the rational basis test.

Quicknotes

EASEMENT The right to utilize a portion of another's real property for a specific use.

EQUAL PROTECTION CLAUSE A constitutional provision that each person be guaranteed the same protection of the laws enjoyed by other persons in like circumstances.

RATIONAL BASIS REVEIW A test employed by the court to determine the validity of a statute in equal protection actions, whereby the court determines whether the challenged statute is rationally related to the achievement of a legitimate state interest.

Bonner v. City of Brighton

Property owner (P) v. Municipality (D)

Mich. Ct. App., 828 N.W.2d 408 (2012).

NATURE OF CASE: Appeal from lower court decision finding that a city ordinance relating to residential blight was unconstitutional because it failed to give property owners a full opportunity to repair their blighted properties prior to demolition by the city.

FACT SUMMARY: Bonner (P) owned two houses in Brighton, Michigan (D), that had been unoccupied for 30 years. Brighton (D) ordered the demolition of the properties because the cost to repair them was more than 100% of the value of the houses. Bonner (P) brought suit alleging that the city ordinance's failure to allow homeowners to repair their homes, regardless of cost, violated substantive and procedural due process.

RULE OF LAW

(1) To comport with substantive due process, legislative acts in the form of state statutes or municipal ordinances that restrict the use of real property must bear a reasonable relationship to the permissible governmental objective of preserving the public health, morals, or safety.

(2) A procedural due process violation occurs when the government unlawfully interferes with a protected property or liberty interest by failing to provide adequate procedural safeguards, such as proper notice, the opportunity to be heard, or the ability to appeal governmental actions.

FACTS: Bonner (P) owned two houses in Brighton, Michigan (D), that had been unoccupied for 30 years. Brighton's (D) ordinance relating to residential blight states that if the city determines a structure is unsafe and the cost to repair the blighted property is more than 100% of its value, the city may order it demolished "without option on the part of the owner to repair." After Brighton (D) determined Bonner's (P) two houses were unsafe, Brighton (D) ordered the demolition of the properties because the cost to repair them was more than 100% of the value of the houses. Bonner (P) appealed to Brighton's (D) city council. Bonner (P) produced documents and testimony that he could repair the houses for $40,000. The total value of the houses was $85,000. Brighton's (D) city inspectors argued the repair costs would exceed $158,000. The city council ordered the structures demolished. Bonner (P) filed this suit alleging that Brighton's (D) failure to allow him to repair the property, regardless of cost, constituted violations of the Fourteenth Amendment's substantive and procedural due process provisions. The

federal district court below agreed and found the ordinance unconstitutional. Brighton (D) appealed to the Michigan Appeals Court.

ISSUE:

(1) To comport with substantive due process, must legislative acts in the form of state statutes or municipal ordinances that restrict the use of real property bear a reasonable relationship to the permissible governmental objective of preserving the public health, morals, or safety?

(2) Does a procedural due process violation occur when the government unlawfully interferes with a protected property or liberty interest by failing to provide adequate procedural safeguards, such as proper notice, the opportunity to be heard, or the ability to appeal governmental actions?

HOLDING AND DECISION: (Markey, J.)

(1) Yes. To comport with substantive due process, legislative acts in the form of state statutes or municipal ordinances that restrict the use of real property must bear a reasonable relationship to the permissible governmental objective of preserving the public health, morals, or safety. The property owner must demonstrate that the challenged statute or ordinance is arbitrary and unreasonably affects the owner's use and enjoyment of the property. Ordinances are presumed to be constitutional and the rational basis test is deferential to legislative bodies. An ordinance will be declared unconstitutional only if it is an arbitrary fiat, leaving no dispute over its unreasonableness. The portion of Brighton's (D) ordinance barring an owner's right to repair just because the city deems those repairs unreasonable is unconstitutional. A municipality should not infringe on an owner's vested property right by forbidding the right to repair. An owner's reasons for wanting to repair a property, regardless of the cost, should be irrelevant to the municipality. The municipality can order the owner to make the repairs within a certain timeframe and if there is no action, the demolition can go forward. However, the refusal to allow owners to make such repairs is a violation of substantive due process. That portion of the statute has no reasonable relation to the public welfare. The goal is to eradicate blight. Barring owners from making repairs does not further the goal of protecting the public health and safety.

(2) Yes. A procedural due process violation occurs when the government unlawfully interferes with a protected property or liberty interest by failing to provide

Continued on next page.

adequate procedural safeguards, such as proper notice, the opportunity to be heard, or the ability to appeal governmental actions. Any restriction or invasion on one's property interests or fundamental rights must be fundamentally fair. To determine what procedures are constitutionally required, a court should examine: (1) the private interest affected by the governmental action; (2) the risk of an erroneous deprivation of rights under the existing procedural scheme; and (3) any adverse impact on the government if additional safeguards are ordered. Here, the nature of the interest at issue is substantial—the ownership of real property. In addition, the risk of an erroneous deprivation is real as the process ultimately may allow the destruction of the property even though the owner seeks to repair the structures. Finally, allowing the owner to make the repairs, regardless of cost, would only minimally affect the city's interest in the health and welfare of its citizens. Again, if the repairs are not made in a timely fashion, the city can still move forward with the demolition. Because Brighton (D) did not afford this opportunity to Bonner (P), the ordinance also constitutes a violation of procedural due process. Affirmed.

DISSENT: (Murray, J.) The statute should not fail based on a procedural due process claim. The ordinance requires Brighton (D) to provide notice, an opportunity to be heard, and a decision from an impartial decision maker. Bonner (P) was afforded each of those procedural protections in this case. In addition, the ordinance does not violate substantive due process. There are two reasons why the city should be allowed to move forward with demolition where the repairs will cost more than 100% of the property's value. First, under the ordinance, the city council has the discretion to allow the owner to approve repairs. Under this scenario, the substantive due process rights cannot be violated. Because there exists a factual scenario that is constitutional, the ordinance should stand. Second, just because there may be other reasonable means to remove blight from city neighborhoods, this court should be deferential to the manner chosen by the city council. That entity is the policymaking body for the city and courts should be wary when making decisions that override their agreed-upon policies.

▶ ANALYSIS

Municipalities have grappled with residential blight for decades. The problem is even more vexing today as many foreclosed properties now sit unoccupied and unmaintained. Many municipalities like Brighton (D) have sought to add more teeth to their ordinances regarding blight. However, as seen here, doing so often invites constitutional challenges.

Quicknotes

PROCEDURAL DUE PROCESS The constitutional mandate that if the state or federal government acts so as to deny a citizen of a life, liberty or property interest the individual is first entitled to notice and the right to be heard.

SUBSTANTIVE DUE PROCESS A constitutional safeguard limiting the power of the state, irrespective of how fair its procedures may be; substantive limits placed on the power of the state.

Village of Belle Terre v. Boraas

Long Island village (D) v. Lessees (P)

416 U.S. 1 (1974).

NATURE OF CASE: Appeal from an action seeking a declaratory judgment and an injunction.

FACT SUMMARY: Boraas (P) and other co-lessees of a house in the Village of Belle Terre (D) brought this action for an injunction and a judgment declaring an ordinance restricting land use to one-family dwellings unconstitutional.

RULE OF LAW
Zoning legislation does not violate the equal protection clause if it is reasonable, not arbitrary, and bears a rational relationship to a permissible state objective.

FACTS: The Village of Belle Terre (the Village) (D) had restricted land use to one-family dwellings. The word "family" as used in the ordinance meant one or more persons related by blood or a number of persons not exceeding two living together as a single housekeeping unit though not related by blood. The Dickmans (P), owners of a house in the Village (D), leased it to two single males, a single female, and three others, Boraas (P) among them. The Village (D) served the Dickmans (P) with an "Order to Remedy Violations" of the ordinance. Thereupon, Boraas (P) and two of the other tenants, as well as the Dickmans (P), brought this action seeking an injunction and a judgment declaring the ordinance unconstitutional as violative of the equal protection clause. The district court held the ordinance constitutional and the court of appeals reversed. The Village (D) appealed to the United States Supreme Court.

ISSUE: Does zoning legislation violate the equal protection clause if it is reasonable and bears a rational relationship to a permissible state objective?

HOLDING AND DECISION: (Douglas, J.) No. Zoning legislation does not violate the equal protection clause if it is reasonable, not arbitrary, and bears a rational relationship to a permissable state objective. The ordinance now before the Court does not discriminate against unmarried couples in violation of the equal protection clause. The ordinance is not aimed at transients so as to interfere with a person's right to travel. It involves no procedural disparity inflicted on some but not on others. It involves no fundamental right guaranteed by the constitution. Economic and social legislation does not violate the equal protection clause if the law is reasonable, not arbitrary, and bears a rational relationship to a permissible state objective. Boraas (P) argues that if two unmarried people can constitute a family under the ordinance, there is no

reason why three or four may not. But every line drawn by a legislature leaves some out that might well have been included. That exercise of discretion, however, is a legislative, not a judicial, function. A quiet place where yards are wide, people few, and motor vehicles restricted are legitimate guidelines in a land-use project addressed to family needs. This goal is a permissible one. The police power is not confined to elimination of filth, stench, and unhealthy places. It is ample to lay out zones where family values make the area a sanctuary for people. Therefore, the decision of the court of appeals is reversed.

DISSENT: (Marshall, J.) The disputed classification burdens the tenants' fundamental rights of association and privacy guaranteed by the First and Fourteenth Amendments. Therefore, strict equal protection scrutiny should be applied. The First Amendment provides some limitation on zoning laws, which, for example, seek to restrict occupancy to individuals adhering to particular religious, political, or scientific beliefs. Zoning officials properly concern themselves with the uses of land and can restrict the number of persons who reside in certain dwellings. But they cannot validly consider who those persons are or how they choose to live.

▶ ANALYSIS

The freedom of association is often inextricably entwined with the constitutionally guaranteed right of privacy. In *Meyer v. Nebraska*, 262 U.S. 390 (1923), the Supreme Court held that the right to establish a home is an essential part of the liberty guaranteed by the Fourteenth Amendment. In *Stanley v. Georgia*, 394 U.S. 557 (1996), in the concurring opinion, Justice Goldberg stated that the constitution secures to an individual a freedom to satisfy his intellectual and emotional needs in the privacy of his own home. Both these cases were used in the dissent to support the argument of discrimination.

Quicknotes

FREEDOM OF ASSOCIATION The right to peaceably assemble.

RIGHT TO PRIVACY Those personal liberties or relationships that are protected against unwarranted governmental interference.

Moore v. City of East Cleveland

Extended family (D) v. City (P)

431 U.S. 494 (1977).

NATURE OF CASE: Appeal from an action challenging the constitutionality of a housing ordinance.

FACT SUMMARY: Inez Moore (D), who lived with her own son and two grandsons, first cousins to each other, was directed to remove her grandson John from her home in compliance with a housing ordinance of Cleveland (P).

RULE OF LAW

Freedom of personal choice in matters of marriage and family life is one of the liberties protected by the Due Process Clause of the Fourteenth Amendment and any zoning ordinance infringing on these freedoms is subject to strict scrutiny.

FACTS: Inez Moore (D) lived in her Cleveland home together with her son and her two grandsons. The two boys were first cousins. Moore (D) received a notice of violation of a housing ordinance from the City of Cleveland (P) stating that John, her grandson, was an illegal occupant and directing her to comply with the ordinance. Cleveland's (P) housing ordinance limited occupancy of a dwelling unit to members of a single family, but contained an unusual and complicated definitional section that recognized as a family only a few categories of related individuals. Moore's (D) family did not fit into any of these categories. When Moore (D) failed to remove her grandson from her home, Cleveland (P) filed a criminal charge. Moore (D) moved to dismiss, claiming that the ordinance was constitutionally invalid on its face. The motion was overruled, and, upon conviction, Moore (D) was sentenced to five days in jail and a fine. The Ohio Court of Appeals affirmed and the Ohio Supreme Court refused review. Moore (D) appealed to the United States Supreme Court.

ISSUE: Is any zoning ordinance that infringes on a person's freedom of choice in matters of marriage and family life subject to the strict scrutiny of the Due Process Clause?

HOLDING AND DECISION: (Powell, J.) Yes. This Court has long recognized that freedom of personal choice in matters of marriage and family life is one of the liberties protected by the due process clause of the Fourteenth Amendment. When government intrudes on choices concerning family living arrangements, this Court must scrutinize carefully the importance of the governmental interests advanced and the extent to which they are served by the challenged regulation. When thus examined, the Cleveland ordinance cannot survive. The City (P) sought

to justify it as a means of preventing overcrowding, minimizing traffic and parking congestion, and avoiding an undue financial burden on the school system. Although these are legitimate goals, the ordinance serves them marginally at best. For example, the ordinance permits any family consisting only of husband, wife, and unmarried children to live together, even if the family contains a half-dozen licensed drivers, each with his own car. At the same time, it forbids an adult brother and sister to share a household, even if both faithfully use public transportation. The ordinance would permit a grandmother to live with a single dependent son and children, even if his school-age children number a dozen, yet it forces Moore (D) to find another dwelling for her grandson, simply because of the presence of his uncle and cousin in the same household. The decision of the Ohio Court of Appeals is, therefore, reversed.

CONCURRENCE: (Brennan, J.) The Constitution will not tolerate the imposition of one sector of the public's preference for nuclear families by the government upon the rest of society. The tradition of the extended family has a rich history in this country and has allowed waves of immigrants to come to this country and find shelter with their cousins or other relatives. Prohibiting these types of families and living arrangements intrudes upon the family associational rights that have been central to our society.

CONCURRENCE: (Stevens, J.) Long before the Constitution, the common law protected a landowner's right to use his or her property as he or she saw fit. While cities and towns may create permissible zoning plans, those plans and schemes must be exercised within constitutional limits.

DISSENT: (Stewart, J.) To suggest that the biological fact of common ancestry necessarily gives related persons constitutional rights of association superior to those of unrelated persons is to misunderstand the nature of the associational freedoms that the Constitution protects. Freedom of association has been constitutionally recognized because it is often indispensable to effectuation of explicit First Amendment guarantees. The association in this case is not for any purpose relating to the promotion of speech, assembly, the press, or religion.

DISSENT: (White, J.) While Mrs. Moore's (D) interest in having a grandchild live with her is a liberty protected by the Due Process Clause, the requirements of that Clause are satisfied because the ordinance was duly enacted by the municipality and is not lacking a specific purpose. The

Continued on next page.

municipality has the power to maintain the character of the neighborhood for single families. Accordingly, there must be some limit on the definition of family and the number of people who may reside in a single family home. The Moores (D) are also free to live in other parts of the Cleveland metropolitan area, outside of East Cleveland.

▶ *ANALYSIS*

The Supreme Court relied on the *Pierce* case, 268 U.S. 535, to support its decision here. *Pierce* struck down an Oregon law requiring all children to attend the state's public schools, holding that the Constitution excludes any general power of the state to standardize its children by forcing them to accept instruction from public teachers only. The Court, in *Moore*, reasoned that by the same token the Constitution prevents East Cleveland (P) from standardizing its children and its adults by forcing all to live in certain narrowly defined family patterns.

■═■

Quicknotes

FREEDOM OF ASSOCIATION   The right to peaceably assemble.

TAKING   A governmental action that substantially deprives an owner of the use and enjoyment of his or her property, requiring compensation.

■═■

Bennis v. Michigan

Car owners (D) v. State (P)

516 U.S. 442 (1996).

NATURE OF CASE: Appeal from civil forfeiture action.

FACT SUMMARY: Michigan (D) confiscated and sold a car co-owned by Tina (P) and John Bennis as a public nuisance because John engaged in sexual activity with a prostitute in the vehicle.

> ## 🏛 RULE OF LAW
> States may "take" property under civil forfeiture laws without any showing that a co-owner of the property was culpable in the wrongdoing that led to the forfeiture.

FACTS: Tina (P) and John Bennis, a married couple, owned a car together. John was arrested when police observed him with a prostitute in the car. John was convicted of gross indecency, and the car was declared a public nuisance and confiscated by the state pursuant to civil forfeiture laws. Tina (P) complained that Michigan (D) could not take her half interest in the car because she did not know that John would use it to violate the law. The trial court rejected her argument, and the state received the proceeds of the sale. Tina (P) appealed.

ISSUE: May states take property under civil forfeiture laws without any showing that a co-owner of the property was culpable in the wrongdoing that led to the forfeiture?

HOLDING AND DECISION: (Rehnquist, C.J.) Yes. States may take property under civil forfeiture laws without any showing that a co-owner of the property was culpable in the wrongdoing that led to the forfeiture. Since 1827, this Court has recognized that an owner's interest in property may be forfeited by reason of the use to which the property is put, even though the owner had no knowledge of this use. Forfeiture serves a deterrent purpose distinct from any punitive purpose. It prevents illegal uses by preventing further illicit use of the property, and by imposing an economic penalty, rendering illegal behavior unprofitable. The Michigan (D) forfeiture laws at issue are consistent with these principles, especially since the trial court has wide discretion to recognize an innocent co-owner's interests, if they so choose. Therefore, the trial court's action in taking Tina's (P) interest in the car was not unconstitutional. Affirmed.

CONCURRENCE: (Thomas, J.) This case is a reminder that the Constitution does not bar all undesirable results. However, the history of forfeiture as a crime deterrent is well documented.

CONCURRENCE: (Ginsburg, J.) John had just as much of an ownership right as Tina (P) and had her consent to use the car. Furthermore, forfeiture proceedings are equitable in nature in that they permit the state courts to police exorbitant applications of the statute.

DISSENT: (Stevens, J.) Fundamental fairness prohibits the punishment of innocent people. Vicarious liability is limited in situations in which no deterrent function is likely to be served. The absence of any deterrent value in regards to Tina (P) shows that forfeitures can be punitive against those who have not done anything wrong.

DISSENT: (Kennedy, J.) The requirements of due process are not met in this forfeiture. "Nothing in the rationale of the Michigan Supreme Court indicates that the forfeiture turned on the negligence or complicity of petitioner, or a presumption thereof, and nothing supports the suggestion that the value of her co-ownership is so insignificant as to be beneath the law's protection."

▶ ANALYSIS

The dissent makes a very persuasive point. The circumstances of this case show that there was little Tina (P) could have done to prevent John's illegal conduct. Thus, it is difficult to see how there was any deterrent function in the forfeiture of the car. Recent laws mandating eviction from rental properties for drug offenses have caused similar problems for family members who reside at these apartments but were not involved with the drug activities.

■▬▬

Quicknotes

DUE PROCESS The constitutional mandate requiring the courts to protect and enforce individuals' rights and liberties consistent with prevailing principles of fairness and justice and prohibiting the federal and state governments from such activities that deprive its citizens of a life, liberty or property interest.

FORFEITURE The loss of a right or interest as a penalty for failing to fulfill an obligation.

PUBLIC NUISANCE An activity that unreasonably interferes with a right common to the overall public.

■▬▬

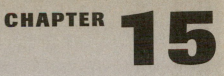
Quick Reference Rules of Law

Kelo v. City of New London

Landowner (P) v. Municipality (D)

545 U.S 469 (2005).

NATURE OF CASE: Appeal from a decision of the Supreme Court of Connecticut allowing a municipality to exercise eminent domain.

FACT SUMMARY: Landowners (Kelo) (P) brought suit against the City of New London (D) alleging that the condemnation of their property by use of eminent domain was an illegal "taking" in violation of the Fifth Amendment.

🏛 RULE OF LAW
A development plan to revitalize an economically distressed city involving the acquisition of property by the power of eminent domain qualifies as a "public use" within the meaning of the Takings Clause of the Fifth Amendment.

FACTS: After having experienced decades of economic decline, the City of New London (the City) (D) approved a development plan to revitalize its downtown and waterfront areas. The City's (D) development agent purchased property toward that aim from willing sellers and utilized eminent domain to acquire additional properties needed in exchange for just compensation. The plan involved Pfizer, Inc., a pharmaceutical company, building a research facility on the property and the City (D) believed this would stimulate the local economy by creating jobs and tax revenue. Nine people (Kelo, et al.) (P) owning 15 properties resisted. Kelo (P), along with the others, brought suit in the circuit court alleging that their property was not blighted but was only condemned because it was located within the development area. Kelo (P) maintained that the "taking" of their property by use of eminent domain violated the "public use" requirement of the Fifth Amendment. The trial court enjoined the "taking" of part of the properties, but the Connecticut Supreme Court held that all of the City's (D) proposed takings were valid. The United State Supreme Court granted certiorari.

ISSUE: Does a development plan to revitalize an economically distressed city involving the acquisition of property by the power of eminent domain qualify as a "public use" within the meaning of the Takings Clause of the Fifth Amendment?

HOLDING AND DECISION: (Stevens, J.) Yes. A development plan to revitalize an economically distressed city involving the acquisition of property by the power of eminent domain qualifies as a "public use" within the meaning of the Takings Clause of the Fifth Amendment. This is not an instance where a municipality is "taking" property for the purpose of transferring it to a private party. Nor is this an instance where the City (D) is planning to open the condemned land to the public. This is a case where the Court must determine if the transfer of condemned property somehow diminishes the public purpose of the taking. The concept of a "public purpose" or the "public welfare" must be painted with a broad and inclusive brush. The City (D) has carefully formulated an economic development plan to provide benefits to the community at large in terms of jobs and increased tax revenue. Promoting economic development has long been recognized as an accepted function of government. The government's pursuit of public purpose will often benefit private parties. This alone is not fatal to the plan because this case does not present the Court with a singular transfer of property from a private citizen to that of a private business enterprise. Nor is there a requirement that there must be reasonable certainty that public benefits will actually flow from the plan. "Because the plan unquestionably serves a public purpose, the 'takings' challenged here satisfy the public use requirement of the Fifth Amendment." This holding does not in any way restrict individual states from imposing additional restrictions to the public use requirement that are much stricter than the federal baseline. The judgment is affirmed.

CONCURRENCE: (Kennedy, J.) The Court holds that a "taking" is upheld if it is rationally related to a conceivable public purpose. The Court should also note that under this rational basis review a "taking" is not appropriate when a transfer of property favors private entities and there is merely an incidental or pretextual public benefit.

DISSENT: (O'Connor, J.) The Court abandons the basic principles in the Bill of Rights and uses the banner of economic development to clothe the illegal transfer of individually owned property to private business entities for any reason the legislature may deem to constitute a public benefit. Nearly any lawful use of private property can be said to generate some incidental benefit to the public, and today's holding expands the use of eminent domain to the point where pretext alone will determine a property's fate. Economic development "takings" are not constitutional.

DISSENT: (Thomas, J.) The proper reading of the public use clause is that it allows the government to take property only if the government owns, or the public has a right to use, the property, as opposed to "taking" it for any purpose whatsoever. Extending the public purpose doctrine to encompass any economic development guarantees that

Continued on next page.

the losses of property will fall disproportionately on poor communities who are the least politically powerful. Urban renewal projects have long been associated with the displacement of minorities and today's holding will further exacerbate these effects.

▶ *ANALYSIS*

The courts have seesawed over the proper interpretation of the public use doctrine. Some have advocated the position of Justice Kennedy that the benefits of the intended use predominate over the private nature of the use. Others have followed the test that the property cannot be "taken" unless the nature of the property justifies the "taking." Others would restrict the doctrine to that of any property being "taken" must then be publicly owned, such as for use in building highways. This view would deny private parties from being somehow incorporated into a public redevelopment plan. It would appear that the Court's vacillation is over. Economic "takings," if benefiting the public in some imagined tangible way are now deemed constitutional. The Court's holding in this case has been one of the most controversial issued in recent times. It has sparked a backlash of state legislation designed to reign in the use of eminent domain.

Quicknotes

EMINENT DOMAIN The governmental power to take private property for public use so long as just compensation is paid therefor.

FIFTH AMENDMENT Provides that no person shall be compelled to serve as a witness against himself, or be subject to trial for the same offense twice, or be deprived of life, liberty, or property without due process of law.

PUBLIC USE Basis for governmental taking of property pursuant to its power of eminent domain so that property taken may be utilized for the benefit of the public at large.

TAKINGS CLAUSE Provisions of the Fifth Amendment to the United States Constitution prohibiting the government from taking private property for public use without providing just compensation therefor.

Tee-Hit-Ton Indians v. United States

Tribe (P) v. Federal government (D)

348 U.S. 272 (1955).

NATURE OF CASE: Appeal from claim of taking under the Fifth Amendment.

FACT SUMMARY: The Tee-Hit-Ton Indians (P) claimed that the United States government's contract to sell Alaskan timber constituted a taking of their property.

🏛 RULE OF LAW
Mere possession does not constitute ownership for the purposes of the Fifth Amendment.

FACTS: The Tee-Hit-Ton Indians (Tee-Hit-Tons) (P) claimed that they had exercised property rights in the Alaskan territories since time immemorial. Before the Russians came to Alaska, the Tee-Hit-Tons (P) communally owned the land, occupied its expanse, and passed ownership rights through the female line. When the Russians came to Alaska, they occupied the same land with the Tee-Hit-Ton's (P) permission. In 1951, the federal government (D) began selling timber in the Alaskan territories to private entities. The Tee-Hit-Tons (P) brought suit under the Takings Clause of the Fifth Amendment of the United States Constitution. The court of claims found no ownership rights. The Tee-Hit Tons (P) appealed, and the United States Supreme Court granted certiorari.

ISSUE: Does mere possession constitute ownership for the purposes of the Fifth Amendment?

HOLDING AND DECISION: (Reed, J.) No. Mere possession does not constitute ownership for the purposes of the Fifth Amendment. The Tee-Hit-Tons (P) claimed that their use of the land differed from other Native Americans because they claimed tribal ownership, and this constitutes ownership requiring compensation. The Alaskan Indians' use of land might be more substantial than that of other North American Indian tribes, but it gives rise only to the level of sovereignty, not ownership. The United States Constitution does not require compensation without a showing of a property right. The Tee-Hit-Tons (P) do not have ownership. Thus their claim must be denied. Affirmed.

DISSENT: (Douglas, J.) The legislative debate surrounding Section 8 of the first Organic Act for Alaska passed in 1884 demonstrates that congressional intent was to prevent any possible invasion into the rights of Indian residents of Alaska except as was necessary to establish title to mining claims in the territory. Congress recognized the claims that the Indians of Alaska had in these lands. That purpose is now totally contradicted by this Court's interpretation that Congress reserved the issue of title to all of these lands for some future day where those rights may be extinguished without compensation.

▶ ANALYSIS

In 1971, Congress passed the Alaska Native Claims Settlement Act, which compensated Alaskan natives for the taking of their lands without recognizing any actual property rights on their part. Congress ultimately reimbursed the tribes $962.5 million in order to extinguish 335 million land claims. It also transferred 40 million acres of federal land as part of the settlement.

Quicknotes

CERTIORARI A discretionary writ issued by a superior court to an inferior court in order to review the lower court's decisions; the Supreme Court's writ ordering such review.

POSSESSION The holding of property with the right of disposition.

PROPRIETARY OWNERSHIP Exclusive ownership or dominion over property held by a particular person in his own right.

Pennsylvania Coal Co. v. Mahon

Surface rights owner (P) v. Coal company (D)

260 U.S. 393 (1922).

NATURE OF CASE: Appeal from the granting of an injunction.

FACT SUMMARY: Mahon (P) desired to prevent the exercise of the mineral rights which the Pennsylvania Coal Co. (D) reserved in a deed transferring certain surface property to Mahon (P).

🏛 RULE OF LAW
Private property may be regulated pursuant to the police power of the state to protect public health, safety, or morals; but if such regulation goes so far as to destroy or appropriate a property right, it becomes a "taking" under the Fifth and Fourteenth Amendments, requiring just compensation therefor.

FACTS: In 1878, Pennsylvania Coal Co. (Coal Co.) (D) transferred certain real property to Mahon (P) by a deed in which Coal Co. (D) reserved the mineral rights on the property and Mahon (P) waived all rights to object to or receive damages for the removal of such minerals. In 1921, the Pennsylvania legislature enacted the Kohler Act, which forbade the mining of coal in such a way as to cause the subsidence of any human habitation. When Coal Co. (D) decided to exercise its mineral rights pursuant to the deed, Mahon (P) instituted an action for an injunction on the grounds that the mining would violate the Kohler Act by causing the subsidence of his home. From a decree granting the injunction, Coal Co. (D) appealed, contending that such an application of the statute would constitute a taking without compensation contrary to due process.

ISSUE: Will an exercise of the police power be upheld if it, in effect, provides for the destruction or appropriation of a private property right?

HOLDING AND DECISION: (Holmes, J.) No. Private property may be regulated pursuant to the police power of the state to protect public health, safety, or morals; but if such regulation goes so far as to destroy or appropriate a property right, it becomes a "taking" under the Fifth and Fourteenth Amendments, requiring just compensation therefor. It is well established, of course, that some property rights must yield to the public interest and the police power. Here, however, the limited public interest in protecting Mahon's (P) surface rights does not justify the total destruction of the mineral rights which Coal Co. (D) reserved in its deed to Mahon (P). As such, the Kohler Act is unconstitutional insofar as it fails to provide for compensation for the taking of Coal Co.'s (D) property rights. The decree that was based upon it is accordingly reversed.

DISSENT: (Brandeis, J.) No taking occurred here. Rather, the state merely exercised the police power to prevent a noxious use of property. The property remains in the possession of the owners.

▶ ANALYSIS

This case illustrates the minority rule. Generally, when a landowner conveys to someone else a right to take minerals underneath the surface of his land, the grantee owes the grantor-landowner the duty to support the surface in its natural state (i.e., without any buildings). Furthermore, generally, ownership of land carries with it the right to have the land supported in its natural state by adjoining land (i.e., the right to have the support of the land undisturbed by excavation on adjoining land). Under this general rule, if an adjoining landowner excavates in such a manner as to cause subsidence on one's own land, he is "absolutely liable" for such subsidence. If, however, there is a structure on the land which subsides "and the land would not have subsided but for such structure," the adjoining landowner is not liable as a matter of law (i.e., he is not "absolutely liable"), but he may be liable for negligent excavation.

━━━

Quicknotes

FIFTH AMENDMENT Provides that no person shall be compelled to serve as a witness against himself, or be subject to trial for the same offense twice, or be deprived of life, liberty, or property without due process of law.

FOURTEENTH AMENDMENT 42 U.S.C. § 1983 Defamation by state officials in connection with a discharge implies a violation of a liberty interest protected by the due process requirements of the U.S. Constitution.

INJUNCTION A court order requiring a person to do or prohibiting that person from doing a specific act.

KOHLER ACT Legislation passed in 1921 that prohibited the mining of coal that would cause the caving in, collapse, or subsidence of a number of specific structures or public facilities.

POLICE POWER The power of a government to impose restrictions on the rights of private persons, as long as those restrictions are reasonably related to the promotion and protection of public health, safety, morals, and the general welfare.

━━━

Penn Central Transportation Co. v. New York City

Railroad company (P) v. City (D)

438 U.S.104 (1978).

NATURE OF CASE: Appeal from action claiming that a statute effected a "taking" of property without just compensation in violation of the Fifth and Fourteenth Amendments of the Constitution.

FACT SUMMARY: Because Penn Central Transportation Co.'s (P) terminal was declared a "landmark" under New York's Landmark Preservation Law, restrictions were placed on the use and alteration of the terminal site.

RULE OF LAW
A landmark preservation statute that restricts the exploitation of sites determined to be "landmarks" does not effect a "taking" of the property so designated for a public use within the meaning of the Fifth Amendment.

FACTS: New York City's Landmark Preservation Law provided for a commission to designate a building as a "landmark" and allowed the property owner to seek judicial review of the decision. Although it opposed designation of its Grand Central Terminal as a "landmark," Penn Central Transportation Co. (Penn Central) (P) did not seek such judicial review of the designation decision nor of the subsequent decision disallowing construction of a multi-story office building over the terminal. The building project was part of a lease agreement with Union General Properties (UGP) under which UGP was to construct the office building and lease it for $3,000,000 a year, also paying $1,000,000 during construction thereof. Claiming that failure to permit construction of the building called for in this 50-year lease agreement had severely restricted the use of its property, Penn Central (P) brought suit in state court. They argued that the application of the Landmark Law had "taken" their property without just compensation in violation of the Fifth and Fourteenth Amendments and arbitrarily deprived them of property without due process of law. Although the trial court granted relief, the court of appeals reversed, finding that there had been no "taking" because the property was not transferred to the control of the City of New York (D), but was simply subject to restrictions on its exploitation. It was also held that no denial of due process had occurred because the same use of the terminal that was presently going on could continue, there had been no showing that a reasonable return on the investment in the terminal could not be realized by continuing such use, and the fact that development rights above the terminal were specifically made transferable, by the Landmark Law, to other property in the vicinity owned by Penn Central (P) provided signif-

icant compensation for any loss of use of the air rights above the terminal itself. From that decision, Penn Central (P) appealed.

ISSUE: If an owner is restricted in the exploitation of his property because it had been designated as a "landmark" under a landmark preservation statute, has there been a "taking" of his property for a public use within the meaning of the Fifth Amendment?

HOLDING AND DECISION: (Brennan, J.) No. The fact that an owner's use or exploitation of his property has been restricted by a landmark preservation statute because it has been designated a "landmark" does not mean that there has been a "taking" of his property for a public use within the meaning of the Fifth Amendment. It is untenable to suggest that a "taking" is established by simply showing that Penn Central (P) has been denied the ability to exploit a property interest that they heretofore had believed was available for development. Nor can diminution in property value, standing alone, establish a "taking." If that were the case, zoning laws could never be upheld. The argument that landmark laws, per se, constitute something akin to discriminatory or "reverse spot" zoning, arbitrarily singling out particular parcels for different and less favorable treatment than neighboring ones, is not compelling. In this case, the landmark legislation involves a comprehensive plan to preserve structures of historic or aesthetic interest wherever they might be found. The decision to designate property as a "landmark" might be somewhat subjective, but it is not arbitrary or unprincipled. Like zoning laws, the Landmark Law may impact more severely on some property owners than others in attempting to promote the general welfare, but that does not in and of itself mean that it "effects" a "taking." In any event, it is not true that Penn Central (P) is solely burdened and unbenefited, the preservation of landmarks being of benefit to all the citizens of New York City both economically and in improving the quality of life in the city as a whole. Nor is this a case where the government has appropriated part of Penn Central's (P) property for its own use, the restrictions on use of the air space above the terminal being akin to the constitutionally valid zoning law that prohibits, for "aesthetic" reasons, two or more adult theatres within a specified area. Here, the basic inquiry is whether or not there has been interference of such magnitude with Penn Central's (P) property as to require an exercise of eminent domain and compensation to sustain it. In that it does not prevent Penn Central (P) from continuing to make reasonable beneficial use of the

Continued on next page.

terminal, the law does not interfere with what must be regarded as Penn Central's (P) primary expectation concerning the use of the parcel. Furthermore, Penn Central's (P) right to the air space above the terminal has not been totally denied. Other plans to build above the terminal might be approved if they harmonized with its character. Most importantly, however, right to exploit the air space above the terminal is transferable to other local parcels on which the desired office building could be constructed. This scheme lessens the severity of impact of the law on the property in question and thereby prevents it from effecting a "taking" under the Fifth Amendment. Affirmed.

DISSENT: (Rehnquist, J.) In this case, only a few property owners must bear the expense associated with the City's (D) desire to preserve a limited number of landmarks. Thus, any analogy to zoning is inappropriate. Zoning places all property owners in an area under similar restrictions for their common benefit as well as for the benefit of the municipality, but such "average reciprocity of advantage" is absent in this case. A few buildings are singled out, all separated from one another, and treated differently from surrounding buildings. In essence, substantial property rights were taken from Penn Central (P). The two exceptions in which such will not constitute a "taking," where the forbidden use constitutes a nuisance or where the prohibition arises from proper zoning laws. Finally, the Landmark Law imposes on a few the cost of preserving landmarks instead of spreading it among everyone. This is precisely the sort of discrimination the Fifth Amendment prohibits, and so the action taken by New York City (D) constituted a "taking" of Penn Central's (P) property. As such, Penn Central (P) is entitled to just compensation, which requires that it receive "a full and perfect equivalent for the property taken" and not simply an approximate compensation. The case should be remanded to determine if the transfer rights afforded by the Landmark Law met this standard of compensation.

▶ ANALYSIS

Many jurisdictions now have what is called "historic zoning" legislation, which obligates owners of historic buildings to preserve and maintain the exterior appearance. Although this imposes a direct financial burden instead of simply limiting use of the property, such laws have consistently been upheld.

■≡■

Quicknotes

NUISANCE An unlawful use of property that interferes with the lawful use of another's property.

TAKING A governmental action that substantially deprives an owner of the use and enjoyment of his or her property, requiring compensation.

■≡■

PruneYard Shopping Center v. Robins

Shopping center (D) v. Political leafleteer (P)

447 U.S. 74 (1980).

NATURE OF CASE: Appeal from decision permitting politically oriented solicitation on private property.

FACT SUMMARY: PruneYard Shopping Center (D) contended that a California decision mandating that it permit political activity on its property violated the Fifth Amendment.

RULE OF LAW

A state may constitutionally mandate that a private property owner allow political activity on his property.

FACTS: Robins (P) and others handed out political materials on retail property owned by PruneYard Shopping Center, Inc. (PruneYard) (D). PruneYard (D) removed them from the property. Robins (P) filed suit, contending that he had a constitutional right to distribute his literature there. The California Supreme Court ruled that, under the California constitution, such a right existed. PruneYard (D) appealed, contending that this ruling deprived it of its property rights, in contravention of the Fifth and Fourteenth Amendments.

ISSUE: May a state constitutionally mandate that a private property owner allow political activity on his property?

HOLDING AND DECISION: (Rehnquist, J.) Yes. A state may mandate that a private property owner allow political activity on his property without violating the Fifth and Fourteenth Amendments. It is true that the right to exclude others is one of the inherent elements of property rights, so long as the property's value is not so diminished that the owner has suffered a "taking." Here, there is no evidence that PruneYard (D) has suffered any diminution in property value, so no taking has occurred. Affirmed.

CONCURRENCE AND DISSENT: (Blackmun, J.) The federal government may be possessed of authority to define what is property.

CONCURRENCE: (Marshall, J.) The rule adopted by the California Supreme Court should be adopted by this Court as well. PruneYard's (D) argument that the state is without power to revise the common law of trespass is without merit. That would return the law to the *Lochner* era, where common law rights were paramount to the detriment of state regulation. On the other hand, there are limits to the extent the state may step in to revise those common law rights.

CONCURRENCE: (Powell, Jr., J.) The state may not compel a person to affirm a belief he does not hold. A property owner may be faced with speakers who wish to use his premises as a platform for views that he finds morally repugnant. The strong emotions evoked by speech in such situations may virtually compel the proprietor to respond. However, the record gives no indication that the customers of this vast center would be likely to assume that Robins's (P) limited speech activity expressed the views of the PruneYard (D) or of its owner.

ANALYSIS

The federal Constitution creates a certain floor, in terms of rights, that states may not go below. States are free to exceed the federal Constitution in terms of rights, if they so choose. The underlying California Supreme Court case here is an example. That Court created a freedom-of-expression right the United States Supreme Court does not recognize.

Quicknotes

DUE PROCESS The constitutional mandate requiring the courts to protect and enforce individuals' rights and liberties consistent with prevailing principals of fairness and justice and prohibiting the federal and state governments from such activities that deprive its citizens of a life, liberty, or property interest.

TAKING A governmental action that substantially deprives an owner of the use and enjoyment of his or her property, requiring compensation.

Loretto v. Teleprompter Manhattan CATV Corp.

Apartment building owner (P) v. TV cable company (D)

458 U.S. 419 (1982).

NATURE OF CASE: Appeal from denial of damages for "taking" of property without just compensation.

FACT SUMMARY: The trial court held that Teleprompter Manhatan CATV Corp.'s (D) governmentally approved installation of cable television equipment on Loretto's (P) building without her permission did not constitute a "taking" of property.

▥ RULE OF LAW
A permanent physical occupation authorized by the government is a "taking" without regard to the public interests it may serve.

FACTS: Teleprompter Manhattan CATV Corp. (Teleprompter) (D) installed its cable television equipment on a building subsequently purchased by Loretto (P). The equipment was permanently fastened to the building and was placed there under authority of the previous owner and the state. Loretto (P) sued, contending this constituted a "taking" of property without due process. The trial court held that this was not a "taking," as cable television served an important public interest. Loretto (P) appealed from entry of summary judgment, and the court of appeals affirmed, upholding the constitutionality of the state statute granting permission to Teleprompter (D). The United States Supreme Court granted certiorari.

ISSUE: Is a permanent physical occupation of property authorized by government a "taking" regardless of the interests served?

HOLDING AND DECISION: (Marshall, J.) Yes. A permanent physical occupation authorized by the government is a "taking" without regard to the public interest served. Although substantial regulation of use is not necessarily a compensable "taking," an actual physical occupation, no matter how slight, must be considered to be a "taking" and requires just compensation. Reversed and remanded.

DISSENT: (Blackmun, J.) Contrary to established precedent, the Court announces a per se "taking" test arising out of physical occupation.

▶ ANALYSIS

The Court distinguished the case of *Penn Central Transportation Co. v. New York City*, 438 U.S. 104 (1978), based on the fact that in that case no actual physical occupation occurred. The state merely prohibited an intended use rather than actually entering the property, and no compensable "taking" was found.

■━■

Quicknotes

TAKING A governmental action that substantially deprives an owner of the use and enjoyment of his or her property requiring compensation.

■━■

Lucas v. South Carolina Coastal Council

Land developer (P) v. State (D)

505 U.S. 1003 (1992).

NATURE OF CASE: Appeal of the denial of a "taking" claim in action for compensation of property value.

FACT SUMMARY: South Carolina's (D) Beachfront Management Act barred Lucas (P) from erecting homes on two parcels of land near the ocean.

 RULE OF LAW
The state must compensate a landowner when a regulatory action denies the owner economically viable use of the land, unless the prohibited use constitutes a nuisance.

FACTS: In 1986, Lucas (P) bought two residential lots near the ocean for $975,000. In 1988, South Carolina (D) enacted the Beachfront Management Act, which sought to counteract coastal erosion. The law restricted new development of beachfront areas and barred Lucas (P) from building homes on his lots as he intended. Lucas (P) brought suit contending that the Act was an unconstitutional "taking" of his property. The trial court ruled that the Act deprived Lucas (P) of any reasonable economic use of the land and was an uncompensated "taking." The South Carolina Supreme Court reversed, holding that the regulation was designed to prevent serious public harm and did not constitute a "taking." Lucas (P) appealed, and the United States Supreme Court granted review.

ISSUE: Must the state compensate a landowner when a regulatory action denies an owner economically viable use of the land?

HOLDING AND DECISION: (Scalia, J.) Yes. The state must compensate a landowner when a regulatory action denies an owner economically viable use of his land, unless the prohibited use constitutes a nuisance. Physical intrusions on property must always be compensated. A regulation that denies all economically beneficial and productive uses of land is the equivalent of physical appropriation and must also be compensated under the Takings Clause. The Court has previously acknowledged that regulations that restrict nuisance-like uses of land may provide an exception to the general rule on takings. The court of appeals attempted to distinguish laws that prevented harmful use from those regulations that confer benefits on the public. This distinction should not provide the basis for our determinations because it is impossible to objectively distinguish the two rationales. The better rule is that the government may only restrict uses that are already unlawful under existing nuisance and property laws. South Carolina's (D) Beachfront Management Act deprived Lucas's (P) land of all economically beneficial use and restricted uses that were previously permissible. Therefore, it was an unconstitutional "taking." Reversed and remanded.

CONCURRENCE: (Kennedy, J.) The trial court's finding that Lucas's (P) land had been deprived of all beneficial use is highly questionable. Furthermore, the nuisance exception should not be the sole justification for severe restrictions when the state's unique concerns for fragile land systems are involved.

DISSENT: (Blackmun, J.) Lucas (P) may continue to use his land for recreation and camping and retains the right to alienate the land. Therefore, the trial court's ruling that the property had lost all economic value is certainly erroneous. The majority opinion today creates regulatory takings in all instances with the limited exception for common law nuisances. In addition, our prior case law has upheld prohibitions without compensation on uses of property that are injurious to the health, morals, and safety of the community.

DISSENT: (Stevens, J.) The majority's categorical approach, which attempts to reduce "takings" to a set formula, does not take into account the complex problems involved in environmental regulation. The determination is properly made by balancing the private and public interests involved.

DISSENT: (Souter, J.) [Justice Souter wrote separately to indicate that he felt the writ of certiorari was improvidently granted because the state supreme court did not review the trial court's factual conclusion that Lucas (P) had been deprived of all viable use of his property. Without such a review by the state supreme court, the Court should have demurred.]

▶ **ANALYSIS**

This case established the Supreme Court's "total takings" rule, meaning that one must be compensated only where the regulatory taking removes all economically viable options for the land. Partial but permanent restrictions of the uses of land were not discussed in the majority opinion.

Continued on next page.

Quicknotes

FIFTH AMENDMENT Provides that no person shall be compelled to serve as a witness against himself, or be subject to trial for the same offense twice, or be deprived of life, liberty, or property without due process of law.

POLICE POWERS The power of a state or local government to regulate private conduct for the health, safety and welfare of the general public.

PUBLIC NUISANCE An activity that unreasonably interferes with a right common to the overall public.

REGULATORY TAKING A governmental action that substantially deprives an owner of the use and enjoyment of his property, whereby the application of a law or regulation deprives the owner of economically viable use of his property, requiring compensation.

Palazzolo v. Rhode Island

Developer (P) v. State (D)

533 U.S. 606 (2001).

NATURE OF CASE: Appeal from state supreme court judgment rejecting a takings claim in an inverse condemnation action.

FACT SUMMARY: Palazzolo (P) brought an inverse condemnation suit against the State of Rhode Island (D) after his development proposals for a parcel of waterfront property were rejected.

RULE OF LAW

A purchaser or successive title holder of land is not barred from bringing a regulatory takings claim by the mere fact that the title was acquired after the effective date of the state regulation alleged to effect the taking.

FACTS: Palazzolo (P) owned a waterfront parcel of land, almost all of which was designated as coastal wetlands prior to his acquisition of the land. After his development proposals for a residential subdivision were rejected, he filed suit in state court claiming the State of Rhode Island's (D) application of its wetlands regulations constituted a taking in violation of the Fifth Amendment's Takings Clause. The Rhode Island Supreme Court rejected the claim that Palazzolo (P) was denied all economically beneficial use of the property since the uplands portion of the property could still be developed. The state court also ruled that because the regulation predated Palazzolo's (P) ownership of the property, he was precluded from bringing a takings claim challenging the regulation. Finally, the court also held that the case was not ripe for adjudication. Palazzolo (P) appealed, and the United States Supreme Court granted certiorari.

ISSUE: Is a purchaser or successive title holder of land barred from bringing a regulatory takings claim by the mere fact that the title was acquired after the effective date of the state regulation alleged to effect the taking?

HOLDING AND DECISION: (Kennedy, J.) No. A purchaser or successive title holder of land is not barred from bringing a regulatory takings claim by the mere fact that the title was acquired after the effective date of the state regulation alleged to effect the taking. The state court was correct in deciding that all economically viable use of the property was not deprived, because the uplands portion of the property could still be developed. The state court erred, however, in determining that the case was not ripe for adjudication. Finally, the state court also was incorrect that post-enactment purchasers can never challenge a regulation under the Takings Clause. The State's (D) sweeping rule, that a purchaser or a successive title holder is deemed

to have notice of an earlier-enacted restriction and is barred from claiming that it effects a taking would absolve the State of its obligation to defend any action restricting land use, no matter how extreme or unreasonable. A State would be allowed, in effect, to put an expiration date on the Takings Clause. This ought not to be the rule. Future generations, too, have a right to challenge unreasonable limitations on the use and value of land. The State's notice justification does not take into account the effect on owners at the time of enactment, who are prejudiced as well. Should an owner attempt to challenge a new regulation, but not survive the process of ripening his or her claim (which, as this case demonstrates, will often take years), under the State's (D) rule the right to compensation may not be asserted by an heir or successor, and so may not be asserted at all. The State's (D) rule also would work a critical alteration to the nature of property, as the newly regulated landowner is stripped of the ability to transfer the interest that was possessed prior to the regulation. The State (D) may not by this means secure a windfall for itself. The rule is, furthermore, capricious in effect. The young owner contrasted with the older owner, the owner with the resources to hold contrasted with the owner with the need to sell, would be in different positions. The Takings Clause is not so quixotic. A blanket rule that purchasers with notice have no compensation right when a claim becomes ripe is too blunt an instrument to accord with the duty to compensate for what is taken. Thus, on remand, the court must address the merits of Palazzolo's (P) *Penn Central Transportation Co. v. City of New York*, 438 U.S. 104 (1978), claim. Affirmed in part, reversed in part, and remanded.

CONCURRENCE: (O'Connor, J.) *Penn Central* still controls. Under that analysis interference with investment-backed expectations is one of a number of factors that a court must examine. The regulatory scheme at the time the property is acquired also shapes the reasonableness of the claimant's expectations.

CONCURRENCE: (Scalia, J.) The investment-backed expectations the law will take into account on remand do not include the assumed validity of a restriction that in fact deprives property of so much of its value that it is an unconstitutional taking.

CONCURRENCE AND DISSENT: (Stevens, J.) Palazzolo (P) is the wrong person to be bringing this action; if anyone is to be compensated it is the owner of the property at the time the regulations were adopted.

Continued on next page.

DISSENT: (Ginsburg, J.) The Rhode Island Supreme Court was correct in finding that the claim was not ripe for several reasons including that Palazzolo (P) had not sought permission for development of the upland portion of the property only.

DISSENT: (Breyer, J.) As Justice O'Connor says in her concurrence, the simple fact that property has changed hands (e.g., by inheritance) does not always and automatically bar a takings claim, nor is the fact that one acquires the subject property after a regulatory law has been enacted dispositive of the issue, although that is a relevant factor.

▶ *ANALYSIS*

The Court here did away with the prior rule under *Lucas v. South Carolina Coastal Council*, 505 U.S. 100. (1992) and *Penn Central* that a purchaser or successive title holder was deemed to have notice of an earlier-enacted restriction and was barred from bringing a takings claim. The Court also held that a state does not avoid the duty to compensate based on a "token interest." So long as a landowner is permitted to build a substantial residence on the parcel, then it is not deemed to constitute a deprivation of all economic value.

Quicknotes

FIFTH AMENDMENT Provides that no person shall be compelled to serve as a witness against himself, or be subject to trial for the same offense twice, or be deprived of life, liberty, or property without due process of law.

INVERSE CONDEMNATION The taking of private property for public use so as to impair or decrease the value of property near or adjacent to, but not a part of, the property taken.

NOTICE Communication of information to a person by an authorized person or an otherwise proper source.

TAKING A governmental action that substantially deprives an owner of the use and enjoyment of his or her property, requiring compensation.

Tahoe-Sierra Preservation Council, Inc. v. Tahoe Regional Planning Agency

Landowners (P) v. Regional planning agency (D)

535 U.S. 302 (2002).

NATURE OF CASE: Appeal from reversal of judgment finding a per se taking of property.

FACT SUMMARY: Tahoe Regional Planning Agency (TRPA) (D) imposed two moratoria, totaling 32 months, on development in the Lake Tahoe Basin while formulating a comprehensive land-use plan for the area. Landowners (P) affected by the moratoria filed suit, claiming that TRPA's (D) actions constituted a taking of their property without just compensation in violation of the Takings Clause.

🏛 RULE OF LAW
A moratorium on development imposed during the process of devising a comprehensive land-use plan does not constitute a per se taking of property requiring compensation under the Takings Clause.

FACTS: Tahoe Regional Planning Agency (TRPA) (D) imposed two moratoria, one, from 1981 to 1983, and a more restrictive one, from 1983 to 1984, totaling 32 months, on development in the Lake Tahoe region while formulating a comprehensive land-use plan of environmentally sound growth for the area. The moratoria were triggered by the increased pollution of Lake Tahoe from accelerating development of the area. During the moratoria, virtually all development was prohibited. Landowners (P) affected by the moratoria filed suit, claiming that TRPA's (D) actions constituted a taking of their property without just compensation in violation of the Takings Clause. The district court found a taking, but the court of appeals reversed. The U.S. Supreme Court granted certiorari.

ISSUE: Does a moratorium on development imposed during the process of devising a comprehensive land-use plan constitute a per se taking of property requiring compensation under the Takings Clause?

HOLDING AND DECISION: (Stevens, J.) No. A moratorium on development imposed during the process of devising a comprehensive land-use plan does not constitute a per se taking of property requiring compensation under the Takings Clause. The attack on the moratoria is only facial. The landowners contend that the mere enactment of a temporary regulation that, while in effect, denies a property owner of all viable economic use of the property gives rise to an unqualified constitutional obligation to compensate for the value of the property's use during that period. The landowners want a categorical rule, but the Court's cases do not support such a rule. The answer to

any given case depends on the particular circumstances of the case, and the circumstances in this case are best analyzed within the framework of *Penn Central Transp. Co. v. New York* (1978). The long-standing distinction between physical and regulatory takings makes it inappropriate to treat precedent from one as controlling on the other. The landowners (P) in this case rely on *First English Evangelical Lutheran Church of Glendale v. County of Los Angeles,* 482 U.S. 304 (1987) and *Lucas v. South Carolina Coastal Council,* 505 U.S. 1003 (1992)—both regulatory takings cases—to argue for a categorical rule that whenever the government imposes a deprivation of all economically viable use of property, no matter how brief, it effects a taking. In *First English,* the Court addressed the separate remedial question of how compensation is measured once a regulatory taking is established, but not the different and prior question whether the temporary regulation was in fact a taking. Nor is *Lucas* dispositive of the question presented. Its categorical rule—requiring compensation when a regulation permanently deprives an owner of "all economically beneficial uses" of his land—does not answer the question whether a regulation prohibiting any economic use of land for 32 months must be compensated. The landowners (P) attempt to bring this case under the rule in *Lucas* by focusing exclusively on the property during the moratoria is unavailing. This Court has consistently rejected such an approach to the "denominator" question. To sever a 32-month segment from the remainder of each fee simple estate and then ask whether that segment has been taken in its entirety would ignore *Penn Central*'s admonition to focus on "the parcel as a whole." Both dimensions of a real property interest—the metes and bounds describing its geographic dimensions and the term of years describing its temporal aspect—must be considered when viewing the interest in its entirety. A permanent deprivation of all use is a taking of the parcel as a whole, but a temporary restriction causing a diminution in value is not, for the property will recover value when the prohibition is lifted. *Lucas* was carved out for the "extraordinary case" in which a regulation permanently deprives property of all use; the default rule remains that a fact specific inquiry is required in the regulatory taking context. Nevertheless, the Court will consider the landowners' (P) argument that the interest in protecting property owners from bearing public burdens "which, in all fairness and justice, should be borne by the public as a whole," justifies creating a new categorical rule. "Fairness and justice" will not be better served by a

Continued on next page.

categorical rule that any deprivation of all economic use, no matter how brief, constitutes a compensable taking. That rule would apply to numerous normal delays—in obtaining building permits, variances, zoning changes, etc.—and would require changes in practices that have long been considered permissible exercises of the police power. Such an important change in the law should be the product of legislative rulemaking, not adjudication. More importantly, the better approach to a temporary regulatory taking claim requires careful examination and weighing of all the relevant circumstances—only one of which is the length of the delay. A narrower rule excluding normal delays in processing permits, or covering only delays of more than a year, would have a less severe impact on prevailing practices, but would still impose serious constraints on the planning process. Moratoria are an essential tool of successful development. The interest in informed decision-making counsels against adopting a per se rule that would treat such interim measures as takings—regardless of the planners' good faith, the landowners' reasonable expectations, or the moratorium's actual impact on property values. The financial constraints of compensating property owners during a moratorium may force officials to rush through the planning process or abandon the practice altogether. And the interest in protecting the decisional process is even stronger when an agency is developing a regional plan than when it is considering a permit for a single parcel. Here, TRPA (D) obtained the benefit of comments and criticisms from interested parties during its deliberations, but a categorical rule tied to the deliberations' length would likely create added pressure on decision makers to quickly resolve land-use questions, disadvantaging landowners and interest groups less organized or familiar with the planning process. Moreover, with a temporary development ban, there is less risk that individual landowners will be singled out to bear a special burden that should be shared by the public as a whole. It may be true that a moratorium lasting more than one year should be viewed with special skepticism, but the district court found that the instant delay was not unreasonable. The restriction's duration is one factor for a court to consider in appraising regulatory takings claims, but with respect to that factor, the temptation to adopt per se rules in either direction must be resisted. Affirmed.

DISSENT: (Rehnquist, C.J.) The relevant time frame here is not, as the majority indicates, 32 months, but rather it is six years because the 1984 Regional Plan that was implemented after the moratoria were lifted also denied landowners (P) all use of their property until 1987, thus extending the period from 1981 to 1987. Neither the takings clause nor the Court's precedent, supports a distinction between "temporary" and "permanent" prohibitions. Such a distinction is tenuous—here, the "temporary" prohibition lasted six years, whereas the "permanent" prohibition in *Lucas* lasted only two years. Using this distinction, the government only has to label its prohibition "temporary" in order avoid compensation. Such a designation would not preclude the government from repeatedly extending the "temporary" prohibition into a long-term ban on all development. Even if a practical distinction between temporary and permanent deprivations were plausible, to treat the two differently in terms of takings law would be at odds with the justification for the *Lucas* rule. The *Lucas* rule is derived from the fact that a total deprivation of use is, from the landowner's point of view, the equivalent of a physical appropriation. Because the rationale for the *Lucas* rule applies just as strongly in this case, the "temporary" denial of all viable use of land for six years is a taking. The majority is concerned that applying *Lucas* here would compel a finding that many traditional, short-term, land-use planning devices are takings. However, the Court has recognized that property rights are enjoyed under an implied limitation. When a regulation merely delays a final land use decision, there are other background principles of state property law that prevent the delay from being deemed a taking, as in the case of normal delays in obtaining building permits, changes in zoning ordinances, variances, and the like. Thus, the short-term delays attendant to zoning and permit regimes are a longstanding feature of state property law and part of a landowner's reasonable investment-backed expectations. But a moratorium prohibiting all economic use for a period of six years is not one of the longstanding, implied limitations of state property law. As is the case with most governmental action that furthers the public interest, here the preservation of Lake Tahoe should be borne by the public at large and not just by a few landowners, and the moratoria constitute a taking that requires compensation.

DISSENT: (Thomas, J.) The majority's conclusion that the temporary moratorium at issue here was not a taking because it was not a "taking of 'the parcel as a whole.'" This position was rejected in the context of *temporal* deprivations of property by *First English*, which held that temporary and permanent takings "are not different in kind" when a landowner is deprived of all beneficial use of his land. Thus, a total deprivation of the use of a so-called "temporal slice" of property is compensable under the Takings Clause unless background principles of state property law prevent it from being deemed a taking. Regulations prohibiting all productive uses of property are subject to *Lucas*'s per se rule regardless of whether the property retains theoretical useful life and value, if and when, the "temporary" moratorium is lifted. Such potential future value, which the majority assures will be recovered upon lifting the moratorium, bears on the amount of compensation due and not on whether there was a taking in the first place.

Continued on next page.

▶ *ANALYSIS*

With this case, the majority of the Court seems to have adopted the approach recommended by Justice O'Connor's concurring opinion in *Palazzolo v. Rhode Island,* 533 U.S. 606 (2001)—namely, an ad hoc approach that evaluates the circumstances of each case using the *Penn Central* framework—and rejected a categorical rule for all regulatory takings cases. The majority also seemed to resolve the "denominator" issue that had hitherto been unsettled in takings jurisprudence.

■■■■

Quicknotes

LAND-USE PLAN General plan for real estate, including local zoning ordinances or real estate development scheme.

PER SE An activity that is so inherently obvious that it is unnecessary to examine its underlying validity. By itself; not requiring additional evidence for proof.

TAKING A governmental action that substantially deprives an owner of the use and enjoyment of his property, requiring compensation.

■■■■

Babbitt v. Youpee

[Parties not identified.]

519 U.S. 234 (1997).

NATURE OF CASE: Review of constitutionality of a federal law.

FACT SUMMARY: Descendants brought suit challenging the escheat provisions of the Indian Land Consolidation Act as unconstitutional.

🏛 RULE OF LAW
Congress may not legislate in such a way as to abrogate the right of persons to pass on property to their heirs.

FACTS: Congress passed the Indian Land Consolidation Act (ILCA) to ameliorate the fractionation problem attendant to an outdated allotment policy that yielded multiple ownership of single parcels of Indian land. The Court invalidated § 207 of the ILCA in *Hodel v. Irving*, 481 U.S. 704 (1987), on the basis that it constituted a "taking" of property without just compensation in violation of the Fifth Amendment. While the suit was pending, Congress amended the section. As amended, the interests in this case would escheat to tribal governments. The descendants of Youpee brought suit challenging the constitutionality of the provision.

ISSUE: May Congress legislate in such a way as to abrogate the right of persons to pass on property to their heirs?

HOLDING AND DECISION: (Ginsburg, J.) No. Congress may not legislate in such a way as to abrogate the right of persons to pass on property to their heirs. The amendment of the statute in this case fails to correct the infirmity of the former § 207. As amended the section still severely restricts the right of an individual to direct the descent of his property. Allowing a decedent to leave an interest only to a current owner severely restricts the number of potential successors.

DISSENT: (Stevens, J.) Section 207 did not constitute an unconstitutional "taking" of Youpee's right to make a testamentary disposition of his property. The federal government has a valid interest in removing impediments to the development of property.

▌ *ANALYSIS*

The concept of "conceptual severance" was developed in order to identify particular strands in the bundle of rights that constituted identifiable interests in property for the purpose of "takings" analysis. When the government changes or modifies a rule that works retroactively to destroy a property interest, such regulation may be viewed as an unconstitutional "taking."

■=■

Quicknotes

DESCENT The transfer of property that occurs when a person dies without a will; usually accomplished in accordance with statute.

HEIRS Those who succeed to one's interest in property pursuant to statute after he dies intestate.

INTESTATE To die without leaving a valid testamentary instrument.

TAKING A governmental action that substantially deprives an owner of the use and enjoyment of his or her property, requiring compensation.

■=■

Stop the Beach Renourishment, Inc. v. Florida Department of Environmental Protection

Beachfront property owners (P) v. State (D)

130 S. Ct. 2592 (2010).

NATURE OF CASE: Appeal from the determination by the state's highest that legislation to restore and maintain beaches, a process that modifies private property boundary lines, did not constitute a judicial taking or violate the due process clause.

FACT SUMMARY: Florida adopted legislation to restore and maintain beaches. With the proposed increase in the width of the beaches, a new boundary line would be created, altering the common law boundary rights of beachfront property owners. After unsuccessfully changing the state's (D) administrative agency's determinations, Stop the Beach (a nonprofit group, hereinafter "Plaintiffs") (P) sought an appeal and rehearing, which were also denied. The Plaintiffs (P) appealed, arguing that the supreme court's decision constituted a judicial taking or violated their rights to due process.

RULE OF LAW

(1) In upholding the state's legislation to restore beaches, a process that modifies private property boundary lines, the court's decision does not constitute a judicial taking or violate the due process clause.

(2) Beachfront property owners do not have a right of accretion superior to the State's right to fill in reclaimed land.

FACTS: The State (D) holds in trust for the public the land permanently submerged beneath navigable waters and the foreshore (the land between the low-tide line and the mean high-water line). Thus, the mean high-water line is the ordinary boundary between private beachfront, or littoral property, and state-owned land. At the center of this case is the right to accretions and relictions. Accretions are additions of alluvions (sand, sediment, or other deposits) to waterfront land; relictions are lands once covered by water that become dry when the water recedes. In Florida, at common law, the beachfront or littoral owner automatically takes title to dry land added to his property; but formerly submerged land that has become dry by avulsion continues to belong to the State.

Florida's Beach and Shore Preservation Act establishes procedures for beach restoration and nourishment projects designed to deposit sand on eroded beaches (restoration) and to maintain the deposited sand (nourishment). Once a beach restoration is determined to be undertaken the State's (D) Board of Trustees of the Internal Improvement Trust Fund (Board) sets what is called "an erosion control line," in reference to the existing mean high-water line.

Once the erosion-control new line is recorded, the common law ceases to apply. Thus, when accretion moves the mean high-water line seaward, the property of beachfront landowners is not extended to that line, but remains bounded by the permanent erosion-control line.

Residents of several jurisdictions sought permits to restore 6.9 miles of beach eroded by several hurricanes that would add about 75 feet of dry sand seaward of the mean high-water line (to be denominated the erosion-control line). Plaintiffs' (P) members, Stop the Beach Renourishment, Inc., a nonprofit corporation formed by owners of beachfront property bordering the project, brought suit against the "State" (D) when the State's Department of Environmental Protection (D) approved the permit. The District Court of Appeal for the First District concluded that the State's (D) order had eliminated the Plaintiffs' (D) littoral rights (1) to receive accretions to their properties and (2) to have their property's contact with the water remain intact. Deciding that this would be an unconstitutional "taking" and would require an additional administrative requirement to be met, the court set aside the order, remanded the proceeding, and certified to the Florida Supreme Court the question whether the Beach and Shore Preservation Act (the Act) unconstitutionally deprived the Plaintiffs (P) of littoral rights without just compensation. The Florida Supreme Court answered in the negative and quashed the remand, concluding that the Plaintiffs (P) did not have a right to the property supposedly taken. The request for a rehearing on the grounds that the decision effected a taking of the Plaintiffs' (P) littoral rights contrary to the Fifth and Fourteenths was denied. The United States Supreme Court then granted certiorari.

ISSUE:

(1) In upholding Florida legislation to restore beaches, a process that modifies private property boundary lines, did the Florida court's decision constitute a judicial taking or violate the due process clause?

(2) Do beachfront property owners have a right of accretion superior to the State's right to fill in reclaimed land?

HOLDING AND DECISION: (Scalia, J.)

(1) No. In upholding Florida legislation to restore beaches, a process that modifies private property boundary lines, the Florida court's decision did not constitute a judicial taking or violate the due process clause. The Takings Clause ("nor shall private property be taken for public

Continued on next page.

use, without just compensation," U.S. Constitution, Amendment 5) applies as fully to the taking of a landowner's riparian rights as it does to the taking of an estate in land. Moreover, though the classic taking is a transfer of property to the state or to another private party by eminent domain, the Takings Clause applies to other state actions that achieve the same thing. Thus, when the government uses its own property in such a way that it destroys private property, it has taken that property. Similarly, our doctrine of regulatory takings aims to identify regulatory actions that are functionally equivalent to the classic taking. Thus, it is a taking when a state regulation forces a property owner to submit to a permanent physical occupation, or deprives him of all economically beneficial use of his property. *Lucas* v. *South Carolina Coastal Council*, 505 U.S. 1003 (1992). Finally, states effect a taking if they re-characterize as public property what was previously private property.

The Takings Clause (unlike, for instance, the Ex Post Facto Clauses) is not addressed to the action of a specific branch or branches. It is concerned simply with the act, and not with the governmental actor. There is no textual justification for saying that the existence or the scope of a state's power to expropriate private property without just compensation varies according to the branch of government effecting the expropriation. Nor does common sense recommend such a principle. It would be absurd to allow a state to do by judicial decree what the Takings Clause forbids it to do by legislative fiat. In sum, the Takings Clause bars the state from taking private property without paying for it, no matter which branch is the instrument of the taking. To be sure, the manner of state action may matter. Condemnation by eminent domain, for example, is always a taking, while a legislative, executive, or judicial restriction of property use may or may not be, depending on its nature and extent. But the particular state actor is irrelevant. If a legislature or a court declares that what was once an established right of private property no longer exists, it has taken that property, no less than if the State (D) had physically appropriated it or destroyed its value by regulation.

Plaintiffs (P) put forward a number of arguments that contradict, to a greater or lesser degree, the principle that the existence of a taking does not depend upon the branch of government that effects it. First, in a case claiming a judicial taking they would add to the normal takings inquiry a requirement that the court's decision have no "fair and substantial basis." To assure that there is no "evasion" of judicial authority to review federal questions, courts have insisted that the nonfederal ground of decision have "fair support." A test designed to determine whether there has been an evasion is not obviously appropriate for determining whether there has been a taking of property. But if it is to be extended there it must mean that there is a "fair and substantial basis" for believing that Plaintiffs (P)

did not have a property right to future accretions which the Act would take away. This is no different from the requirement that Plaintiffs (P) must prove the elimination of an established property right.

Next, Plaintiffs (P) argue that federal courts lack the knowledge of state law required to decide whether a judicial decision that purports merely to clarify property rights has instead taken them. But federal courts must often decide what state property rights exist in nontakings contexts. A constitutional provision that forbids the uncompensated taking of property is quite simply insusceptible of enforcement by federal courts unless they have the power to decide what property rights exist under state law.

Plaintiffs (P) also warn against depriving common-law judging of needed flexibility. That argument has little appeal when directed against the enforcement of a constitutional guarantee adopted in an era when, courts had no power to "change" the common law. But in any case, courts have no peculiar need of flexibility. It is no more essential that judges be free to overrule prior cases that establish property entitlements than that state legislators be free to revise pre-existing statutes that confer property entitlements, or agency heads pre-existing regulations that do so. And insofar as courts merely clarify and elaborate property entitlements that were previously unclear, they cannot be said to have taken an established property right.

For its part, Plaintiffs (P) propose an unpredictability test, arguing that a judicial taking consists of a decision that "'constitutes a sudden change in state law, unpredictable in terms of relevant precedents.'" The focus of Plaintiffs' (P) test is misdirected. What counts is not whether there is precedent for the allegedly confiscatory decision, but whether the property right allegedly taken was established. A "predictability of change" test would cover both too much and too little. Too much, because a judicial property decision need not be predictable, so long as it does not declare that what had been private property under established law no longer is. A decision that clarifies property entitlements (or the lack thereof) that were previously unclear might be difficult to predict but it does not eliminate established property rights. And the predictability test covers too little, because a judicial elimination of established private-property rights that is foreshadowed by dicta or even by holdings years in advance is nonetheless a taking.

Plaintiffs' (P) argue that the state supreme court took two of the property rights of the Plaintiffs (P) by declaring that those rights did not exist: the right to accretions and the right to have littoral property touch the water. There is no taking unless Plaintiffs (P) can show that, before the state supreme court's

Continued on next page.

decision, littoral-property owners had rights to future accretions and contact with the water superior to the State's (D) right to fill in its submerged land. Though some may think the question close, the showing cannot be made.

Two core principles of state property law intersect in this case. First, the State (D) as owner of the submerged land adjacent to littoral property has the right to fill that land, so long as it does not interfere with the rights of the public and the rights of littoral landowners. Second, if an avulsion exposes land seaward of littoral property that had previously been submerged, that land belongs to the State (D) even if it interrupts the littoral owner's contact with the water.

(2) No. Beachfront property owners do not have a right of accretion superior to the State's right to fill in reclaimed land. The issue here is whether there is an exception to this rule when the State (D) is the cause of the avulsion. Prior law suggests there is not. Thus, state law has allowed the State (D) to fill in its own seabed, and the resulting sudden exposure of previously submerged land was treated like an avulsion for purposes of ownership. The right to accretions was therefore subordinate to the State's (D) right to fill. The state supreme court decision is consistent with these background principles of state property law. It did not abolish the Plaintiffs' (P) right to future accretions, but merely held that the right was not implicated by the beach-restoration project, because the doctrine of avulsion applied.

Plaintiffs (P) also contend that the State (D) took their littoral right to have their property continually maintain contact with the water. Plaintiffs (P) argue instead that they have a separate right for the boundary of their property to be always the mean high-water line. The state supreme court states that "there is no independent right of contact with the water" but it "exists to preserve the upland owner's core littoral right of access to the water." Because the state supreme court's decision did not contravene the established property rights of Plaintiffs (P), the State (D) has not violated the Fifth and Fourteenth Amendments. Because the Florida Supreme Court's decision did not contravene the established property rights of Plaintiffs (P), Floirida has not violated the Fifth and Fourteenth Amendments. The judgment of the Florida Supreme Court is therefore affirmed.

CONCURRENCE: (Kennedy, J.) The analysis of the principles that control ownership of the land in question, and of the rights of Plaintiffs (P) as adjacent owners, is correct. This case does not require a determination whether, or when, a judicial decision determining the rights of property owners can violate the Takings Clause of the Fifth Amendment. This separate question notes certain difficulties that should be considered before accepting the theory that a judicial decision that eliminates an established property right constitutes a violation.

If a judicial decision, as opposed to an act of the executive or the legislature, eliminates an established property right, the judgment could be set aside as a deprivation of property without due process of law. The Due Process Clause, in both its substantive and procedural aspects, is a central limitation upon the exercise of judicial power. When courts act without direction from the executive or legislature, they may not have the power to eliminate established property rights by judicial decision. Courts, unlike the executive or legislature, are not designed to make policy decisions about "the need for, and likely effectiveness of, regulatory actions." The Court would be on strong footing in ruling that a judicial decision that eliminates or substantially changes established property rights, which are a legitimate expectation of the owner, is "arbitrary or irrational" under the Due Process Clause.

CONCURRENCE: (Breyer, J.) There is no unconstitutional taking of property occurred in this case. Parts of the plurality unnecessarily address question of constitutional law that are better left for another day.

▶ ANALYSIS

The Court's plurality opinion held that the adjacent beachfront property owners could not show they had rights to the future exposed land and contact with the water superior to the State's (D) right to fill in submerged land. The State's (D) right to modify Plaintiffs' (P) boundaries was consistent with the doctrine of avulsion. It did not, however, view the Plaintiffs' rights to future accretions to be forbidden. This was a key determination before deciding whether the Florida Supreme Court effectuated a taking without just compensation in violation of the Fifth and Fourteenth Amendments.

■≡■

Quicknotes

TAKING A governmental action that substantially deprives an owner of the use and enjoyment of his property, requiring compensation.

TAKINGS CLAUSE Provision of the Fifth Amendment to the United States Constitution prohibiting the government from taking private property for public use without providing just compensation therefor.

■≡■

Koontz v. St. Johns River Water Management District

Landowner (P) v. State agency (D)

133 S. Ct. 2586 (2013).

NATURE OF CASE: Appeal from state supreme court decision holding that state agency's order requiring landowner to pay for improvements to wet lands not attached to land owner's property was not unlawful.

FACT SUMMARY: Koontz (P) sought develop a portion of wetlands he owned to build an office building. To mitigate the environment impact, the Water Management District (the District) (D) allegedly ordered him to convey several acres of his undeveloped property to the state as a conservation easement. In addition, the District (D) allegedly required Koontz (P) to hire contractors and fund repairs to District-owned wetlands several miles away.

🏛 **RULE OF LAW**
Under the unconstitutional conditions doctrine, a government agency may condition the approval of a permit on the landowner's dedication of property to the public only if there is a nexus or rough proportionality between the property the government agency demands and the social costs of the permit applicant's development plans.

FACTS: Koontz (P) sought to develop a portion of wetlands he owned to build an office building. Specifically, Koontz (P) planned on developing 3.7 acres of property. He offered an additional, contiguous 11 acres to the state as a conservation easement to mitigate the environmental impact. The Water Management District (the District) (D) allegedly ordered him to decrease the size of the development and convey 14 acres to the state as the conservation easement. In addition, the District (D) allegedly required Koontz (P) to hire contractors and fund repairs to District-owned wetlands several miles away. Koontz (P) believed the demands were excessive and brought suit in a Florida state court against the District (D). The suit alleged the District's (D) demands constituted a taking without just compensation pursuant to the particular Florida statute. He did not file a Fifth Amendment takings claim. A state trial court found the District's (D) demands that Koontz (P) fund repairs to other District-owned wetlands lacked a nexus and rough proportionality to the environmental impact of Koontz's (P) proposed development. Eventually, the Florida Supreme Court reversed. The United States Supreme Court granted Koontz's (P) petition for further review.

ISSUE: Under the unconstitutional conditions doctrine, may a government agency condition the approval of a permit on the landowner's dedication of property to the public only if there is a nexus or rough proportionality

between the property the government agency demands and the social costs of the permit applicant's development plans?

HOLDING AND DECISION: (Alito, J.) Yes. Under the unconstitutional conditions doctrine, a government agency may condition the approval of a permit on the landowner's dedication of property to the public only if there is a nexus or rough proportionality between the property the government agency demands and the social costs of the permit applicant's development plans. The doctrine protects landowners' Fifth Amendment right to just compensation for property the government takes during a permitting process. The rationale for the doctrine is that permit applicants, in need of various building and environmental permits to proceed, are vulnerable to governmental coercion. The permit is likely worth more than the uninhabitable land the government seeks to take. By forcing a landowner to deed over a certain portion of land for conservation purposes, the government may force a landowner to give up land voluntarily than normally would require just compensation under the Fifth Amendment. Accordingly, while governments may order landowners to remedy or mitigate the environmental impacts of their projects, a government may not leverage its ability to grant a permit to pursue other governmental interests that lack a nexus to the environmental impacts of the project in question. That is the case here. Allegedly forcing Koontz (P) to fund repairs for wetlands unrelated to his project does not bear a nexus to the impacts of his particular project. The Florida Supreme Court did not analyze this case using these principles. Accordingly, the matter is reversed and remanded for the state courts to determine if the District (D) actually made the demand to Koontz (P) to repair the unrelated wetlands. Reversed and remanded.

DISSENT: (Kagan, J.) The majority has mischaracterized the actions of the District (D) in this case. If the District (D) ordered Koontz (P) to repair the unrelated wetlands, that is a monetary obligation, not the taking of real property. Accordingly, the unconstitutional conditions doctrine does not apply. This court has already decided that the Fifth Amendment does not apply when the government requires a private entity to make a monetary contribution as opposed to taking real property. The fear is that this decision may prohibit municipalities from applying various land-use fees that have been common for decades.

Continued on next page.

▶ *ANALYSIS*

Taxes and fees upon land are not considered takings. The minority argued the District's (D) actions were more of a permissible tax or fee upon the landowner and were independent of the permitting process. The majority's analysis focused on the District's (D) actions as a whole, finding that its' alleged order that Koontz (P) turn over additional lands and repair others constituted an unconstitutional condition in the permitting process.

■━■

Quicknotes

TAKINGS CLAUSE Provision of the Fifth Amendment to the United States Constitution prohibiting the government from taking private property for public use without providing just compensation therefor.

■━■

Common Latin Words and Phrases Encountered in the Law

A FORTIORI: Because one fact exists or has been proven, therefore a second fact that is related to the first fact must also exist.

A PRIORI: From the cause to the effect. A term of logic used to denote that when one generally accepted truth is shown to be a cause, another particular effect must necessarily follow.

AB INITIO: From the beginning; a condition which has existed throughout, as in a marriage which was void ab initio.

ACTUS REUS: The wrongful act; in criminal law, such action sufficient to trigger criminal liability.

AD VALOREM: According to value; an ad valorem tax is imposed upon an item located within the taxing jurisdiction calculated by the value of such item.

AMICUS CURIAE: Friend of the court. Its most common usage takes the form of an amicus curiae brief, filed by a person who is not a party to an action but is nonetheless allowed to offer an argument supporting his legal interests.

ARGUENDO: In arguing. A statement, possibly hypothetical, made for the purpose of argument, is one made arguendo.

BILL QUIA TIMET: A bill to quiet title (establish ownership) to real property.

BONA FIDE: True, honest, or genuine. May refer to a person's legal position based on good faith or lacking notice of fraud (such as a bona fide purchaser for value) or to the authenticity of a particular document (such as a bona fide last will and testament).

CAUSA MORTIS: With approaching death in mind. A gift causa mortis is a gift given by a party who feels certain that death is imminent.

CAVEAT EMPTOR: Let the buyer beware. This maxim is reflected in the rule of law that a buyer purchases at his own risk because it is his responsibility to examine, judge, test, and otherwise inspect what he is buying.

CERTIORARI: A writ of review. Petitions for review of a case by the United States Supreme Court are most often done by means of a writ of certiorari.

CONTRA: On the other hand. Opposite. Contrary to.

CORAM NOBIS: Before us; writs of error directed to the court that originally rendered the judgment.

CORAM VOBIS: Before you; writs of error directed by an appellate court to a lower court to correct a factual error.

CORPUS DELICTI: The body of the crime; the requisite elements of a crime amounting to objective proof that a crime has been committed.

CUM TESTAMENTO ANNEXO, ADMINISTRATOR (ADMINISTRATOR C.T.A.): With will annexed; an administrator c.t.a. settles an estate pursuant to a will in which he is not appointed.

DE BONIS NON, ADMINISTRATOR (ADMINISTRATOR D.B.N.): Of goods not administered; an administrator d.b.n. settles a partially settled estate.

DE FACTO: In fact; in reality; actually. Existing in fact but not officially approved or engendered.

DE JURE: By right; lawful. Describes a condition that is legitimate "as a matter of law," in contrast to the term "de facto," which connotes something existing in fact but not legally sanctioned or authorized. For example, de facto segregation refers to segregation brought about by housing patterns, etc., whereas de jure segregation refers to segregation created by law.

DE MINIMIS: Of minimal importance; insignificant; a trifle; not worth bothering about.

DE NOVO: Anew; a second time; afresh. A trial de novo is a new trial held at the appellate level as if the case originated there and the trial at a lower level had not taken place.

DICTA: Generally used as an abbreviated form of obiter dicta, a term describing those portions of a judicial opinion incidental or not necessary to resolution of the specific question before the court. Such nonessential statements and remarks are not considered to be binding precedent.

DUCES TECUM: Refers to a particular type of writ or subpoena requesting a party or organization to produce certain documents in their possession.

EN BANC: Full bench. Where a court sits with all justices present rather than the usual quorum.

EX PARTE: For one side or one party only. An ex parte proceeding is one undertaken for the benefit of only one party, without notice to, or an appearance by, an adverse party.

EX POST FACTO: After the fact. An ex post facto law is a law that retroactively changes the consequences of a prior act.

EX REL.: Abbreviated form of the term "ex relatione," meaning upon relation or information. When the state brings an action in which it has no interest against an individual at the instigation of one who has a private interest in the matter.

FORUM NON CONVENIENS: Inconvenient forum. Although a court may have jurisdiction over the case, the action should be tried in a more conveniently located court, one to which parties and witnesses may more easily travel, for example.

GUARDIAN AD LITEM: A guardian of an infant as to litigation, appointed to represent the infant and pursue his/her rights.

HABEAS CORPUS: You have the body. The modern writ of habeas corpus is a writ directing that a person (body) being detained (such as a prisoner) be brought before the court so that the legality of his detention can be judicially ascertained.

IN CAMERA: In private, in chambers. When a hearing is held before a judge in his chambers or when all spectators are excluded from the courtroom.

IN FORMA PAUPERIS: In the manner of a pauper. A party who proceeds in forma pauperis because of his poverty is one who is allowed to bring suit without liability for costs.

INFRA: Below, under. A word referring the reader to a later part of a book. (The opposite of supra.)

IN LOCO PARENTIS: In the place of a parent.

IN PARI DELICTO: Equally wrong; a court of equity will not grant requested relief to an applicant who is in pari delicto, or as much at fault in the transactions giving rise to the controversy as is the opponent of the applicant.

IN PARI MATERIA: On like subject matter or upon the same matter. Statutes relating to the same person or things are said to be in pari materia. It is a general rule of statutory construction that such statutes should be construed together, i.e., looked at as if they together constituted one law.

IN PERSONAM: Against the person. Jurisdiction over the person of an individual.

IN RE: In the matter of. Used to designate a proceeding involving an estate or other property.

IN REM: A term that signifies an action against the res, or thing. An action in rem is basically one that is taken directly against property, as distinguished from an action in personam, i.e., against the person.

INTER ALIA: Among other things. Used to show that the whole of a statement, pleading, list, statute, etc., has not been set forth in its entirety.

INTER PARTES: Between the parties. May refer to contracts, conveyances or other transactions having legal significance.

INTER VIVOS: Between the living. An inter vivos gift is a gift made by a living grantor, as distinguished from bequests contained in a will, which pass upon the death of the testator.

IPSO FACTO: By the mere fact itself.

JUS: Law or the entire body of law.

LEX LOCI: The law of the place; the notion that the rights of parties to a legal proceeding are governed by the law of the place where those rights arose.

MALUM IN SE: Evil or wrong in and of itself; inherently wrong. This term describes an act that is wrong by its very nature, as opposed to one which would not be wrong but for the fact that there is a specific legal prohibition against it (malum prohibitum).

MALUM PROHIBITUM: Wrong because prohibited, but not inherently evil. Used to describe something that is wrong because it is expressly forbidden by law but that is not in and of itself evil, e.g., speeding.

MANDAMUS: We command. A writ directing an official to take a certain action.

MENS REA: A guilty mind; a criminal intent. A term used to signify the mental state that accompanies a crime or other prohibited act. Some crimes require only a general mens rea (general intent to do the prohibited act), but others, like assault with intent to murder, require the existence of a specific mens rea.

MODUS OPERANDI: Method of operating; generally refers to the manner or style of a criminal in committing crimes, admissible in appropriate cases as evidence of the identity of a defendant.

NEXUS: A connection to.

NISI PRIUS: A court of first impression. A nisi prius court is one where issues of fact are tried before a judge or jury.

N.O.V. (NON OBSTANTE VEREDICTO): Notwithstanding the verdict. A judgment n.o.v. is a judgment given in favor of one party despite the fact that a verdict was returned in favor of the other party, the justification being that the verdict either had no reasonable support in fact or was contrary to law.

NUNC PRO TUNC: Now for then. This phrase refers to actions that may be taken and will then have full retroactive effect.

PENDENTE LITE: Pending the suit; pending litigation under way.

PER CAPITA: By head; beneficiaries of an estate, if they take in equal shares, take per capita.

PER CURIAM: By the court; signifies an opinion ostensibly written "by the whole court" and with no identified author.

PER SE: By itself, in itself; inherently.

PER STIRPES: By representation. Used primarily in the law of wills to describe the method of distribution where a person, generally because of death, is unable to take that which is left to him by the will of another, and therefore his heirs divide such property between them rather than take under the will individually.

PRIMA FACIE: On its face, at first sight. A prima facie case is one that is sufficient on its face, meaning that the evidence supporting it is adequate to establish the case until contradicted or overcome by other evidence.

PRO TANTO: For so much; as far as it goes. Often used in eminent domain cases when a property owner receives partial payment for his land without prejudice to his right to bring suit for the full amount he claims his land to be worth.

QUANTUM MERUIT: As much as he deserves. Refers to recovery based on the doctrine of unjust enrichment in those cases in which a party has rendered valuable services or furnished materials that were accepted and enjoyed by another under circumstances that would reasonably notify the recipient that the rendering party expected to be paid. In essence, the law implies a contract to pay the reasonable value of the services or materials furnished.

QUASI: Almost like; as if; nearly. This term is essentially used to signify that one subject or thing is almost analogous to another but that material differences between them do exist. For example, a quasi-criminal proceeding is one that is not strictly criminal but shares enough of the same characteristics to require some of the same safeguards (e.g., procedural due process must be followed in a parole hearing).

QUID PRO QUO: Something for something. In contract law, the consideration, something of value, passed between the parties to render the contract binding.

RES GESTAE: Things done; in evidence law, this principle justifies the admission of a statement that would otherwise be hearsay when it is made so closely to the event in question as to be said to be a part of it, or with such spontaneity as not to have the possibility of falsehood.

RES IPSA LOQUITUR: The thing speaks for itself. This doctrine gives rise to a rebuttable presumption of negligence when the instrumentality causing the injury was within the exclusive control of the defendant, and the injury was one that does not normally occur unless a person has been negligent.

RES JUDICATA: A matter adjudged. Doctrine which provides that once a court of competent jurisdiction has rendered a final judgment or decree on the merits, that judgment or decree is conclusive upon the parties to the case and prevents them from engaging in any other litigation on the points and issues determined therein.

RESPONDEAT SUPERIOR: Let the master reply. This doctrine holds the master liable for the wrongful acts of his servant (or the principal for his agent) in those cases in which the servant (or agent) was acting within the scope of his authority at the time of the injury.

STARE DECISIS: To stand by or adhere to that which has been decided. The common law doctrine of stare decisis attempts to give security and certainty to the law by following the policy that once a principle of law as applicable to a certain set of facts has been set forth in a decision, it forms a precedent which will subsequently be followed, even though a different decision might be made were it the first time the question had arisen. Of course, stare decisis is not an inviolable principle and is departed from in instances where there is good cause (e.g., considerations of public policy led the Supreme Court to disregard prior decisions sanctioning segregation).

SUPRA: Above. A word referring a reader to an earlier part of a book.

ULTRA VIRES: Beyond the power. This phrase is most commonly used to refer to actions taken by a corporation that are beyond the power or legal authority of the corporation.

Addendum of French Derivatives

IN PAIS: Not pursuant to legal proceedings.

CHATTEL: Tangible personal property.

CY PRES: Doctrine permitting courts to apply trust funds to purposes not expressed in the trust but necessary to carry out the settlor's intent.

PER AUTRE VIE: For another's life; during another's life. In property law, an estate may be granted that will terminate upon the death of someone other than the grantee.

PROFIT A PRENDRE: A license to remove minerals or other produce from land.

VOIR DIRE: Process of questioning jurors as to their predispositions about the case or parties to a proceeding in order to identify those jurors displaying bias or prejudice.

Casenote® Legal Briefs